RUNNING & GROWING A BUSINESS

QuickStart Guide®

RUNNING & GROWING
A BUSINESS

QuickStart Guide®

The Simplified Beginner's Guide to
Becoming an Effective Leader,
Developing Scalable Systems, and
Profitably Growing Your Business

Ken Colwell, PhD, MBA

Editors: Bryan Basamanowicz, Jesse Hassenger, Marilyn Burkley
Cover Illustration and Design: Katie Donnachie, Nicole Daberkow, Copyright © 2022 by ClydeBank Media LLC
Interior Design & Illustrations: Katie Donnachie, Brittney Duquette, Copyright © 2022 by ClydeBank Media LLC

First Edition - Last Updated: July 4, 2023

ISBN: 9781636100630 (paperback) | 9781636100647 (hardcover) | 9781636100678 (audiobook) | 9781636100661 (ebook) | 9781636100654 (spiral bound)

Publisher's Cataloging-In-Publication Data
(Prepared by The Donohue Group, Inc.)

Names: Cowell, Ken, author.
Title: Running & growing a business QuickStart guide : the simplified beginner's guide to becoming an effective leader, developing scalable systems and profitably growing your business / Ken Colwell, PhD, MBA.
Other Titles: Running and growing a business QuickStart guide | Running & growing a business Quick Start guide
Description: [Albany, New York] : ClydeBank Business, [2022] | Series: QuickStart Guide | Includes bibliographical references and index.
Identifiers: ISBN 9781636100630 (paperback) | ISBN 9781636100647 (hardcover) | ISBN 9781636100654 (spiral bound) | ISBN 9781636100661 (ebook)
Subjects: LCSH: Small business--Management. | Entrepreneurship. | Leadership. | Strategic planning. | Success in business.
Classification: LCC HD62.7 .C69 2022 (print) | LCC HD62.7 (ebook) | DDC 658.022--dc23

Library of Congress Control Number: 2022933989

Author ISNI: 0000 0004 6515 9581

For bulk sales inquiries, please visit www.go.quickstartguides.com/wholesale, email us at orders@clydebankmedia.com, or call 800-340-3069. Special discounts are available on quantity purchases by corporations, associations, and others.

Copyright © 2022
www.quickstartguides.com
All Rights Reserved

ISBN-13: 978-1-63610-063-0 (paperback)
ISBN-13: 978-1-63610-065-4 (spiral bound)

OVER
850,000

READERS **LOVE** *QuickStart Guides.*

Really well written with lots of practical information. These books have a very concise way of presenting each topic and everything inside is very actionable!

— ALAN F.

The book was a great resource, every page is packed with information, but [the book] never felt overly-wordy or repetitive. Every chapter was filled with very useful information.

— CURTIS W.

I appreciated how accessible and how insightful the material was and look forward to sharing the knowledge that I've learned [from this book].

— SCOTT B.

After reading this book, I must say that it has been one of the best decisions of my life!

— ROHIT R.

This book is one-thousand percent worth every single dollar!

— HUGO C.

The read itself was worth the cost of the book, but the additional tools and materials make this purchase a better value than most books.

— JAMES D.

I finally understand this topic ... this book has really opened doors for me!

— MISTY A.

Contents

PART III – STRATEGIC ISSUES IN GROWING YOUR BUSINESS

BEFORE YOU START READING, DOWNLOAD YOUR FREE DIGITAL ASSETS!

 Business Valuation Workbook

 Due Diligence Checklist

 Ken's Business Brokers List

 Delegation Decision Matrix

TWO WAYS TO ACCESS YOUR FREE DIGITAL ASSETS

Use the camera app on your mobile phone to scan the QR code
or visit the link below and instantly access your digital assets.

SCAN ME

or

go.quickstartguides.com/rungrow

VISIT URL

Introduction

Anyone interested in reading about how to run and grow their business will find plenty of content out there offering advice, tips, or narratives about the best ways to do it. Some of this material is good, some of it is trite, and some of it is downright awful. So, if I'm asking you to read my stuff, the obvious questions are: Why should you? What sets me apart from any number of other would-be experts? Before we get to the real meat of this QuickStart Guide, let me tell you a little bit about my background and why I think my unique perspective will help you navigate complex issues more easily than you could on your own—or by turning to the myriad blog posts, newsletters, podcasts, etc., that deal with these topics.

A few years ago, I was approached by the publishers of the QuickStart Guides to write about starting a business. I did, and to my gratification, *Starting a Business QuickStart Guide* became an immediate bestseller. *Running and Growing a Business QuickStart Guide* is my follow-up, reflecting the next significant hurdle for a founder after a successful launch.

I believe my first book succeeded due to both my experience in academia and my fluency in the practical, nuts-and-bolts aspects of entrepreneurship. This combination allows me to use relevant, real-world examples to illustrate tried-and-true models from the domains of operations, human resources, and strategic management in addition to entrepreneurship. Hopefully, this will demystify these concepts for you. I also don't pull any punches and am very blunt about what works and about the mistakes I've seen founders make over the years. My hope is that this will make for an enjoyable and educational read.

I also write for readers who did not start out as entrepreneurs—as I didn't myself. I'm a Gen-Xer; my dad was a corporate wage slave and I assumed I would be too. So when I graduated from university, I started working in a series of "normal" jobs in finance. I ended up as a managing director at a major brokerage firm in San Francisco and also acquired (sorry, Elon!) an MBA. But I wasn't in San Francisco at just any time; I was there in the mid-to-late 1990s. In other words, during the dot-com boom and bust. It was the first time I'd been exposed to the startup world, and I was at ground zero. My company wasn't a startup, but we were making a major push into online brokerage and disrupting the relatively sleepy world of personal finance while basically inventing high-volume e-commerce as we went along.

The whole firm experience left me burned out. I was tired of the middle manager's life of going to meeting after meeting, trying to get support and resources for the things I wanted to do. I wanted a way out, but I still wasn't thinking of starting my own business. In those days, tech deals needed massive amounts of capital to scale, which venture capital (VC) firms and other private equity organizations were happy to provide to the right people. I didn't have the technical background or expertise. It wasn't for me.

Several of my MBA professors had suggested academia as a career path, so I started to ask more questions about it. It sounded awesome: freedom to pursue whatever research projects I wanted, tenure for job security, and a good salary to boot. So I went to the University of Oregon to get my PhD in strategic management and entrepreneurship.

As I was studying and observing the dot-com bubble in real time, my advisor and I realized that private equity (PE) investors were pivoting. They had been roasted in the press for their extravagant bets on what seemed to be worthless e-commerce plays. I remember in particular people laughing about VC funding for five online pet stores. Who in the world would buy pet kibble online? (I write this as I await my latest Chewy order.) On the other hand, when pets.com was buying sock puppet ads for the Super Bowl, we all probably should have predicted that the bubble would burst.

Once I got my PhD, I joined the faculty of Drexel University in Philadelphia as an assistant professor of strategy and entrepreneurship. At a school like Drexel, a professor's job is to produce high-quality research and teach a few courses each term. After a while, I found that I hated the research part of the job. I was too practical and impatient with the long time it took to get published and the politics it took to get into the best journals. I found myself drifting toward work at the entrepreneurship center, helping students who were interested in starting businesses, and taking student teams to national business plan competitions. Even though we were well into the internet age, it still took a lot of money to begin and scale a tech startup, and budding entrepreneurs needed business plans with extensive details to pitch to potential investors.

Because I wasn't enthusiastic about the major part of my job—academic research—I knew I had to find a new gig. By this time, I had acquired a decade of experience in the startup ecosystem. I'd met a lot of entrepreneurs, and I began to understand what made them tick and what deals were fundable and workable. With my foot already in the academic door, I got a job running the entrepreneurship program at the University of Miami School of Business. Freed of research responsibilities, I could focus on what I really loved: tapping into the local entrepreneurial ecosystem and getting my students involved in it.

Tapping into that ecosystem was also very educational for me. It was the first time I had really interacted with entrepreneurs on a personal basis, rather than as research subjects. I began to better understand how they thought and what motivated them. Because I was trained as a business researcher, I was able to recognize and characterize behaviors that led to successful outcomes in a way that was different from those without this background. I was also able to apply standard tools of strategic management (like external analysis of the firm environment and internal analysis of firm competencies and capabilities) to the entrepreneurial context and show how they were meant to be used: to help managers make more effective decisions. As you will see over and over in this book, these tools can help you understand not only what needs to be done, but why. This realization led me to run an entrepreneurial consulting program with my students, helping local entrepreneurs, and eventually to found my own consulting firm, Innovative Growth Advisors.

After a few years at UMiami, I felt I was ready for my next challenge in academic administration, so I became a dean. People misunderstand what a dean does—and those misperceptions aren't helped by depictions of deans in movies as evil despots out to foil students' fun. In reality, they are unit managers for fairly large organizational entities, managing academic programs with (in my case, anyway) thousands of students and millions of dollars in annual revenue. I have been dean of business schools at three universities as of this writing, and I've tried to take the lessons of entrepreneurship and apply them to academia. In other words, to use the tools of creativity and innovation to attract new students and to help existing ones graduate and get good jobs.

During these twenty-plus years, I've been both an observer and a participant in the startup ecosystem in many ways—studying it as an academic, teaching it to students, acting as a consultant to help students and others start and grow their own businesses, and running my own ventures. This varied background has provided me with insight into what works and what does not. My perspective on business growth and success is very much my own and quite distinct from that of the others who currently write, speak, think, and publish in this field.

Speaking of twenty-plus years of close observation, I've seen radical changes in the startup world over the last two decades. Gone are the days when you needed to raise millions of dollars and live in San Francisco or one of the other entrepreneurial hot spots. You can live wherever you like and start a business on your phone sitting in your local coffee shop. There are apps to resolve every startup headache—supply chain issues, finding vendors and employees, payments, accounting, everything. And your venture doesn't have to involve big tech or big science to scale. It has never been easier to *start* a business. But in the end, you'll still have to deal with some very fundamental issues if your business is going to *succeed*.

That's where this book comes in. It addresses the critical topics of personal health, management style, organizational design, and strategic management at three levels of analysis: the individual founder (you), the organization (your business), and your strategic context (the economic environment). That may seem a bit daunting, but don't worry—I've provided numerous real-world examples of companies, many of which you've heard of, dealing with these issues. It is my sincere hope and objective that the perspectives gained and refined through your reading of this book will lead to successful outcomes for both your business venture and your general well-being. Good luck on the journey!

One note on terminology: "Growth" and "scaling" are technically two different concepts, though they are similar and I treat them as such. "Growth" refers to any incremental revenue increase, and "scaling" is a specific type of growth in which revenue increases much more rapidly than costs. Scaling is often the goal of company founders and brings with it a unique set of challenges, because organizational complexity increases very rapidly with scaling. This book addresses the challenges of scaling, but the ideas and techniques I discuss work no matter what level of growth you seek. So I use the terms "growing" and "scaling" somewhat interchangeably throughout the text, because while that distinction does exist between the two terms, the general concepts surrounding them have the same basic relevance to your business.

Chapter by Chapter

» This book is divided into three parts: Getting Yourself Ready for Growth (part I), Maneuvering for Growth (part II), and Strategic Issues in Growing Your Business (part III). You may be tempted to skip over the material in part I to get to the more nuts-and-bolts stuff in parts II and III. Resist that temptation. If you are going to truly scale your business, you need to look at *yourself* with the same scrutiny you apply to your business.

» So, before diving into the strategic and operational issues required for rapid expansion, you need to ask a personal (and potentially uncomfortable) question: *Am I ready for this?* In chapter 1, "Reflecting," I'll help you look in the mirror to find the answer. We'll examine how mindsets that fuel personal growth—such as curiosity and accountability—are essential to support your company's growth. I'll also share ways you can develop these mindsets.

» Continuing the emphasis on your foundational role, chapter 2, "Balancing," explores the link between your health and your company's health. I'll show you ways to preserve your mental and physical well-being as you grapple with growth. Rapid expansion creates plenty of upheaval, and this chapter will provide a path to balance.

» Personal development is also central to chapter 3, "Laughing," which reveals how lessons from the world of comedy can help you think in more flexible ways. Stress management amid business challenges is part of that. But as you'll see, the tools of the comedy trade can also enhance your ability to effectively communicate, collaborate, and find creative solutions for complex problems.

» Part II kicks off with chapter 4, "Leading," where we'll build on the earlier exploration of great leader characteristics and look at facets of leadership that affect a firm's growth. You'll learn how aspects of leadership such as delegation and transparency will shape your ability to create and execute a compelling vision for your company.

» Leadership earned its own chapter, but it's not the only management ability you'll need to transform your business. We examine other essentials for your manager's toolkit in chapter 5, "Management Skills That Accelerate Growth." That includes strong communication skills and an organizational structure that fosters agility.

» You're not flying solo as a leader. You have a team to support you, and that team will need to expand significantly to drive your business goals. That's why chapter 6, "Hiring," is devoted to finding people who can fuel your growth. Your ability to recruit and keep valuable employees will help determine your company's fate.

» The people in your organization matter a great deal for your growth. So do operational tools—especially the ones that don't exactly sound sexy, like policies and procedures. But these are exactly the kinds of tools that will help your business reach exciting heights. In chapter 7, "Create Scalable Systems and Processes," we'll learn why that's the case, as we look at the importance of documentation that helps you respond quickly and gives you the ability to track performance closely while measuring what's meaningful.

» After exploring the ways you and your organization must be equipped for rapid growth, our discussion shifts in part III to address strategies for pursuing that goal. In chapter 8, "Growing and Scaling," we'll examine approaches such as expanding existing product lines, exploring new product categories, and making acquisitions. Any form of expansion requires careful assessment, because a painful gap exists between "can" and "should."

» While it's great to have ideas for how to grow your business, you need to create something more concrete. You need a plan that allows you to execute your strategy. Chapter 9, "Planning," is all about helping you develop a strategic plan that's flexible and guided by a well-crafted mission, with relevant goals that let you monitor progress.

» The best-laid business plans will languish if they lack enough money. To help you avoid that problem, we look at an array of funding sources in chapter 10, "Funding." These options for debt and equity are a critical step on the path to growth, because investments from friends and family won't be sufficient to support your new phase.

» Unpredictable events can destroy much—or all—of your hard-earned growth if you don't have strategies in place to respond. That's why I added a coda, titled "We Live in a VUCA World." The acronym stands for volatility, uncertainty, complexity, and ambiguity. Those things often require abrupt changes, and you'll find guidance here for making effective decisions when the stakes are high. You'll also see how the unofficial US Marine Corps mantra applies to navigating chaos and protecting the health of your company.

PART I

GETTING YOURSELF READY FOR GROWTH

| 1 |
Reflecting

Chapter Overview
- » Growth Mindset
- » Persistence
- » Accountability

Success is not an accident. Success is actually a choice.

– STEPH CURRY

When speaking to people who are interested in starting a business, I find that they often have one of two distinctly different thought processes about learning entrepreneurial skills through training or mentoring. On one hand, many people think that it's unnecessary because entrepreneurs are born, not made. These people often have a fixed idea of what successful entrepreneurs look and act like, and they don't believe *they* have what it takes. On the other hand, a good percentage of nascent entrepreneurs also think training and mentoring is a waste of time for them, but it's because they already know everything there is to know and don't need to learn anything else in order to be successful. In my view, both of these types of people are exhibiting fixed mindsets. They both think they have an innate set of skills and abilities that can't be changed very much. They're both wrong. This chapter is about avoiding a fixed mindset and focusing on a growth mindset instead.

The Growth Mindset

When you picture yourself, you may imagine a set of physical characteristics, like height, weight, hair and eye color, etc., alongside a set of mental characteristics—personality, intelligence, skills, and abilities. As people move into adulthood, they tend to think these qualities are fixed. This leads many to have self-limiting beliefs:

"No matter what I do, I can never lose weight. I guess it's just my metabolism."

Or how about:

"I'm not one of those techie types. I could never start an e-commerce business."

And yet we all know people who have experienced very positive physical transformations or learned new skills that helped them in their lives and careers. Are these people just part of the lucky few, or can anyone improve their natural skills and abilities beyond whatever innate limitations they may have?

According to Stanford University psychologist Carol Dweck, your answer to that question has profound implications for your life, because it determines what you accomplish. In her book *Mindset*, Dweck explores this idea in detail. Grounded in more than twenty years of research, her work emphasizes the role of two different mindsets—fixed and growth—and their extensive power to shape our lives:

1. A *fixed mindset* stems from the belief that your qualities are carved in stone. It's a mindset that drives people to prove themselves repeatedly. Dweck has observed many people who are consumed by the desire to prove themselves in their careers and relationships. In every situation, they feel compelled to reaffirm something about their intelligence, personality, or character. As Dweck notes, when people with fixed mindsets encounter challenges, they ask questions focused on personal validation: *Will I succeed or fail? Will I look smart or stupid? Will I be accepted or rejected? Will I feel like a winner or a loser?*

2. A *growth mindset* comes from the belief that your qualities can be enhanced through focused, sustained effort. This doesn't mean people with a growth mindset believe that everything and anything is possible. They don't expect to will themselves into becoming the next Einstein or Michael Jordan. Rather, they believe their true potential is unknown, because it's not possible to predict exactly what years of dedicated effort will yield. In the words of William Shakespeare, "We know what we are, but not what we may be." Unlike with a fixed mindset, the desire to learn eclipses the need for approval. People with a growth mindset reframe mistakes and failures. They don't feel anxious because they're afraid they might look stupid. Instead, challenging situations spark their enthusiasm and willingness to improve by practicing new skills and seeking new information.

These mindsets have particular relevance for entrepreneurs focused on expansion. That's because in business, as in life, the only constant is change. To navigate the ever-shifting terrain of industry trends, customer needs, and the economy, you'll need to develop new skills and improve existing ones. Your company won't be able to adapt (a topic we'll further explore in chapter 11) unless you have a growth mindset.

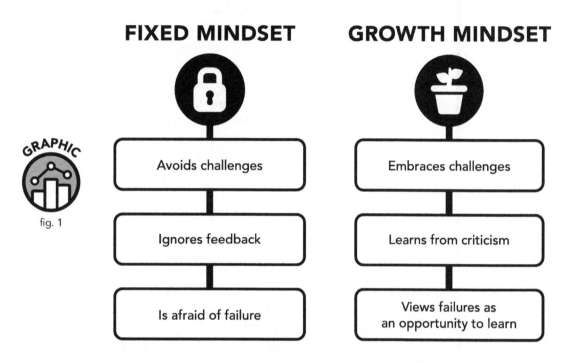

FIXED MINDSET

- Avoids challenges
- Ignores feedback
- Is afraid of failure

GROWTH MINDSET

- Embraces challenges
- Learns from criticism
- Views failures as an opportunity to learn

GRAPHIC

fig. 1

One essential quality of a growth mindset is persistence, which we'll cover in more detail later in this chapter. As the leader of a growing company, you will find yourself repeatedly stretched to the limit. By cultivating a growth mindset, entrepreneurs do more than endure challenging times. They find ways to thrive and use their passion as fuel during a struggle.

EXAMPLE

How the Fixed Mindset of "CEO Disease" Will Keep You in the Dark: When company leaders have an overwhelming need to feel smart, they often end up with "CEO disease." They insulate themselves from honest feedback. Travis Kalanick—the cofounder of Uber who was forced to resign as CEO in 2017—provided a memorable demonstration of this, thanks to a dashcam that recorded him arguing with an Uber driver. When the driver complained that he'd lost nearly $100,000 due to Uber's lowering of rates, Kalanick lost his temper. Before storming out of the vehicle, he told the Uber driver, "Some people don't like to take responsibility for their own shit. They blame everything in their life on somebody else. Good luck!" Instead of listening with an open mind and genuine interest in how the company's decisions affected the lives of its frontline workers, Kalanick lashed out when his leadership was criticized.

If you want to see a cure for CEO disease in action, look to Fadi Ghandour, the cofounder of the Dubai-based delivery and logistics firm Aramex. When Ghandour arrived in Dubai at two a.m. after a trip, he stepped outside the CEO cocoon: instead of using a luxury car service, he had one of his company's package couriers pick him up at the airport and drive him to his hotel. He used that time to ask the courier detailed questions about his work. As he listened closely, Ghandour discovered that operational issues hindered the courier's ability to make on-time deliveries.

He immediately scheduled an all-hands meeting of local management. Ghandour ensured that several couriers also attended, so he could ask them questions and allow the managers to hear their descriptions of ongoing work problems.

The tone of the meeting was just as important as the content. The CEO didn't call out managers and blame them for overlooking problems. Instead, the meeting focused on gathering information and learning. The experience compelled Ghandour to create a new company policy: all executives must occasionally work as couriers, so they can detect problems early by appreciating the challenges faced by frontline workers.

Think for a moment about those two CEO examples, Travis Kalanick at Uber and Fadi Ghandour at Aramex, and consider which one reflects your mindset when you're faced with criticism. As a leader, what's your capacity for listening to complaints and learning from them? Your initial feeling might be defensiveness, and that's OK, as long as you don't let that feeling control your next move. Instead of a knee-jerk reaction ("jerk" being the operative word here), you can choose to pause for a moment and respond to criticism with a sense of curiosity.

Cultivating the Growth Mindset

The real difference between a fixed mindset and a growth mindset is how much control you believe you have over your own future. People with fixed mindsets believe their future is something that happens to them and they just have to cope with whatever comes up around the bend. People with a growth mindset believe their future is something they can create. That may seem like a minor difference, but it leads to a profound difference in how you live your life and approach difficult situations. Here's the good news: although one mindset often dominates much of our behavior, we are all a mix of both—and Dweck outlines steps we can take to shift the balance toward a growth mindset:

» Start by accepting that we all have a combination of fixed and growth mindsets.

» Learn to recognize what triggers your fixed mindset. This could be failure, criticism, deadlines, or disagreements. What are the events or situations that make you feel your abilities are fixed and, as Dweck says, transport you to "a place of judgment rather than to a place of development"?

» Understand what happens after the arrival of your fixed-mindset "persona"—meaning the inner voice that urges you to avoid challenges and ruthlessly criticizes when you fail at something. This could mean giving your fixed-mindset persona a name, such as a person in your life, a character in a book or movie, or just a name you don't like, to remind yourself that that's not who you want to be. Think about how this persona influences the way you think, feel, and act. How does that affect you and the people around you? As you become more familiar with your fixed-mindset persona, don't judge it. Instead, focus on observing it.

» Recognize that your fixed-mindset persona was created to keep you safe. That's why it fears uncertainty and also why it will limit what you can accomplish. Instead of trying to block that fixed-mindset inner voice, note when it shows up. Explore what it's saying—don't try to silence it immediately, because that will just make it stick around longer. Allow your mind to settle down a bit, then respond to the inner voice by reflecting on the changes you'll make, based on whatever setback you just experienced. With this approach, you can slowly teach your fixed-mindset persona to think in a different way. Failure is not a permanent condition, unless you fail to believe you have the capacity to change.

We can't eliminate our fixed-mindset triggers entirely. Instead, the goal is to gradually learn to remain in a growth-mindset place, despite the inevitable triggers. And recognizing that everyone struggles with a fixed-mindset persona in their daily lives can strengthen the compassion we feel for others. It might sound small, but this is a quality that can really help your teams thrive. A growth mindset helps create conditions for success.

In 2020, payment processing company Fattmerchant was on *Inc.*'s 5000 list for the second year in a row, with more than 1,000 percent growth. Here's what makes that remarkable achievement even more notable: Ten years earlier, founder and CEO Suneera Madhani had no interest in starting a company. Because her father was an entrepreneur, she saw firsthand how unpredictable that path could be. But she recognized a widespread customer need. She wanted to change the perception that payment processors are a "necessary evil" by offering customers a flat fee (on top of the credit-card interchange rate) and a monthly subscription, so they wouldn't be trapped in long-term contracts. She envisioned technology that would bring all the customer's transactions—whether online, in-store, or mobile—on to one platform and provide data analytics to help improve business performance.

A year after she founded her company in 2014, Madhani joined a tech accelerator in Orlando to help develop the technology needed to bring all customer transactions onto one platform and, ultimately, to integrate that platform with other applications, such as QuickBooks. By 2018, her company had reached $10.3 million in annual revenue.

Madhani's growth mindset played a critical role in transforming her clear vision into an entrepreneurial reality. "I didn't go to CEO school, but I always know how to raise my hand and ask for help, and I know how to get the right resources together," she told *Middle Market Growth* magazine. "That has probably been my biggest reason for my personal success."

Other Important Mindsets

A growth mindset isn't the only essential attribute shared by successful entrepreneurs. To facilitate your growth as a leader, you must also cultivate curiosity, optimism, and self-awareness. All three of these relate to the growth-mindset development process, because they reflect the power of continuous learning. Curiosity will keep you constantly seeking new ideas and perspectives. Optimism allows you to see opportunities in challenging situations and find the motivation to take calculated risks. Self-awareness helps you to thoroughly assess personal strengths and weaknesses, identifying areas for improvement you never knew existed. Let's look at each of these mindsets in detail, to better understand how they can affect your business performance.

Optimism

I have not failed. I've just found 10,000 ways that won't work.
— THOMAS EDISON

When entrepreneurs thrive during tough times, they're often drawing strength from another powerful mindset: optimism. Optimistic business leaders increase their chances of success by refusing to dwell on setbacks. Instead, they see mistakes as opportunities to learn and as building blocks for growth. It's a source of fortitude that can help you overcome daunting challenges. Having this attitude helps you recognize that lack of success in the moment isn't the same thing as failure in the long term.

Let's face it: you had to have some optimism when you started your business in the first place. You knew perfectly well that most new businesses fail, so the odds were not in your favor. But you believed that some combination of factors—your killer product, your solid plan, your dogged determination, etc.—were going to lead you to beat those odds. And you were right. As Henry Ford once said, whether you think you can or think you can't, you're right.

Optimism doesn't mean sitting back and believing everything will be fine. That's not optimism; that's denial. Rather, it means believing in yourself and your team (which is why our exploration of hiring practices in chapter 6 is so critical). Optimism is a reflection of faith in your ability to problem-solve and to make choices that strengthen your brand's reputation and integrity. Your business challenges won't disappear just because you have optimism. But they won't feel quite so insurmountable. (Optimism is also essential for grit, a quality we'll examine a little later.)

Although many entrepreneurs aspire to be "disruptors," few deserve that title as much as Henry Ford. He revolutionized an entire industry. But there's something most people don't know about his historic disruption: the biggest steppingstones to the Ford Motor Company came in the form of two huge business failures.

Ford moved beyond his entrepreneurial disasters by not treating them as disasters. In that regard, optimism played a significant role. Ford didn't believe things would magically work out. Instead, he trusted his ability to learn and solve problems.

In his book *Mastery*, author Robert Greene describes Ford's not-so-successful foray into auto manufacturing and how it shaped his ultimate success. In the late 1890s, Ford founded the Detroit Automobile Company, with funding from a prominent Detroit businessman. High hopes were soon replaced with a constellation of setbacks. Ford's prototyped car had to be reworked, and some parts were too heavy or of poor quality. As Ford refined his design, stockholders grew impatient. A year and a half after the company launched, the board of directors dissolved it.

From this failure, Ford concluded that his auto design had tried to address too many consumer needs. His next car would be smaller and lightweight. Ford's Detroit investor gave him a second chance with this approach, and they formed the Henry Ford Company. But Ford soon felt pressured to get his design into production quickly. As he tried to set higher standards for the industry, he became increasingly frustrated with businesspeople who lacked design knowledge and yet continued to interfere with his process. Ford left the company less than a year after it was founded.

Industry observers had no doubt that Ford's auto manufacturing days were over. With so much money at risk, second chances in the industry rarely happened—and a third chance was out of the question. But Ford seemed "blithely unconcerned," writes Greene. "He told everyone that these were all invaluable lessons to him—he had paid attention to every glitch along the way, and like a watch or an engine, he had taken apart these failures in his mind and had identified the root cause: no one was giving him enough time to work out the bugs." As Ford saw it, the investors kept mucking up his clear vision of the process. Instead of allowing him to perfect his design, they kept offering mediocre ideas in areas they didn't understand.

In addition to optimism, Ford also had luck. He managed to find a like-minded investor who agreed to stay out of the production process of Ford's new business: the Ford Motor Company.

By focusing his efforts on how to do better next time, Ford remained undaunted in the face of failure. As Greene writes in *Mastery*, it's a curse to have a flawless first attempt: "You will fail to question the element of luck, making you think that you have the golden touch. When you do inevitably fail, it will confuse and demoralize you past the point of learning."

As your company experiences growing pains, you will need to inspire others during difficult times, and optimism can have a powerful effect. Winston Churchill understood this well. Throughout World War II, Churchill delivered speeches filled with the painful reality Britain faced—and then followed those sobering facts with words of optimism, explaining why he expected the nation would prevail.

It's crucial to note, however, that Churchill did include those sobering, painful realities before unleashing his optimistic reassurances. So a word of caution here: too much optimism can be a problem, especially for someone running a business. Being overly optimistic can lead you to be too aggressive and take too many risks, because you believe they'll pay off no matter what. It can also lead you to continue to follow unfruitful paths with the confidence that things will turn around "any time now." This impulse is often driven by the "sunk cost fallacy," defined as our reluctance to abandon a course of action because we've already invested heavily in it (whether that's time, effort, money, or all of the above). The longer we hold on to a belief, the harder it becomes to admit we're wrong. That's why entrepreneurs need to maintain an open mind and continually interrogate their opinions. Otherwise, the sunk cost fallacy will compel them to stick with a plan that no longer serves their business.

This is where self-awareness comes in (see below). If you know that optimism is one of your blind spots, you need to take steps such as those outlined in the "Self-Awareness" section to ensure that this positive mindset does not turn into a negative for you.

Curiosity

Research is formalized curiosity. It is poking and prying with a purpose.
– ZORA NEALE HURSTON

No matter how smart you are today, much of your knowledge could be obsolete by next year. Technological innovation and changes to other aspects of your business environment—the economy, geopolitical upheavals, supply chain disruptions, shifts in customer taste, or any number of other things—could require abrupt changes in the way you conduct business. That's why many of the greatest entrepreneurs are also relentlessly curious. They understand that if they don't continue to learn, they put their business at a disadvantage. When asked to name a trait that would most help CEOs succeed, Dell CEO Michael Dell responded, "I would place my bet on curiosity."

If you aren't continually seeking new information and perspectives, it will hinder your company's ability to evolve by distancing you from the people who determine your success—namely, your employees and your customers. Peter Drucker, one of the most influential management thinkers of all time, emphasized the need for curiosity throughout his career. In particular, he underscored the critical importance of having a curious mind that reflects carefully on what to ask. As Drucker wrote, "The important and difficult job is never to find the right answers. It is to find the right question. For there are few things as useless—if not dangerous—as the right answer to the wrong question."

This includes the uncomfortable territory of questioning the beliefs you already have and how you might be wrong about them. (Accepting that you will be wrong about many business decisions is a fundamental aspect of accountability, a topic we'll discuss later in this chapter.) We often spend too much energy proving we're right and not enough being curious about whether we've led ourselves astray.

By not clinging so tightly to the desire to be correct, we can remain curious about how our assumptions might be incorrect. As a result, we improve our ability to stay ahead of business threats, and we adapt more quickly when they emerge.

EXAMPLE

The founder of IKEA, Ingvar Kamprad, excelled at staying relevant by being relentlessly curious about his customers. Kamprad wanted to stay in touch with the next generation of buyers. So when he was in his seventies, he continued to organize and attend conferences for teens. To remain connected with the consumers he served, he preferred to fly economy, even though he was one of the richest people in the world. He also preferred to take public transportation. "I see my task as serving the majority of people," he once said in an interview. "The question is, how do you find out what they want, how best to serve them? My answer is to stay close to ordinary people, because at heart I am one of them."

I don't think it's coincidental that so many top entrepreneurs are lifelong learners and voracious readers. That includes Patrick Collison, cofounder of Stripe, the enormously successful payments company that was worth $95 billion by March 2021. On his personal website, Collison includes a list of the hundreds of physical books he owns. It's worth noting that his reading diet isn't restricted to books about business and technology. Instead, the list reveals his wide-ranging interests, including fiction, biography, history, and religion. Jeff Bezos, the founder of Amazon whose tenure there was marked by relentless experimentation with explicit lack of negative consequences for failure, closed his farewell speech when he stepped down as CEO in 2021 by exhorting his 1.3 million employees to "let curiosity be your compass."

For further proof of entrepreneurs whose curiosity and avid reading fueled their business success, look to Microsoft founder Bill Gates. He developed a twice-yearly ritual called Think Week, which he engaged in for more than twenty years. For Think Week, Gates retreated to an unassuming waterfront cottage at a secret location and spent nearly every waking moment reading and thinking, sometimes for eighteen hours straight. No visitors were allowed, except for the caretaker who brought him two meals a day (fun fact: he relied on Diet Orange Crush to fuel his marathon reading sessions). These blocks of uninterrupted reading and thinking allowed Gates to evaluate tech trends and developments —with some guidance from Microsoft employees. Two months before a scheduled Think Week, Microsoft would submit an open call for papers from any employees who had suggestions for Gates. His technical assistant would collect the papers and decide which ones deserved Gates's review. Gates read dozens of papers during each Think Week; his record was 112.

By allowing himself time to explore these ideas, at a place away from home and work, Gates could bring additional clarity to his strategic vision for the company. The results of Think Week had the ability to shape the future of Microsoft, as well as the tech industry. For example, a Think Week in 1995 inspired Gates to write "The Internet Tidal Wave," a lengthy internal memo that spurred Microsoft to develop its internet browser and defeat Netscape.

Self-Awareness

It's not only the most difficult thing to know one's self, but the most inconvenient.

– JOSH BILLINGS

Many of you are reading this chapter thinking you demonstrate a solid growth mindset, exude optimism, and practice and encourage curiosity in your organization. But do you? When is the last time you took an unflinching inventory of your strengths, weaknesses, bad habits, and biases? For many entrepreneurs, the honest answer would be "never." Or maybe they'd consider a one-time personality assessment their good-enough foray into self-awareness. This would be a mistake. The cultivation of self-awareness is not a one-and-done activity. It requires regular self-inquiry and ongoing receptiveness to criticisms that sting but may hold deep truths about your behavior.

Those deep truths may lead you to some unpleasant revelations—even the possibility that you may not be the best leader for your company in the long term. Developing self-awareness can produce discomfort, but that's the nature of any process that leads to meaningful growth. As with optimism and curiosity, the benefits are substantial. When entrepreneurs have a high level of self-awareness, they have a clearer understanding of where they can contribute to the company's growth, how their actions affect those around them, and what changes they can make to improve their performance. Here are a few steps you can take in that direction:

Conduct a 360-Degree Review

In *360-degree reviews* (aka 360s), candid feedback is gathered from a wide array of people you interact with: colleagues, direct reports, sometimes even friends and family. These 360s can be conducted through online surveys or in-depth interviews. Because the feedback usually contains some painfully honest criticism, it should always be delivered in aggregate, as an anonymous series of responses to each question, so a respondent's name is never connected to a comment they made. If you choose to do a 360, make sure the company you hire will provide more than a summary report. The results of the report will likely reveal some unflattering but accurate aspects of your behavior. When that information isn't delivered with the proper context, it's easy to feel attacked and defensive, and it's much harder to remember that 360s provide a valuable opportunity for self-reflection.

360-DEGREE REVIEW

GRAPHIC

fig. 2

CUSTOMERS

MANAGEMENT

SUBORDINATES

TEAM MEMBERS

COLLEAGUES

YOURSELF

IMPORTANT

One common blind spot for business leaders—and everyone else, for that matter—is how emotions influence decisions. Dan Ariely, MIT professor of behavioral economics and author of *Predictably Irrational*, observes that we consistently underestimate the role emotions play in our choices. "I think we assume or believe that we are rational but we're not. The interesting thing about irrationality is that it works on us in ways that we don't recognize," he said in an interview. "It is the mistake that we make repeatedly as individuals."

Ariely points out how odd and problematic it is for people to assume they have the capacity to always think rationally. "Where is this assumption coming from? When we look at our physical existence, we don't assume that we can jump tall buildings and lift everything," says Ariely. "We're realistic because we have a physical reality and we realize what we can do and can't do. But when it comes to our minds, we assume that we're intellectual supermen. And that's a very strange and dangerous idea."

In chapter 6, we'll talk about the importance of having a board of advisors. Ariely's findings reinforce how essential that is for evaluating decisions—because as smart as you are, you're not as rational as you think.

Hire an Executive Coach

You may think, "I've been running my company just fine for years. I don't need a coach." If so, you're in good company, because that's the same reaction Google CEO Eric Schmidt had in 2002, when board member and venture capitalist John Doerr told him, "You need a coach." After Schmidt questioned how that could possibly help an established CEO, Doerr replied that in his experience, everyone can use a coach. Schmidt ended up working with Bill Campbell, an ex-football coach who used his skills to coach a long list of tech leaders, including Steve Jobs at Apple, John Donahoe at eBay, Dick Costolo at Twitter, and Sheryl Sandberg at Facebook. Schmidt became so convinced of Campbell's value as an executive coach that he even coauthored a book about his management lessons, called *Trillion Dollar Coach: The Leadership Playbook of Silicon Valley's Bill Campbell*.

Schmidt is one of many leaders who have discovered that an executive coach can help to reveal a common blind spot: namely, that we are pretty bad at seeing ourselves as others see us. The right coach will identify behaviors that are undermining your hard work. You'll have a guide to help you learn from constructive criticism instead of reacting defensively or falling into the pit of self-flagellation.

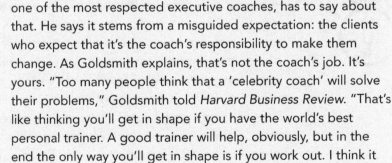

Want to know one of the biggest mistakes clients make when working with an executive coach? Here's what Marshall Goldsmith, one of the most respected executive coaches, has to say about that. He says it stems from a misguided expectation: the clients who expect that it's the coach's responsibility to make them change. As Goldsmith explains, that's not the coach's job. It's yours. "Too many people think that a 'celebrity coach' will solve their problems," Goldsmith told *Harvard Business Review*. "That's like thinking you'll get in shape if you have the world's best personal trainer. A good trainer will help, obviously, but in the end the only way you'll get in shape is if you work out. I think it was Arnold Schwarzenegger who said, 'Nobody got muscles by watching me lift weights.'"

Learn from the People Around You

Even without a 360-degree review, you can still draw fodder for self-reflection from those around you. This approach is emphasized by Goldsmith, who considers himself a facilitator. He says that most of what his clients learn comes from colleagues, friends, and family. "What I generally teach people is, the real coach isn't me; it's the people around you," Goldsmith says. "If you want to have a better relationship with your customers, who needs to be your coach? Your customers. If you want to have a better relationship with your coworkers, who needs to be the coach? Your coworkers."

If you want to develop a specific skill—listening, for example—Goldsmith has this advice: don't ask a coach to explain how to be a great listener. Instead, ask the people around you this question: What are some ways I can do a better job of listening to you? The result, says Goldsmith, will be specific, concrete ideas that relate to communicating with those individuals. Instead of receiving generic communication tips from a coach, you'll understand how the people in your life perceive you as a listener, says Goldsmith. "Even though they're not experts on the topic of listening, they actually know more about how you listen, or don't, than you do, or certainly than a coach does."

A candid assessment of personal flaws can give you more patience as a company leader. You'll have more tolerance for the shortcomings of others when you have more awareness of your own.

Give Credit to Luck

If you become a wildly successful entrepreneur, remember this: there will always be people who are smarter than you, or work harder, but don't make it. Luck always plays a role. It's an uncomfortable truth that some entrepreneurs have trouble admitting.

The influence of luck comes up regularly on *How I Built This*, the popular podcast about successful entrepreneurs. The host, Guy Raz, ends every episode by asking entrepreneurs how much luck played a role in their success, compared to work, skill, or intelligence. Raz has said he asks this question not because he believes there's a right or wrong answer, but because it forces the entrepreneur to take a moment to reflect. When Raz asked it of Rod Canion, founder of Compaq Computer, the entrepreneur paused and shared a particularly self-aware response:

If you'd asked me that in the late eighties, I would probably have said it was 90 percent intelligence and insight and work, and 10 percent luck. But I would say today it was the other way around. That tells you how perspective changes with time.

– ROD CANION,
founder of Compaq Computer

MY TAKE

When I was an entrepreneurship professor, every time an entrepreneur visited my university to speak with my students, I always asked how luck played a role in their success. Here's what I discovered: the least self-aware entrepreneurs are the ones who can't identify a single way that luck played a role. There are even trite sayings about it that come up again and again: "luck is where preparation meets opportunity," or how about "the harder I work, the luckier I get." If you find yourself saying or even thinking these things, then you should take a step back and reevaluate. You've had much more luck in your life than you realize.

Recognize Blind Spots

To truly develop self-awareness, we must accept that no matter how thoroughly we analyze our strengths and weaknesses, blind spots will always exist. One entrepreneur who understands this well is Rand Fishkin. His book, *Lost and Founder: A Painfully Honest Field Guide to the Startup World*, even has a chapter called "Self-Awareness Is a Super-Power." Fishkin grew his company Moz to $45 million in annual revenue. He also worked with a therapist and an executive coach after struggling with depression for years and finally seeking help (we'll examine the importance of protecting your mental health in chapter 2). Through his executive coach, Jerry Colonna, Fishkin learned significant lessons about self-awareness. "First and foremost," writes Fishkin, "no one is self-aware. And equally, no founder is fully self-aware."

If you believe you've achieved absolute self-awareness, that in itself is a blind spot. The goal is to maximize self-awareness and minimize self-deception, which can come in the form of rationalizations about our behavior or unrealistic assessments of our abilities. As physicist Richard Feynman once said, "The first principle is that you must not fool yourself—and you are the easiest person to fool."

Persistence

Success is not the absence of failure; it's the persistence through failure.
— AISHA TYLER

It's easy to feel enthusiastic about your business when things run smoothly. But what happens when a crisis hits? You might think, "I already know what that feels like! I faced lots of challenges to launch my business."

Although it's true that starting a business takes determination, the process of growing one requires an even higher level of commitment. As the size of your head count and customer base increases, so will a new array of obstacles. When things go wrong in this phase of your business, you'll find there's a much bigger wrench jamming up a much more complicated machine.

Staying in Love with Your Work

What does it take for leaders to stay committed to their vision during high-stakes, high-stress situations, where the complex machinery of their business threatens to grind to a halt?

Here's the short answer: grit. In her TED Talk on that subject (which has received more than 23 million views), author Angela Duckworth defines **grit** as "passion and perseverance for very long-term goals." For entrepreneurs, that typically means sticking with their primary business goal for years.

The fundamental nature of grit reflects a challenge that's particularly relevant for entrepreneurs working to expand their business. Although it's thrilling to launch a company, you'll experience plenty of tough times when the thrill is gone. That's when tenacity requires more than gritting your teeth and enduring. To stay focused, you'll need to see deeper meaning behind your business plans.

Perseverance is not a long race; it is many short races one after the other.
— WALTER ELLIOT

Interest and Purpose

Like any relationship, staying in love with the business you worked so hard to build takes two elements: interest and purpose.

» **Interest.** This refers to the thing you truly enjoy doing and thinking about. For entrepreneurs, this could be their industry or the main product or service that launched their company, but it doesn't have to be. Some entrepreneurs are in love with the process of discovering and exploiting new opportunities and are indifferent to the industry itself. After the initial spark of "this is something I'd like to spend a lot of time thinking and learning about," interest goes through several stages as we gain more knowledge and skills. This is why I'm so adamant that making money cannot be the primary goal of your venture. It simply won't hold your interest in the long run, and you won't be successful. The money will come if you can execute your plan effectively. You won't do so if it bores you.

When we are in the later stages of exploring a particular interest, a critical element keeps enthusiasm alive: our interests thrive when we have a crew of encouraging supporters, which can come in the form of peers, mentors, friends, or family. Why is this so important for sustaining our interests? There are two reasons: Encouraging supporters provide the ongoing stimulation and energy needed to reinforce and bolster how much we like something; and they provide positive feedback, which makes us feel happy, competent, and secure.

» **Purpose.** For many entrepreneurs, a desire to help other people is not the primary motivator for launching a business. The original spark for your business may simply have emerged from something you enjoy. Regardless, you'll likely experience a growing appreciation for how your work can contribute to the greater good.

The desire to connect with and help others is crucial for sustaining long-term passion. Think about situations where you found the strength to rise above seemingly insurmountable challenges. You'll likely reach this realization: your ability to beat the odds had some connection to a deep need to assist others.

This level of focus brings to mind a core principle for success in business (and life): begin with the end in mind. When your growing business encounters setbacks, you'll make more effective choices if you have clarity about what you want to build.

Why "No" Is a Launchpad for Learning

When you take steps to grow your business, expect to hear a steady stream of "no." "No" can come from investors who don't want to give you funding, potential customers who aren't interested in your new service, or distribution deals that never materialize. In fact, sometimes it seems as though everyone is betting against you. "No" doesn't feel great, but successful entrepreneurs don't take it personally. Instead of feeling rejected, they reframe "no" as an opportunity to improve. They focus on ways to learn from "no" and transform it into "yes."

Since rejection is so common, it's no surprise that highly successful businesspeople often start out in sales. (Serial entrepreneur Mark Cuban and Spanx's CEO/founder Sara Blakely are two examples.) Sales experience does help entrepreneurs develop a wide range of essential skills, including communication—but one of the most transformative aspects of a sales job is this: the top salespeople fail more than they succeed. In the daily soundtrack of their work lives, "no" is on heavy rotation. The key to emotional resilience lies in how we interpret, and react to, the sound of "no." As entrepreneurs feel more at home with "no," they see it as part of the process of growing a business, not a reflection of their self-worth.

Grit is great—if your persistence points in the right direction. There's nothing noble (or useful) about sticking to your vision with blind, unquestioning zeal. Be willing to reevaluate what you're pursuing. Sometimes "no" is the right answer, and it's up to you to know when.

How a Strong Mission Fueled Persistence for Bevel: When entrepreneurs persist despite repeated setbacks, it's not a sign of blind optimism. It often stems from a sense of purpose and reflects a belief about two things: their customers (or potential customers) face a meaningful problem, and their business has the ability to solve it.

That was the case with Tristan Walker, who founded Walker & Company Brands in 2013 to provide health and beauty products to people of color. Walker's first product line, Bevel, focused on the shaving needs of Black men. He wanted to help that underserved market avoid the problem of razor bumps, a common occurrence when curly facial hair grows back into the skin and causes inflammation. Walker envisioned products that weren't just functional but also beautifully designed—including a safety razor, a packet of blades, shaving cream, and a brush.

He had a clear sense of purpose. He saw a significant problem faced by a large group of underserved consumers and had a vision for solving it.

But when he spoke with investors, few of them shared that vision. After meeting with sixty investors to ask for funding, all but three said no.

When Walker wasn't able to get as much funding as he wanted, or the sales volume he wanted, what kept him going?

His persistence was grounded in the nature of the customer problem he identified. This relates directly to our earlier discussion of grit in this chapter: Walker had an intention to contribute to the well-being of others. He also firmly believed that if he didn't solve the problem, nobody would. As he persisted, his company grew, and in 2017 it was purchased by Proctor & Gamble, which reportedly paid somewhere between $20 million and $40 million. Less than five years after dozens of investors rejected the product idea, Bevel was being carried by large retail chains such as Walmart and Target. "I never started this company to get wealthy; I started this company to serve," Walker said in an interview with Recode. "I started this company to realize that vision of making health and beauty simple for people of color."

Take These Steps to Avoid a "Contempt Attack." During times of crisis, strong leaders show a high level of persistence and resilience. Unfortunately, they can forget that their employees won't necessarily display the same level of commitment. This can create extreme frustration for leaders, particularly in the midst of high stress and uncertainty. It can cause them to lash out. Executive coach Carol Kauffman has a term for this behavior: "contempt attack." As with panic attacks, the feelings that trigger contempt attacks emerge abruptly and hijack your thoughts. If you start to have such feelings about your colleagues, you need to stop, look in the mirror, and take a deep breath. You're not being constructive or fair.

Accountability

Blame is just a lazy person's way of making sense of chaos.
                                                        – DOUGLAS COUPLAND

When things go wrong with your growing business—and they will, with great regularity—what kind of leader will you be? We'll address leadership in chapter 4, but I do want to touch on one aspect of leadership here because it is critical for your success in life as well as business: personal accountability.

Some entrepreneurs make excuses. They respond to a crisis by looking for people or circumstances to blame. But leaders who position their businesses to thrive don't waste time and energy playing the blame game. Instead, they take responsibility for their choices and learn from the situation.

There are two false narratives that come into play here, and both of them are toxic. The first is that some factor completely outside of your control was to blame for the negative outcome. "The economy turned on me," "Those damned politicians," or "Facebook/Amazon changed their policy again," and so on. OK, so what contingency plans did you have? What reserves did you maintain to tide you over? What new opportunities arose as a result of the changing conditions, and how quickly did you pivot to take advantage of them?

The second is even worse: subtly or overtly blaming an individual or team. "The R&D guys aren't moving fast enough," "Why can't that salesperson hit her numbers," or "Our marketing sucks." Really? Who hired and trained those people? Were they given the tools they need to succeed? Were their goals clearly laid out to them, and were they reasonable goals? (Look for more on goal setting in chapter 9.)

Successful entrepreneurs recognize that accountability is an essential leadership quality. That's because leaders who lack it will undermine not only their own integrity, but the company's as well. Accountability builds trust with customers, employees, and investors. It also encourages innovation, by focusing efforts on problem-solving and improvements instead of blame.

Leaders show accountability for their missteps when they communicate three things:

» They describe the mistake they made and who it affected.
» They express what they learned from that mistake.
» They share the steps they will take to avoid making that mistake again.

NOTE

Strong leaders take the blame—and they do the opposite for success. When things go well, they praise others publicly and privately, while downplaying their own role. The best leaders are the ones who take less than their share of credit for success. They see themselves as part of a team, not the lone hero who makes victories possible.

Exercising Humility

Whenever an awards ceremony takes place, you'll always hear recipients use the phrase "I'm so humbled … " It's too bad we can't hand those people a dictionary along with their award, to stop them from abusing that word; in real life, being humbled typically doesn't come with the positive reinforcement and support of an award. So what does humility really mean? Forget the award-ceremony usage and see how the Cambridge dictionary defines it: *the quality of not being proud because you are aware of your bad qualities*. That dictionary's definition even includes an example sentence about accountability: *He doesn't have the humility to admit when he's wrong.*

The inability to admit you're wrong is an understandable temptation, particularly for entrepreneurs who find themselves under enormous amounts of pressure. Leaders don't necessarily shrug off accountability deliberately. Sometimes we deceive ourselves into believing others are at fault, because it's too painful to admit our own flaws. That's why humility is an important aspect of self-awareness.

Humility matters because without it, leaders risk crossing the line between self-confidence and arrogance. Studies show that humility in leaders improves team performance.

In part, that's because leaders with humility will readily admit their mistakes. Humility makes accountability possible. As organizational psychologist and author Adam Grant says, "Humility isn't having a low opinion of yourself. One of its Latin roots means 'from the earth.' It's about being grounded." Research shows that humility is revealed through three actions:

» Recognize your own shortcomings and limitations.
» Appreciate others' strengths, give credit where it's due, and highlight the team's success over your individual achievements.
» Show openness to learning from others.

These qualities fuel both business and personal growth. As Grant notes, "Humility stops us from resting on our laurels. It prevents us from getting complacent. It keeps us focused on learning." Remember earlier in this chapter when we explored the value of a growth mindset? Without humility, you won't achieve that.

Don't find fault, find a remedy.

– HENRY FORD

Leaders who show accountability help to protect and build their teams. That's something Doug Lynch understands well. He's seen how accountability is essential for both pro athletes and entrepreneurs to perform at the highest levels. Lynch played professional ice hockey for fifteen years and then went on to start several businesses, including sports apparel company Zenkai Sports, which he cofounded with a friend who worked at Nike for fourteen years. The company raised $500,000 in its first six months, and by 2021 it had major contracts with organizations such as the Canadian Olympic cycling team and the NHL Officials Association. "When you're part of a pro sports team, you have to be accountable for your role and for when you screw up. I screwed up thousands of times in my career," he said in an interview. "When you're an entrepreneur, you're accountable to yourself, your team, employees, and contractors for the decisions or mistakes you make."

CrossFit – A Case Study in Lack of Awareness and Accountability: Greg Glassman wasn't just the founder and CEO of a successful company; he was a leader in one of the biggest exercise trends of the twenty-first century. His business, CrossFit, focused on high-intensity, full-body workouts, and CrossFit gyms often instilled exercisers with a strong sense of community. Glassman's business even spawned a series of athletic competitions called CrossFit Games. Launched in 2000, the company had about fourteen thousand affiliate gyms around the world by 2020. That year, Glassman was forced to step down as CEO and relinquish his ownership of the company. His swift downfall related directly to his lack of accountability. He failed to recognize significant cultural shifts in society, and then refused to acknowledge that he and his company were overdue for some much-needed changes.

In June 2020, a Seattle CrossFit owner wrote a long letter to CrossFit leadership, stating that her gym was unlikely to renew its CrossFit affiliation. Previously, this particular gym owner had been dubbed by the company's leadership as "the conscience of CrossFit," because of her efforts at counseling the brand on trans inclusion. But as demands for social justice and police reform swept through the country that year, CrossFit leadership was silent. As the gym owner wrote in her letter, CrossFit had displayed "incoherent brand identity that is losing value, absent leadership at a time when leadership is most important, and a moral ambiguity that doesn't jibe with the zeitgeist or our own values."

When a company's leadership receives a message like that, from an affiliate that had enthusiastically supported the brand for nearly a decade (as was the case with this gym owner), it signals a pressing need for reflection. It should prompt some uncomfortable but necessary discussions about reevaluating the company's actions. An accountable leader would see that letter and recognize it was time for a course correction.

Glassman didn't see it that way. To him, the letter wasn't constructive criticism. It was an unjustified, hurtful attack. He responded with this: "You think you're more virtuous than we are. It's disgusting," he wrote. "You're doing your best to brand us as a racist and you know it's bullshit. That makes you a really shitty person."

During the next few days, Glassman continued his meltdown by making offensive comments about the Black Lives Matter movement. On Twitter, he belittled the pandemic and the death of George Floyd, a man whose death at the hands of police became national news, as "FLOYD-19." In a Zoom call (with audio published by BuzzFeed), Glassman said, "We're not mourning for George Floyd. Can you tell me why I should mourn for him? Other than that it's the white thing to do … "

Glassman then issued this apology (although "non-apology" would be a more accurate description): "I, CrossFit HQ, and the CrossFit community will not stand for racism. I made a mistake by the words I chose yesterday. My heart is deeply saddened by the pain it has caused. It was a mistake, not racist but a mistake."

The response was not surprising. Many companies, including Reebok, quickly announced an end to their partnerships with CrossFit. Superstar athletes did the same. Within three days of Glassman's "FLOYD-19" tweet, about five hundred gyms announced plans to drop their CrossFit affiliations. Glassman stepped down as CEO on June 9 and sold his full ownership in the company that same month.

Accountability—or lack of it—has a powerful influence on company culture. You lead by example when you respond to mistakes. When leaders blame others, they set the tone for employees' behavior. Blaming seems not only acceptable but encouraged. This creates a culture of fear, in which employees are unwilling to take risks and try new things. It also makes them unwilling to admit their own mistakes. Departments are more likely to protect their own interests. Instead of collaborating, they will criticize other departments such as sales, marketing, or product development. The result: a company that misses opportunities for growth, because it's too busy wasting time and energy on finger-pointing.

When you work to develop the mindsets we've discussed in this chapter, you'll find that as they inspire you to learn and overcome challenges at your growing company, they will do the same for your employees, with you leading by example.

Chapter Recap

» To provide strong leadership and make ambitious choices for your company, you'll need to stay grounded in healthy mindsets. Leaders with a growth mindset see challenging situations as opportunities to improve. They trust their ability to learn, gain new skills, and find solutions. Viewing setbacks through this lens of optimism helps leaders move beyond setbacks. Conversely, a fixed mindset creates fear of failure and a strong need for approval, leading to the desire to play it safe. When leaders have a fixed mindset, they focus on "looking good" instead of learning and approaching situations with an open mind. Uber cofounder Travis Kalanick demonstrated this mindset when he chose to berate an Uber driver who criticized the company's policies.

» We all have a mix of growth and fixed mindsets. Instead of trying to silence the inner voice of your fixed mindset, focus on noticing when it shows up. Don't judge it. Guide your thoughts back to a growth mindset by considering other ways to view mistakes, for example. Set aside thought patterns of worry and fear by considering what you can learn from failures.

» By constantly asking thoughtful questions and seeking new information, you will help your business evolve and compete. This means not only remaining curious about your customers' needs and industry trends, but also expanding your knowledge of unrelated fields and relentlessly questioning your own assumptions.

» It's not easy for an entrepreneur to conduct a candid assessment of their strengths and weaknesses. When you uncover uncomfortable truths about your leadership abilities, let that self-awareness provide a clear-eyed view of how you can work better with others and boost your company's growth.

» When a crisis hits, a leader's true worth is revealed. Ineffective leaders play the blame game by pointing fingers at events or people. This creates a culture of fear and stifles innovation. Successful leaders know better—they demonstrate accountability by discussing their mistakes. As a result, they build trust with customers, employees, and investors.

| 2 |
Balancing

Never get so busy making a living that you forget to make a life.
– DOLLY PARTON

In this book, we're exploring how to keep your business healthy as it expands. It's not easy, but you'll find it much harder to grow your business if you don't maintain your own health.

Founding and running a business means providing critical guidance for its strategy and mission. You're the captain of the ship, and that requires a steady hand and clear vision. If you're on the edge of burnout, your ship risks drifting off course and running into icebergs.

Living a balanced life protects your company's core asset: you. Although we will explore several guiding principles for achieving balance, this is the most important takeaway: don't equate your business with your life. Entrepreneurs often fall into this trap. After all, beyond the enormous amount of time and energy you've devoted to the business, it's something you built. It feels personal.

Conventional work-life balance with rules such as "weekends are for family" or "after six p.m. I shut off my phone" will never work for someone running a growing business. But although an entrepreneur's work life and personal life do intersect repeatedly, they are not the same thing. Your value as a person is independent from the business value you create and from your company's successes and failures.

At this point, you may be thinking that all this personal stuff sounds too woo-woo and new-age-y. After all, you're reading this book to get serious about making your company bigger and better. But consider this: if you focused your attention on just one part of your business and neglected the others, how well do you think it would do? That approach would prevent it from operating at full potential and would eventually run it into the ground. The same is true of your life. Though the business world often glorifies a hustle-and-grind culture, it is not a path to sustainable growth. It is a path to burnout.

The pursuit of a balanced life will always be a work in progress. Balance is not something you find one day and never have to think about again. Rather, it's like a garden; it needs constant care, and sometimes the weeds take over. This is why you need to experiment with habits, routines, and guiding principles to find those that fit your life best. With that in mind, let's examine some approaches that have helped other successful entrepreneurs seek balance.

The Five Balls of Life—Coca-Cola CEO Emphasizes the Importance of Personal: In a 1996 Georgia Tech commencement address that ultimately went viral, former Coca-Cola CEO Brian Dyson invites us to imagine life as a game in which we are juggling five balls in the air: "You name them work, family, health, friends and spirit. And you're keeping all of these in the air. You will soon understand that work is a rubber ball. If you drop it, it will bounce back. But the other four balls—family, health, friends and spirit—are made of glass. If you drop one of these, they will be irrevocably scuffed, marked, nicked, damaged or even shattered. They will never be the same. You must understand that and strive for balance in your life."

Protect Your Physical Health

The quality of your sleep, diet, and exercise all affect your performance as the leader of your growing organization. Obvious, right? Here's the problem: entrepreneurs frequently overlook the obvious and neglect the role of their physical health. Does this sound familiar? If you're like most people who work hard to grow their business, many aspects of your physical health are at the bottom of a long to-do list.

Instead of falling into that trap, begin today to make your physical health a bigger priority. To get you started on that path, here are two areas for improvement that are often underappreciated but that thriving entrepreneurs need to build into their schedules.

Get More Rest

We all know sleep is important, and yet we are so willing to sacrifice it on the altar of ambition and major goals. That's because we fool ourselves into believing that we'll achieve even more if we cut back on sleep. Suddenly we've added more waking hours to our day, and we can cross so much more off our to-do lists!

Here's what many entrepreneurs don't realize (until it's too late): when they cut back on sleep, they're slowly sabotaging their health, as well as the quality of their work and decisions.

Be regular and orderly in your life, so that you may be violent and original in your work.

— GUSTAVE FLAUBERT

Entrepreneurs are constantly thinking of ways to grow their business, but their ability to innovate decreases as their fatigue level increases. Studies have shown that a good night's sleep improves problem-solving abilities. More sleep allows you to be more productive, while sleep deprivation can make you think as clearly as a drunk person. I'm not kidding. Research indicates that if you sleep only four or five hours a night for a week, you will have impairment similar to a blood alcohol level of 0.1%. This hinders your ability to think rationally and analytically. And like a drunk who doesn't think he's slurring his words, you probably won't recognize how lack of sleep has muddled your thinking.

Personal mantras like "You snooze, you lose" and "I'll sleep when I'm dead" are losing their appeal as more successful entrepreneurs speak out about the value of sleep. Leo Widrich, cofounder of the social media management platform Buffer, has said that he sleeps about seven and a half to eight hours each night. His company, which launched in 2010, reached $21 million in revenue in 2020. Another entrepreneur who makes rest a top priority is author and podcast host Tim Ferriss, who has said he functions best, mentally and physically, when he gets a total of nine hours of sleep each day. That includes seven and a half hours of sleep at night and, whenever possible, a ninety-minute afternoon nap. In an *Entrepreneur* interview, Ferriss made it clear that he doesn't view sleep deprivation as an entrepreneurial badge of honor: "Generally speaking, if you feel like you have to cut down on sleep to get done what you need to get done, it's not that you don't have the time; you don't have clear enough priorities."

Get Outside

Research suggests that spending time outdoors has a host of benefits. It promotes relaxation as well as problem-solving and creativity. Even if it's just for five or ten minutes per day, exposure to nature creates a sense of well-being. You'll experience a decrease in levels of cortisol (known as the "stress hormone") and an increase in dopamine (known as the "happy hormone"). If you're able to combine outdoor time with regular exercise, all the better; although all forms of exercise will improve your health, outdoor exercise has particular benefits.

You can also use your time outdoors as a meditative practice. The Japanese even have a term for it: *shinrin-yoku*, or "forest bathing." This practice was developed in the 1980s specifically to counter tech burnout and has become increasingly popular in the West in the decades since. There are now certified forest bathing guides, but at its essence it involves completely immersing yourself in a natural setting and fully exploring it using all your senses. It might sound strange, but researchers have studied it a number of times and have consistently found it to offer health benefits.

If you don't have mobility issues, walking outside is an excellent daily health habit. And although a walk through a forest or other natural area is ideal, it's not always convenient. Fortunately, a walk through a park or a little bit of gardening can have similar benefits. That was the finding of a study with more than 1,200 participants, which also showed that the biggest improvements in self-esteem and mood came in the first five minutes of exposure to nature. Keep that in mind if you associate a walk outside with a major time commitment.

Because you spend so many hours each day immersed in the challenges of your business, and most likely gazing at various screens, stepping outside can help you step outside of your head. Your world can shrink when you're too focused on business challenges, and being outside helps you shift your perspective. It forces you to take a break from staring at your problems under a microscope. Instead, you can lift up your head, literally and metaphorically, and appreciate the wider world.

Protect Your Mental Health

> *You're imperfect, and you're wired for struggle, but you are worthy of love and belonging.*
>
> — BRENÉ BROWN

Here's an idea mentioned at the start of this chapter, and one that bears repeating due to its outsized impact on entrepreneurs' mental well-being: although your work life and personal life are connected, they are two different things. Your value as a person is independent from the business value you create and your company's successes and failures.

If you are experiencing anxiety and depression, you're not alone. And if you're not experiencing it now, chances are you will at some point while your business grows. Entrepreneurship has never been easy, but it's even more complex and stressful in the twenty-first century, as rapid changes in technology and globalization affect so many industries. It's no surprise that, compared to people who don't start a business, entrepreneurs are 30 percent more likely to experience depression.

Our mental health affects the quality of our physical health (and vice versa). Case in point: when we experience mental anguish, it can sabotage our sleep. Rand Fishkin, founder and former CEO of software company Moz, describes this problem—and his struggles with depression—in his memoir *Lost and Founder*. See if his description of "the loop" in his head feels familiar:

> *I remember weeks on end where I was the most tired, worn-out, poorly functioning version of myself I'd ever been, barely able to keep my eyes open during meetings ... But when I'd climb into bed, 'the loop' would begin— an awful circle of thoughts fixated on how much I'd messed up and how it could never be fixed, and all the opportunities and wonderful things I and all the people around me would miss out on as a result.*

The good news is, you can take steps to stop the loop and other thought patterns that sabotage your mental health (and your health in general). If you remember nothing else from this chapter, remember this: your company's worth will fluctuate, but that does not change your fundamental worth as a person. Let's explore some ways to help maintain that perspective.

Make an Appointment with a Therapist

Running a company can be an isolating endeavor. It's lonely when you feel everything is riding on your choices and actions. Many entrepreneurs have found that therapy is an effective way to combat this feeling and maintain mental health. That includes Rand Fishkin, the founder mentioned above who built Moz into a $45 million software company. It took years for him to acknowledge he was depressed. After he did, he started seeing a therapist, a decision that played a critical role in helping to restore his mental health.

Anand Kulkarni, CEO of startup Crowdbotics, sought a therapist when his business was growing rapidly. As Kulkarni told *Inc.* magazine, "The kind of problems you face when you're running a business aren't always things you can productively unburden on your co-founders when they may be having the exact same problems. Your employees are looking to you as a leader to solve their problems, so you don't always want to share the company's problems with them. At some point, your friends and significant others get tired of listening to the same problems over and over again." Kulkarni felt one benefit immediately after seeking therapy: "Being unburdened by just having someone to tell the things that were concerning me."

Find a Community of Other Founders/CEOs

Belonging to a group of other founders and CEOs is extremely useful for sharing leadership strategies and tactics, but these groups are critical for another reason. They allow you to share your struggles with people who have similar challenges, and they provide a constant reminder that you're not the only one grappling with acute growing pains. These group interactions can occur online or in person. What's most important is to find a group you trust and can interact with regularly. Added bonus: you will likely discover ways to support other leaders in the group, and that in itself will increase feelings of well-being.

There are countless groups, communities, masterminds, etc., out there for business owners. They are often touted as necessary for accountability and success, but they can also boost your mental stability by giving you access to people who are going or have gone through the same things you have. It can be helpful to have people like that as a sounding board, but be careful. Some of these groups are full of tech bros who just want to brag about their successes. If all the posts on their Facebook page are about how they're "killing it," that group may not be the best use of your time or money. Groups like the Entrepreneurs' Organization (EO)

act much more like a support group than a place to crow about how awesome they are. Per their website, "We help entrepreneurs achieve their full potential through the power of life-enhancing connections, shared experiences and collaborative learning."

It is much easier to find entrepreneurial affinity groups in some communities than in others. Start by asking entrepreneurs you respect if there are any groups they recommend. Online, search Facebook, LinkedIn, or Reddit and ask for appropriate groups or subreddits, and ask members in your area for suggestions.

Ask Friends and Family to Help You Watch for Signs of Depression

You're probably familiar with many of the symptoms of depression, such as major fluctuations in sleep, weight, appetite, or energy; significant loss of interest in things you used to enjoy doing; and increased feelings of worthlessness. The problem is, depressed people are often not the best observers of their own behavior. That's why it's important to enlist the help of friends and family members, who can watch for early warning signals that an overworked founder might miss. This also gives your loved ones the green light to talk about a potentially sensitive topic. They might be reluctant to tell you they're observing signs of depression unless you encourage them to do so in advance.

Cultivate Stronger Relationships

There's a pragmatic reason to protect your relationships with friends and family: you will need their support to endure the turmoil of entrepreneurship. One entrepreneur who has observed this repeatedly is Nicole Moore, a wellness center founder and licensed marriage and family therapist. Moore has experienced the stabilizing force of relationships in her own career, as well as with the entrepreneurs she counsels. "Entrepreneurs give so much and create so much value in the world, but I noticed that there was often a big gap in their interpersonal lives as they focused on work to the exclusion of rich and deep personal connections," Moore said in an interview with Thrive Global. That lack of positive emotional connection puts entrepreneurs' well-being at risk. When a company crisis hits, they're more likely to fall into isolation, stagnation, and even depression. Strong relationships provide stability and help entrepreneurs stay grounded. As Moore observed, "If you have a crazy day at work but you have a friend to call and let off some steam with, or a supportive spouse, it can make all the difference in feeling like you're not actually out on a limb all alone."

Many entrepreneurs have discovered that "work-life balance" isn't a useful way to think about personal relationships, because it creates unrealistic expectations about "doing it all." Angie Hicks, cofounder of Angie's List (now called Angi), is one of those entrepreneurs. She rejects the notion of work-life balance. Instead, she believes in work-life choice. As Hicks told *Entrepreneur* magazine, "No one is superhuman, you can't do everything. It's about making the right choices for you at the right time. I made a commitment a long time ago, I'm at home for dinner with my family. We may not have good food, we might be having carryout, but it's important that we're together. Somebody once told me, no matter how much your boss cares about you, no matter who they are, they are never going to ask you if you are at your kid's orchestra concert. You have to remember to make those choices and make sure those things are a priority for you."

As a founder of a growing company, you will be pulled in many directions, which could lead you to unwittingly neglect some of the relationships you value most. To avoid that mistake, consider these tips:

Block Off Time on Your Calendar for Family and Friends

Do you find yourself thinking, "Well, maybe I'll call (friend or family member) later today," before putting it off again when you run out of time? Do you regularly cancel plans because work gets in the way? Try scheduling blocks of time for phone calls or in-person visits with friends and family, and treat them as you would an important business meeting. Resist the temptation to reschedule because it's "just" a personal event and not business.

Schedule Reminders about Life Events

When you ask people about things that matter to them—like a vacation they just took or an upcoming medical procedure—it shows they matter to you. But because you have a lot of work issues on your mind, don't rely on your memory; put these dates on your calendar, whether the event is big or small; and don't limit it to the usual stuff like birthdays and anniversaries. If someone is going on a trip, record their departure and return dates, so you can wish them bon voyage and later ask about highlights from their vacation. It only takes a minute out of your day to send them a quick message about an upcoming event or to ask how they're feeling.

Have Better Conversations

Although it's wonderful to strengthen relationships by doing activities together, like playing sports or attending a concert, sometimes the most valuable shared experience you can have is a great conversation. But when your attention is consumed by work challenges, the quality of your personal conversations can quickly degrade. Here are some suggestions to address that problem:

» **Put your phone away.** For in-person conversations, *put your phone away* are four of the most important words in the English language. You can even turn it into a game: the first person to pull out their phone has to buy dinner, or a round of drinks, etc.

» **Notice your conversational bad habits, and address them.** Marissa King, professor of organizational behavior at the Yale School of Management, notes this common conversation misstep: when someone shares a personal problem, the other person often responds with a "me too" story—as in, "I'm sorry to hear about your medical issue, I had a similar problem when … " Although "me too" stories are often well-intentioned, they take the focus off the original speaker, who likely had more to say about their life challenge. King says that another well-intentioned misstep is the tendency to jump in too early with follow-up questions. Although follow-up questions can show we care, we often fool ourselves into thinking that we're being good listeners, when we've actually interrupted the other person's desire to share their full story. Instead, try being silent and waiting until you feel the speaker is ready to take a break.

» **"Want me to just listen—or do you want advice?"** This is a question King uses in her conversations. You can change the way you word it, but the idea is to let the other person know you're happy to stay in listening mode unless they ask for your opinion. This helps us resist the urge to fix things and instead focus on allowing the speaker to say more about how they feel.

To avoid making your loved ones feel alienated while you're deeply immersed in business growth, entrepreneur and *Shark Tank* investor Lori Greiner suggests finding opportunities for their involvement with your company. As she told *Entrepreneur,* "It's best to try to include them as much as you can, even if that means having them help you design or name an invention together. What you do as an entrepreneur, make it inclusive to the people you love. As busy as you are, they still need you."

When examining your relationships, look for the bad as well as the good. Some relationships build you up and make you feel happy and motivated. Others are toxic and seem to tear you down and derail your success. As it says in Proverbs 27:17, "As iron sharpens iron, so one person sharpens another." Make sure to find relationships that sharpen you rather than dull you.

Seek Mindfulness

Mindfulness has become a widespread buzzword. You've probably heard it described as "being in the moment," but that definition is a bit too vague to be useful. What does "being in the moment" look like in our daily lives, and why does mindfulness matter for entrepreneurs?

To greet the challenges of growing a business, you can't waste time and energy dwelling on past regrets or worrying about future unknowns. Instead, effective entrepreneurs focus on the present. It's difficult to listen to an employee, for example, if your attention is divided between them and worrying about a big presentation due the next day.

Mindfulness requires focused attention and the ability to quiet your mind. Another way to think about it is the difference between broadcasting and receiving. Since you are the leader of your business, your default mode is likely broadcasting: you make decisions, create plans, and share them. In broadcast mode, you're sending out signals. With mindfulness, you are in receiving mode. The idea is to pick up weak signals through the noise. We can hear the *words* someone is saying—a customer expressing their frustration, for instance. But if we aren't listening mindfully, we can miss their true meaning entirely and fail to understand what matters most.

Innovative opportunities do not come with the tempest but with the rustling of the breeze.

–PETER DRUCKER

As Hal Gregersen, MIT Leadership Center's former executive director, observes in his book *Questions Are the Answer*, "The basic idea is to take things that have been part of your life's backdrop and pull them to the forefront of your mind for a time … Being mindful means paying more attention to the things you don't normally notice, the things you take for granted, and the questions you stopped asking long ago. It is, in short, the opposite of being mindless."

Increase Mindfulness with Meditation

Although it's important to reflect on the past and plan for the future, it's easy to become mired in unproductive patterns like dwelling on mistakes and dreaming (or worrying) about the future. How do we avoid getting yanked forward and backward and instead stay grounded in the present? Meditation, which has been shown to lower blood pressure and boost creative thinking, is one method that has worked for many successful entrepreneurs. You'll read about more approaches later in this section.

At this point, you may be rolling your eyes if you've grown weary of people insisting that you try meditation. Meditation isn't the only way to cultivate mindfulness, and it might not be a good fit for you. But if you haven't explored it yet, consider that many entrepreneurs feel meditation helps to fine-tune these essential skills:

» **Learning to detect your invisible thought patterns**. As your business grows, it's critical to listen carefully to your customers, employees, and investors. Some entrepreneurs fail to recognize that it's also vital to listen to your own thoughts. We all have an inner monologue. Sometimes we hear it clearly, but much of the time it's constant background noise that goes unnoticed. When we try meditation—for example, just the act of focusing our attention on our breath—we often hear that ongoing monologue for the first time. It can take the form of rumination or harsh criticism or other unproductive patterns that drain our energy. We can recognize how it's holding us back. This matters, because we can't take steps to fix a problem if we're unaware it exists. Meditation also helps us notice how much our thoughts jump around; this is often referred to as the "monkey mind."

» **Building persistence with "begin again."** Those two words represent one of the most powerful lessons of meditation. When we try to focus our attention on our breath, we will likely achieve mindfulness for a nanosecond. Before we know it, we'll start thinking about what's for dinner or how we're going to address a work crisis. We'll notice our mind has wandered, and then we'll return to focusing on our breath, only to have the same distracted thinking occur again and again. Even if we meditate for just a few minutes, this mental tug-of-war can take place dozens of times. As prominent meditation instructor and author Sharon Salzberg explains, the most important moment in meditation is when you notice your mind has wandered. Then you must ask yourself to let go and start again. Salzberg notes that the "secret ingredient" for making this process work—the ability to begin again, over and over—is self-compassion. In that sense, meditation is an exercise in resilience and persistence, qualities that are vital for entrepreneurs who are constantly trying new ideas to grow their business. Many ideas will fail, but thriving entrepreneurs know how to set those failures aside and begin again.

Thoughts are things! This is a great truth … The power to think as you wish to think is the only power over which you have absolute control.

– NAPOLEON HILL

» **Choosing to respond, not react.** By helping you stay grounded in the present and aware of your previously hidden thought patterns, meditation trains you to have more control over your emotions. The goal is to avoid getting yanked around by "the malevolent puppeteer of our ego"—a vivid, relatable descriptor from news anchor and mindfulness aficionado Dan Harris (he hosts a podcast called 10% Happier and wrote a best-selling book with the same name). This doesn't mean meditation will keep you from losing your temper ever again. But it does increase your ability to control your thoughts and emotions, rather than being controlled by them and reacting in a way you will later regret. When first responders are asked about the impressive, cool-headed ways they handle emergencies, they often reply, "My training kicks in." Meditation can have a similar effect. Think of it as training for your everyday interactions. When we meditate, we practice viewing the world without having a knee-jerk emotional reaction to it. The benefits of this approach are summed up nicely in the following quote, often attributed to Viktor Frankl: "Between the stimulus and the response there is a space, and in this space lies our power and our freedom."

The R.A.I.N. Technique for Mindfulness: This acronym, first created about twenty years ago by Michele McDonald, is a useful tool for remembering four steps of mindfulness, particularly if you're feeling overwhelmed (figure 3).

» **Recognize** what's going on. Note how you're feeling, whether it's anxious, angry, jealous, etc.

» **Allow** your experience to exist, just as it is. Don't start judging your emotions ("I shouldn't feel this way," "I hate feeling this way") or telling yourself a story about those feelings.

» **Investigate with curiosity.** See how your emotions inhabit your body. Are you experiencing tightness in certain muscles, heat in your face, etc.?

» **Non-identification** — Recognize that you are not your emotions. You may feel envy, anger, frustration, or shame. Those feelings do not reflect your identity. Although the emotion you're feeling may be extremely uncomfortable, remember that it's simply a phase you will pass through. It's taking place in this moment, and it's temporary.

fig. 3

RECOGNIZE	**ALLOW**	**INVESTIGATE**	**NON-IDENTIFICATION**
what's going on.	the experience to be there, just as it is.	with kindness.	lets painful thoughts come and go.

How Meditation Affects the Lives of Three Prominent Entrepreneurs

1. **Oprah Winfrey** wrote a blog post about the power of meditation and how it has shaped her life. Here's an excerpt:

   The voice in your head is so constant: I need to do _____. I am _____.

   It's easy to mistake that voice for you until you've been "still" enough to know otherwise.

   It's a sad and confusing predicament to be lost in the world—I know, because I've experienced time and again what that disconnectedness feels like. You start believing what the world has to say about you, whether it's the world in your head or the world outside. That outside world is constantly trying to convince you you're not enough. But you don't have to take the bait. Meditation, in whatever form you choose, helps you resist.

What I know for sure, and have had to learn through much trial and error: The voice that truly matters is the silent voice of awareness, consciousness, aliveness.

2. **Ray Dalio,** founder of Bridgewater Associates, the largest hedge fund in the world, has done transcendental meditation for more than forty years. If Dalio experiences anxiety that he can't shake, he uses meditation to achieve calmness. He says meditation allows him to deal with anxiety like "a ninja in a fight." Although he doesn't meditate every day, he does do it on the majority of days, twice a day. Dalio notes that frequency matters: "It's like yoga. If you practice it, it becomes easier to get into."

3. **Marc Benioff,** CEO and founder of Salesforce, meditates daily. His goal: quiet the noise in his mind, so that stillness will allow him to detect subtle changes in the world around him. He begins each meditation session with an emphasis on gratitude and notes the things he's thankful for, then focuses on forgiveness. He also mentally notes things that are bothering him, along with his disappointments and anxieties, and then sets them aside. The point is to clear his mind of the negative clutter that would otherwise consume his thoughts. This creates space for new insights, so he can perceive things that would normally be lost in the noise of worry and problem-solving.

Write It Down

It's hard to focus attention in a mindful way if you're cluttering your memory bank unnecessarily with mental notes about your latest inspiration. As you generate new ideas for goals, remember to store them someplace other than your head. That advice comes from an entrepreneur who has a bit of experience with business growth: Sir Richard Branson, founder of the Virgin Group, which now comprises more than four hundred companies. In a 2006 interview, Branson said the most important item he travels with is a notebook in his back pocket. "I could never have built the Virgin Group into the size it is without those few bits of paper."

Branson reinforced his dedication to this habit in a company blog post. "I go through dozens of notebooks every year and write down everything that occurs to me each day," he said. "An idea not written down is an idea lost. When inspiration calls, you've got to capture it."

DETOUR

Empty Your Anxieties onto the Page: In addition to Sir Richard Branson's advice for capturing inspiration, there's another way entrepreneurs can benefit from writing down their thoughts. As their lives become increasingly complex, it provides a way to unload anxieties and maintain a healthy perspective during times of enormous stress.

This was the case for Guy Raz, host of the radio show *How I Built This*. Raz has interviewed hundreds of entrepreneurs and has an entrepreneurial spirit himself—at one point in his career he was producing three shows, with two more in the works. During that time, he also experienced weeks of sleepless nights. He worried about everything. As he describes in his book *How I Built This*, Raz felt as if "the world was collapsing" around him.

Relief finally came during yet another sleepless night, when his wife took out a notebook and asked him to share what was on his mind. "I poured out everything in my head, and she wrote every word of it down," says Raz. "The act of emptying my anxieties onto the page was itself a therapeutic act that helped me get back to sleep, but the real salvation came three months later when Hannah pulled out the notebook and read my list of worries back to me. Not a single item on that list was relevant any longer! Not one of my worries had materialized in any meaningful way."

Remember earlier in this chapter, when founder and CEO Rand Fishkin described the loop in his head that kept him awake, even when he was exhausted? Guy Raz was able to interrupt his own "loop" by unloading his worst fears on the page. That experience stuck with him. In his book, Raz has a recommendation for entrepreneurs who experience emotional anguish like his, which he calls "a period of crippling anxiety and despair that no one could possibly understand what you're dealing with, that everything is riding on the decisions you make, that it's all up to you."

This is his advice: "When that happens, I want you to pull out a notebook and write those worries down. I want you to trap them on the page, so that you can look at them the next day, the next week, the next month, the next year, and realize that while every challenge and crisis you face in the pursuit of your idea feels like it could be the end of it all, it's not."

START JOURNALING: Journaling is one of the best techniques there is to keep yourself present. It's easy, free, and there are no rules. Just pick a time—first thing in the morning or when you're winding down after work are great options—and your favorite writing medium. Whether you're using pen and paper or one of the many available journaling apps, make sure you commit to writing each day. Write about whatever is on your mind. It can be things that are making you anxious, ideas for future projects, or just how you're feeling. There's no set length. It can be a few sentences or a page or more, depending on the day, how you feel, and how much time you have. Volume isn't important, but frequency is—so do it every day. The act of writing clears your mind and allows you to see things in perspective. Try it!

Develop Time-Management Routines

If you don't pay appropriate attention to what has your attention, it will take more of your attention than it deserves.

– DAVID ALLEN

It's critical to develop effective processes and systems to help your business grow (a topic we will cover in detail in chapter 7). You need to make a similar evaluation when figuring out the best way to structure your day, beyond how you get work done. There are many time management systems you can try, and it will likely take some experimentation to find a good fit. To get you started, here are two popular systems:

The Value of "Important" vs. "Not Urgent"

Some entrepreneurs pride themselves on plowing through a long to-do list each day. But checking off list items isn't the same thing as progress. These entrepreneurs mistakenly equate "busy" with "productive," and soon find themselves overextended. They're running as fast as they can but feel like they're not getting closer to their goals. Why does this happen? Usually, the problem stems from spending too much time doing things and not nearly enough time questioning whether they're the right things.

As an astute observer of human behavior, Stephen Covey saw that most people lack an effective approach to priorities. In his book *The 7 Habits of Highly Effective People*, Covey suggests we basically spend our time in one of four ways. As you can see in his time management matrix in figure 4, the factors that define our daily activities are "urgent (or not)" and "important (or not)":

fig. 4

TIME MANAGEMENT MATRIX

	URGENT	NOT URGENT
IMPORTANT	**I** **ACTIVITIES:** • Crises • Pressing problems • Deadline-driven projects	**II** **ACTIVITIES:** • Prevention activities • Relationship building • Recognizing new opportunities • Planning, recreation
NOT IMPORTANT	**III** **ACTIVITIES:** • Interruptions, some calls • Some emails, some reports • Some meetings • Proximate, pressing matters • Popular activities	**IV** **ACTIVITIES:** • Trivia, busywork • Some emails • Some phone calls • Time wasters • Pleasant activities

Source: *The 7 Habits of Highly Effective People*

As Covey notes, effective people think preventively. They minimize problems, which allows them to focus on opportunities. These people spend most of their time in quadrant II, and the result is:

» Vision and perspective
» Balance
» Discipline
» Control
» Fewer crises

Covey's time management matrix underscores a common pitfall for creating priorities: people typically spend most of their time on urgent stuff but not important stuff. That's a problem, because "important" and "not urgent" represent the heart of effective personal management. This quadrant includes things like building relationships, long-range planning, exercising, preventive maintenance, and preparation—as Covey says, "all those things we know we need to do, but somehow seldom get around to doing, because they aren't urgent."

MY TAKE

I was introduced to Covey's work during my first supervisory training program at Charles Schwab & Co. more years ago than I care to admit. All of the seven habits are useful, but a few really stood out to me and became guiding principles of my life. The time management matrix is one of them, and it gets more and more useful for founders and other businesspeople as our attention gets crowded with more and more distractions. As I write this, I am on a browser with more than fifty tabs open. I have thirty-four messages in Microsoft Teams that I have not read, as well as a note on Facebook Messenger. I have ten other apps open. My inbox contains 384 notes. It would be easy for me to start looking at these things. Some of them might even be urgent. But I am writing a book that doesn't need to be finished today, tomorrow, or by the end of the week. The book (and writing in general) is very important to me, but because it is not urgent I can, hopefully, do a good job with it.

Getting Things Done

Also known as *GTD*, Getting Things Done® is a productivity system developed by David Allen. He wrote a book about it with the same title. Allen's method includes five basic steps, as described on his GTD site:

» **Step 1 — Capture**: Write, record, or gather any and everything that has your attention into a collection tool.

» **Step 2 — Clarify**: Is it actionable? If so, decide the next action and project (if more than one action is required). If not, decide if it is trash, reference, or something to put on hold.

» **Step 3 — Organize**: Park reminders of your categorized content in appropriate places.

» **Step 4 — Reflect**: Update and review all pertinent system contents to regain control and focus.

» **Step 5 — Engage**: Use your trusted system to make action decisions with confidence and clarity.

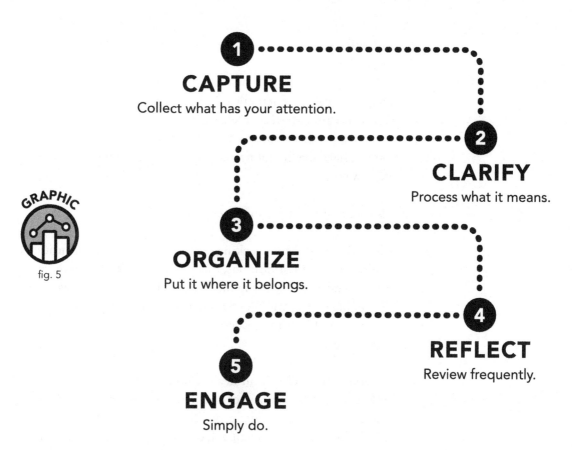

1 CAPTURE
Collect what has your attention.

2 CLARIFY
Process what it means.

3 ORGANIZE
Put it where it belongs.

4 REFLECT
Review frequently.

5 ENGAGE
Simply do.

GRAPHIC

fig. 5

Use Time-Management Fundamentals to Create Your Own System

Stephen Covey's matrix and David Allen's GTD represent two essential concepts of effective time management. You need a way to sort out what's important and a method to track and encourage progress on the stuff that matters. A wide array of time-management systems will promise to make you a productivity wizard. Whatever method you choose, make sure it's grounded in the two basic ideas I just mentioned: decide what's important, and design habits that keep your important tasks moving along.

One successful entrepreneur who's done this is Mathilde Collin, CEO and cofounder of Front, a company that has raised more than $138 million in venture capital funding. With more than two hundred employees at her company, Collin has plenty of responsibilities to juggle. She also has a reputation for having a disciplined approach to business, including her work calendar. In an interview, Collin describes the time management tricks that have helped her most.

To ensure that you stay focused on the right stuff, she recommends asking these questions:

» Does your calendar actually reflect the priorities you're orienting your team around every single week?
» Is there an activity you aren't spending enough time on?
» Do you have the discipline and the built-in time to disconnect and step away?

She also shares these time-management tips:

» **Limit the time spent checking email and opt out of notifications.** Collins has quit notifications, except for her calendar reminders. She also takes a very disciplined approach to email. "I have two 30-minute dedicated slots in my calendar every day to go through my inbox and I try my hardest to not look at it outside of those times," she says.

» **Reserve time to clear your head.** Collin has experimented with various ways to optimize her calendar and says the most valuable change she's made is adding something she calls "stepping back time." Says Collin, "It's half a day each week where I allow myself only a notebook—no computer—to really concentrate on a key issue. I tinkered with this quite a bit, splitting it up into an hour a few times a week, for example, but I found that made it harder to focus."

» **Analyze the way you use your time—and learn from it.** "At the end of every single week I have my [assistant] send me an analysis of my calendar," says Collin. "It's split by the type of activity, such as interviewing, selling, managing and so on. This is how I flagged that I need to step up my hiring efforts. I also look at it on a team level to see if I'm spending too much time with any one group and neglecting another."

LIFE IS A GRAND EXPERIMENT. Experimentation is a key part of business growth. The same holds true for your personal habits and routines. As you try some of the approaches in this chapter for the first time, they may feel unnatural. To overcome that initial resistance, adopt a spirit of experimentation. See if applying a new habit changes the way you feel throughout the day. Collect data on it for at least a week, then evaluate whether that method is a good fit for you. And keep this in mind: when you're dissatisfied with the quality of your daily experience, the biggest mistake you can make is not to experiment with new ideas. Always remember this quote (source unknown but often misattributed to Albert Einstein): "The definition of insanity is doing the same thing over and over again and expecting different results."

Chapter Recap

» If you want to grow a healthy business, you need to start by protecting your own health. Entrepreneurs who don't pay close attention to their physical and mental health are putting themselves at high risk for burnout. And that puts the company at risk too.

» A lack of sleep is not a badge of honor. If you think you don't have time to sleep, you need to reevaluate your to-do list. Some entrepreneurs think they can still be productive with just a few hours of rest, but they don't realize they've hit a point of diminishing returns. Lack of sleep impairs your ability to think clearly and make choices that help your company grow.

» Although entrepreneurship can be incredibly rewarding, the stress and long hours often take a toll on mental health. Founders are more likely to experience depression than people who don't start a business. If it happens to you, don't isolate yourself and try to "push through the pain." Instead, seek support, whether it's from a therapist, a community of other entrepreneurs, or family and friends.

» With mindfulness, you cultivate a focused attention that allows you to not only detect subtle cues in communication but also become more aware of your own thought patterns and how they shape your behavior. When you learn to quiet your mind, you improve your ability to pick up weak (but meaningful) signals in the noise.

| 3 |
Laughing

Chapter Overview
» Using Improv for Training and Communication
» Sources and Uses of Humor in the Workplace

A sense of humor is part of the art of leadership, of getting along with people, of getting things done.

– PRESIDENT DWIGHT EISENHOWER

When people talk about work and play, they often assume those two things shouldn't overlap. Playing, after all, is what you do when you're *not* at work, right? But while it may sound counterintuitive, a playful, humor-filled approach to business will help you get serious about growth.

Plenty of studies emphasize the overall health and wellness benefits of a sense of humor, such as laughter's ability to relieve stress. But there are also business-specific reasons for entrepreneurs to embrace playfulness and humor: these qualities boost creativity and foster the right mindset to solve common challenges in communication, leadership, and team building.

As you'll see in some of the examples throughout this chapter, self-deprecating humor is the safest option for business leaders. This does not mean you'll be developing an office stand-up routine. This chapter will not make you the funniest person in the room—which is not a useful goal to have in the workplace, where some attempts at humor can be risky. Unless you know your audience well, jokes can backfire. Instead, consider this advice from Peter McGraw, a behavioral economist who's studied how lessons of comedy can apply to business: "I don't want you to be funny. I want you to think funny."

What does "think funny" mean? It's not far off from the intention behind Apple's famous slogan, *Think different*. We can take lessons from comedy to help us question and rethink our deeply ingrained patterns of thought and behavior. This matters because, as your company grows, you will face increasingly complex problems. When you're stuck, new perspectives can help you get unstuck. If we "think funny," we can also uncover ways to strengthen fundamental elements of business success. That includes how effective listening informs better communication and collaboration. As you'll see, a playful mindset is a tool used by "serious" businesspeople, including insurance companies and successful investors. Let's explore how it can help you face the complexities that accompany a growing business.

You don't want the wrong joke to derail your reputation and business. If you really want to include one in a speech, email, or social media post, consider running it by trusted friends or family members who can accurately assess whether your humor might be offensive. The point is to get perspectives beyond your own. This means your humor sounding board should include people who are significantly different from you in aspects like race, gender, and sexual orientation.

Improve Your Leadership with Improv

In *improvisational comedy*, or improv, the performers don't have scripts. Instead, they use audience suggestions to create scenes and dialogue. The performers' choices are guided by the fundamental rules of improv, which we'll examine here. Chicago's The Second City is famous for being a groundbreaking home of improv and a training ground for comedians like Bill Murray, Tina Fey, Keegan-Michael Key, and Gilda Radner. But in addition to training aspiring performers, The Second City has taught thousands of executives to produce better work, by working better together.

The corporate training division is called Second City Works. With more than $18 million in revenue, its clients have included State Farm, P&G, and Major League Baseball. Kelly Leonard, executive director of learning and applied improvisation at Second City Works, explains that companies ask for their help because improv comedy relies on "soft skills writ large." The same elements that drive growing businesses—effective collaboration, communication, leadership, and adaptability—are also necessary for improv performers.

Improv comedy revolves around teamwork. As your company expands and adds more employees, teamwork can become a bigger challenge. Second City's Leonard knows this well. When asked about the main reason companies contact Second City Works for training, Leonard sums it up in two words: dysfunctional teams. These teams often need help with listening and collaborating.

Listening to Your Teammates

To overcome obstacles to growth, you'll need to foster a sense of unity among employees. This means maximizing collaboration and minimizing clashes, by breaking the toxic habits that become ingrained in many workplaces. A major element of improv, the need for intensely focused listening, is at the core of the problem for many dysfunctional teams. "What we're doing is having people unlearn the bad practices they've gotten themselves into," says Leonard. "Every business problem is a communication problem. And human beings are really bad communicators—like, stunningly bad communicators."

Here's something that distinguishes great leaders: they are great listeners. But this can be particularly challenging at a growing company, because your attention gets pulled in many new directions. And it's a universal truth that most of us are pretty bad listeners most of the time. Listening is often shorthand for *I'm thinking about what I'm going to say next and how my words can make me look good or prove I'm right*. We can't listen fully and absorb critical information if we're thinking two steps ahead or pondering our to-do list.

Thinking back to chapter 2, you'll recall that to achieve the benefits of mindfulness, you must focus on the present moment. The same concept applies to effective listening. If your attention is divided when someone is sharing their thoughts, you will miss opportunities to learn what's most important to them.

String of Pearls — An Improv Exercise for Better Listening: This is one of many listening-focused activities that The Second City uses to train its improv performers and its corporate clients. The description below comes from the Second City book *Yes, And: How Improvisation Reverses "No, But" Thinking and Improves Creativity and Collaboration*.

» **Exercise:** Have the group stand in a line facing forward. The person at one end of the line is given the first sentence of a story, and the person at the other end, the last sentence. The first person repeats the given opening sentence, and then, going down the line, each participant improvises a succeeding line of dialogue until the last, who says the line he was given—the point being to make the progression from first to last as logical as possible.

> » **Point of Focus:** Listening. This is an excellent exercise to help people listen more closely and think harder about what others are saying before speaking themselves.

Making Conversations More Productive with "Yes, And"

In addition to lazy listening, Second City Works' Kelly Leonard says a harmful communication habit is the tendency to include "no" in our responses, often because we want to maintain control in conversations. This instinct can become even stronger if things start to feel a little out of control in your growing business.

In improv, performers are trained to avoid saying no when one of their teammates makes a statement. Here's why: during an improv performance, if someone says, "I can't believe you're riding a hippopotamus," and a performer responds with, "No, I'm riding a horse," it drains the momentum from the scene.

The same holds true with business conversations, because "no" tends to create tension and drain collaborative energy. A more productive approach can be found in a core improv principle: instead of saying no, reply with "Yes, and … " This phrase encourages collaboration by creating a connection between the other person's perspective and yours. With "yes, and," you don't blindly accept an idea. You build on it.

Whether it's the improv stage or the workplace, "no" stops the flow of ideas, while "yes, and" sparks creativity. Holly Mandel has observed this dynamic firsthand for more than twenty years. After performing and teaching at The Groundlings, an L.A. improv and sketch comedy troupe, she went on to found iMergence, which provides corporate education based on improv principles.

As Mandel introduces improv fundamentals to clients—a list that includes Netflix, P&G, Adidas, and IBM—she watches those concepts transform collaboration skills.

"When I lead these sessions, typically people start out scared to make mistakes," Mandel told *Slate* in an interview. "They self-edit. Maybe there's a hierarchy in the office where some people never get heard and some people squelch the conversation. Maybe the boss is scared to look stupid, so he acts too cool for the exercise." But as the workshops progress, she sees camaraderie build between coworkers. "They start to hear each other," Mandel said. "They gain the confidence to speak freely and take risks."

You may be tempted to use a phrase that looks like a compromise: "Yes, but." That's a mistake, because it won't accomplish the same goals as "Yes, and." When you respond with "Yes, but," you push the other person's ideas away. It starts out positive but ends on a negative and makes people feel defensive.

So much of improv relies on of being receptive to ideas, and that concept is essential for growing a business. As your company gets bigger, you may be exposed to more criticism from employees or customers. In response, your mind can turn into a clenched fist, pounding on the table and insisting it's right. Instead, try to make your mind like an open hand, receptive to new perspectives and ready to grab hold of opportunities as they arise.

The "Yes, and" technique may feel uncomfortable at first. But before you reject it outright, try this experiment. Spend five minutes having a conversation using "Yes, and," and have another five-minute conversation employing "Yes, but." See if that shift in style makes the conversations feel different or have different outcomes.

Years before he served as CEO of Twitter, Dick Costolo worked in comedy. He trained at The Second City in Chicago and performed onstage with comedians who would later move on to *Saturday Night Live*. Although Costolo's career took a different path, he continued to use improv comedy lessons for more effective leadership. That included a mindset focused on listening and accepting. "If you start improvising that you're washing the dishes, and a minute later I walk over and turn on the TV where the sink is supposed to be, the audience feels the scene's been ruined," Costolo told *Bloomberg News*. With that in mind, Costolo urged his managers to listen and respond with openness to their employees' perceptions. "When they deny there's an issue and reflexively defend the status quo, it creates misery for people."

Shifting Out of Autopilot with Stand-Up

Unlike improv performers, stand-up comedians work alone on stage (although self-aware comedians know they need a behind-the-scenes team of friends, family, and mentors to support them and help them grow). Despite this different performance environment, they share the same foundation for success. As with improv, the best comedians have a refined ability to see the world in unexpected ways. Great entrepreneurs have this skill as well.

One exercise for cultivating that mindset is to observe how the best comedians construct their jokes. Although "disruption" is a business term that's been overused in recent years, it does represent the engine that powers many jokes. Talented comedians excel at disrupting our predictable thought patterns, challenging our assumptions about the world and compelling us to consider new perspectives. Growth-minded entrepreneurs do this regularly in their companies as they challenge assumptions about industries and consumer behaviors. With that in mind, let's examine some of the ways comedians shift our thought patterns out of autopilot.

Take a Detour with Unexpected Connections

To make us laugh, comedians subvert our expectations. They recognize when we have assumptions about what they'll say next—and then they take the joke in a new direction. They disrupt our underlying thought patterns and make us pay attention by playing with our expectations.

As an example of how this works, consider this joke by comedian Anthony Jeselnik about his strict parents:

My mom and dad once made me smoke an entire pack of cigarettes. An entire pack of cigarettes in one sitting. Just to teach me an important lesson about brand loyalty.

Jeselnik is a master of misdirection. He knows that our brains expect the lesson to be connected to aversion therapy—in this case, making someone smoke a lot of cigarettes at once so they feel sick and never want another one. He uses our predictable thought patterns to his advantage and jolts our awareness by taking us down an unexpected path.

To make those unexpected connections, you need a combination of creativity and rigorous analytical thinking. Here's what Jeselnik shared about his process in an interview: "I think of myself almost like a miner. I'm mining for gold. I'm going to search this area of 'getting caught smoking cigarettes.' How many different ways can that go?" He also observes that in some of the best jokes, the punchline gets as far away from the premise as possible while still maintaining a connection. As Jeselnik says, it's like trying to increase the distance between two live wires and still get a spark.

Q: Are there ways you can play with the deeply ingrained thought patterns of your customers or employees? Not to shock them, but to delight them? What assumptions surrounding your company or industry can you upend?

Explore a Different Point of View

Humor can invite us to imagine distorted realities that defy the laws of physics. It can also open our minds to different interpretations of the physical realities we encounter every day. See how comedian Mitch Hedberg accomplished this with three of his jokes:

» *I like an escalator, man, because an escalator can never break. It can only become stairs.*

» *My friend asked me if I wanted a frozen banana, I said, 'No, but I may want a regular banana later … so, yeah.'*

» *I like to play blackjack. I'm not addicted to gambling. I'm addicted to sitting in a semicircle.*

Hedberg shows us new ways to view everyday objects and events from his creative point of view. This mental flexibility relates directly to problem-solving abilities. In their *Harvard Business Review* article, "Find Innovation Where You Least Expect It," authors Tony McCaffrey and Jim Pearson explain that entrepreneurs' creativity can be limited by a psychological bias called "functional fixedness." This occurs when people view objects only in terms of their traditional purposes. "When we see a common object, we automatically screen out awareness of features that are not important for its use," the article's authors note. "This is an efficient neurological tactic for everyday life, but it's the enemy of innovation."

As a result, business leaders can overlook solutions hiding in plain sight. One way to remove those blinders is to change our default mode for describing things. According to McCaffrey and Pearson, "When told that a candlewick is a string, for instance, almost everyone recognizes that it could be used to tie things together." One approach they recommend is describing things in terms of generic parts. For example, instead of "candlewick," or even "string," think "fibrous strands covered in wax." As the authors note, this avoids "unintentionally narrowing people's conception of it, opening them to more ideas for its uses."

This ability to look at ideas and objects in new ways is a major part of joke-writing. It helps comedians examine not only the perspectives of people but of inanimate objects as well. Jerry Seinfeld does this regularly, and his skydiving joke is one example:

The thing I wonder about in skydiving is why do they even bother with the helmets? You jump out of a plane 20,000 feet in the air and that chute doesn't open, I got news for you: The helmet is now wearing you for protection. Later on the helmet's talking to the other helmets going, "Boy, it's a good thing that he was there, or I would have hit the ground directly."

As silly as it might sound, the ability to imagine how a skydiving helmet might "feel" helps us develop a sense of empathy. As we'll discuss further in chapter 4, the starting point for empathy is the effort to understand people's needs and point of view. When you expand your mind to think about specific ways other people experience their daily lives, it can help you remember to put customers and employees at the center of your most important conversations. Of course, the process doesn't end there. Empathy means more than genuine concern for others' well-being; it requires that you act on that concern. In chapter 4, we'll discuss more about how empathy really means "compassion in action." But thinking like a comedian and exploring different points of view is an essential first step.

Think of the tools that professional comedians use to structure their jokes—exploring different points of view and delighting us by disrupting our predictable thought patterns—as power yoga for your imagination. You're not trying to be a better joke writer. Rather, you're looking for ways to train your mind for both strength and flexibility. If you can take your thoughts off autopilot, you pave the way for innovation.

Michael Dubin, founder of Dollar Shave Club (DSC), built his direct-to-consumer razor business from nothing into the second-biggest men's razor company in the world (behind Gillette) before selling it to Unilever for around $1 billion in early 2021. Dubin studied (you guessed it) improv at the Upright Citizens Brigade in New York City, but the explosive growth of his brand was fueled by his hilarious commercials that became viral videos. The first one has been viewed over 27 million times on YouTube and is full of outrageous misdirections and sight gags. (Go ahead, click on it. I guarantee you'll watch it multiple times.) But Dubin used those same tools for a serious business purpose. In an industry dominated by one brand that sold premium-priced razor blades via retail stores, DSC entered the market by selling low-priced blades directly to consumers via a subscription model. How's that for misdirection?

Opening Doors with Self-Deprecating Humor

When Elon Musk hosted *Saturday Night Live*, he used the opportunity to make fun of his monotone speaking voice. "Sometimes, after I say something, I have to say, 'I mean that,' so people really know that I mean it. That's because I don't always have a lot of intonational variation in how I speak. Which I'm told makes for great comedy," Musk said in his monologue. The joke got big laughs, but it represents more than just comedy-show fodder. When leaders take aim at their own flaws, it can convey emotional intelligence and help forge stronger relationships.

There's even research that shows leaders have a particular advantage if they know how to poke fun at themselves. As Stanford professors and coauthors Jennifer Aaker and Naomi Bagdonas note in their book *Humor, Seriously,* one study found that when leaders use self-deprecating humor, employees rate them higher in both trustworthiness and leadership ability. By highlighting flaws, self-deprecating humor makes leaders more human and more relatable. As a result, this helps them cultivate a quality that's highly prized by many companies: authenticity.

Q: If you have an open-door policy, think about how to use a playful mindset to become more approachable. How can you open the door wider with humor?

Laugh at Your Own Mistakes

Self-deprecating humor includes the ability to laugh when you slip on a metaphorical banana peel. But not every personal mistake is something we can (or should) laugh about immediately. You've probably heard of the humor formula "tragedy + time = comedy." Some disasters need breathing room before you can appreciate the funny parts.

As a general rule, humor can help us choose the way we view failures. We can shift our mindset and stop running away from our mistakes. Instead, we can seek ways to learn from them. But we won't achieve that without a workplace culture that embraces mistakes. By laughing at their own screw-ups, leaders can help foster a safe place for others to admit to errors.

One big proponent of this approach is Spanx founder and CEO Sara Blakely, who has this motto: "If you can laugh about it, you can learn from it." Blakely's ability to reframe her failure stems from one of her dad's dinner table traditions. During family meals, he regularly posed the question, "What did you fail at this week?" Every time Blakely shared her latest fail, her dad had the same response: a high-five accompanied by "Way to go!" As Blakely once told an audience, "If I didn't have something that I had failed at, he actually would be disappointed."

Her father gave her a lasting gift: the ability to retrain her thinking about failure. As Blakely explained, "Failure for me became about not trying, instead of the outcome."

Blakely has instilled her father's ethos into her own company. She puts it into practice at company-wide "oops meetings," where she encourages employees to use humor as they discuss their recent mistakes. To do this, she kicks off the meeting by sharing a recent failure of her own. She then cues up a song that reflects her mistake, starts dancing, and invites employees to join her. Once, after she told employees about her strategic error of staying in a product category too long, she invited them to dance along with her to "Mr. Roboto" (a fitting song that also outstays its welcome).

Blakely has summed up the benefits of oops meetings with the saying, "Better things happen when you're not paralyzed by fear."

Some leaders think they should focus on preventing mistakes. But the most effective leadership comes from understanding that mistakes will happen. The goal is to correct them as quickly as possible. As your company's leader, you set the tone for how errors are perceived. If your employees feel afraid to share, it will take you longer to discover and correct mistakes.

"Product Roast" Provides a Safe Way to Share Criticism: What if your sales kept rising and customers seemed happy, but your company got a bit complacent about product or service improvements? A few years ago, that was a real concern for Basecamp founder and CEO Jason Fried. Right before a big internal meeting, Fried was wishing he could jump-start the company's enthusiasm for new product features. While channel surfing one night, he ended up watching a comedy roast for Joan Rivers.

That led to an aha moment: what if Basecamp did a product roast and encouraged employees to let the insults fly, so they could speak openly about design flaws?

The product roast was different from the company's usual product meeting, because all departments attended, including designers, programmers, and customer service representatives. "Everyone had an opportunity to rip on something without worrying about hurt feelings," Fried told *Inc.* magazine. "People understood the spirit of the roast and felt free to take a jab."

The day after Basecamp's product roast, the company began fixing some of the issues that were raised. But it didn't stop there. During the following weeks, the company started to solve "some deeper problems that emerged through the laughs," said Fried. As he described it, the roast hit all the right notes: "It brought us together, generated some laughs, broke the ice on the first day of a long week together, highlighted a bunch of issues, and motivated us to dig in."

Breaking the Tension with a Sense of Humor

When your business grows, so does the likelihood of new crises. As more stressful situations arise, here's the question you must consider: How will you handle that stress, and how will you help your employees cope with it?

A panicked mind can't problem-solve. That's why it's critical to seek levity in tough situations. This holds true especially when you're overtired, overworked, and don't feel particularly funny. When you find ways to laugh, you won't necessarily feel instantly relaxed, but the humor will nudge you toward a less anxious state of mind. It points the way to a less dire perspective. That in itself will help you think more clearly in the most stressful situations.

Yoda as a Stress Buster: *"Create lasting value with a sense of purpose and a sense of humor."* That's part of the mission statement of DNS Capital, a family office for the Pritzkers, one of the wealthiest families in the United States. As chairman and CEO of DNS (which stands for "Does Not Suck"), Michael Pucker embodies that emphasis on humor. Case in point: his LinkedIn profile photo is a modified version of Edvard Munch's The Scream, featuring Homer Simpson.

In his role of overseeing more than a dozen companies (including Beyond Meat) that are part of DNS investments, he's playful with a purpose. "Humor has a funny way of breaking down walls in a big hurry and making people comfortable," he told *Middle Market Growth* magazine. That includes helping his portfolio company executives maintain a positive outlook in difficult situations.

When he noticed that the CEO at one of his companies was uncharacteristically stressed, Pucker took action. He superimposed a photo of the CEO on a picture of Yoda, added a wise Yoda-ism, and sent it to the CEO and some of his employees. "They needed a release. They needed to laugh at themselves," said Pucker. For him, humor represents the cornerstone of a solid business relationship. "If you're not putting yourself in someone else's shoes, you're not doing a really good job of building a relationship. It's a lot easier to build those relationships when you're not taking yourself too seriously. A good way to not take yourself too seriously is through humor and fun."

Humor can also boost your negotiating skills. This observation comes from Chris Voss, someone who knows a few things about how to succeed at high-stakes negotiations. A former FBI hostage negotiator, Voss now runs a consulting firm that guides businesses through important deals. In his best-selling book *Never Split the Difference: Negotiating As If Your Life Depended On It*, Voss has this to say about overcoming negotiation challenges: "Humor and humanity are the best ways to break the ice and remove roadblocks."

Share the Truth in Unexpected Ways

QUOTE

Humor is the good-natured side of a truth.

– MARK TWAIN

Truth is a gold mine for humor, and stand-up comics know this well. The next time you watch a comedy performance, note the moments that get the biggest laughs or applause. Chances are, they're grounded in truths about the human experience. It doesn't matter if those truths are trivial or profound. By giving voice to something that might normally go unspoken, comics make us laugh.

Humor grounded in truth can serve a larger purpose in your business. It can be a vehicle for delivering uncomfortable truths, as highlighted earlier in this chapter with the role of levity in sharing mistakes.

Humor can also forge connections and lighten tense moments, by openly stating the truth in an unexpected way. One example of this comes from Connor Diemand-Yauman, a serial entrepreneur and one of the instructors for the "Humor: Serious Business" course at the Stanford Graduate School of Business. When Diemand-Yauman joined a large nonprofit as their co-CEO, his first all-hands Zoom call was scheduled during a particularly divisive time in the United States. He wanted to reassure his employees and also show that he recognized the hardship and challenges faced by the country. That's no easy task for a CEO, especially one that has recently joined an organization. But Diemand-Yauman found a way to accomplish those communication goals through humor.

During the first part of the Zoom call, he shared his screen. Then, when it was time for someone else to speak, he pretended to accidentally leave his screen-share on. As employees on the Zoom call wondered what he was about to unwittingly share, Diemand-Yauman pulled up Google and typed into the search field "things inspirational CEOs say in hard times."

The employees burst out laughing, and Diemand-Yauman was able to show how much he wanted to reassure them. In that moment of levity, he did more than ease tension. He made himself vulnerable by sharing the unspoken truth that CEOs don't always know what to say in difficult situations, and they worry about finding the right words.

You don't have to be the quickest wit in the room. The easiest way to have more humor at work is not to try to be funny—instead, just look for moments to laugh.

– DICK COSTOLO,
former Twitter CEO

Leaders don't need to tell jokes, but they should show a sense of humor. This can take the form of laughing at other people's jokes, being quick to laugh at oneself, or creating opportunities for levity. As Stanford professors and coauthors Jennifer Aaker and Naomi Bagdonas note in their book, *Humor, Seriously*, one study showed that managers with a sense of humor (regardless of whether others considered them "funny") were rated by subordinates as 23 percent more respected and 25 percent more pleasant to work with. Being quick to laugh at yourself is better than being quick-witted. By looking for ways to bring laughter and playfulness to your entire organization, you can strengthen problem-solving abilities, collaboration, and effective communication in general.

Chapter Recap

» By applying lessons from comedy, entrepreneurs can strengthen their communication skills and think in more flexible ways to help address the thorny challenges of growing a business.

» Improv performers create entertaining scenes onstage through the power of "Yes, and ... " After affirming another performer's statement, they build on it with more ideas. Leaders can use the same technique in conversation to foster a collaborative dynamic.

» The best joke-writers disrupt our way of thinking. They make unexpected connections between things or situations and encourage us to explore different points of view. By shaking up our predictable thought patterns, they take our minds out of autopilot. This can provide inspiration for more flexible ways of thinking about the world and, more specifically, the problems faced by your growing business.

» When leaders can laugh openly at their mistakes, employees will feel more comfortable bringing their own errors to light. When workers don't fear how failures will be received, they're more likely to share problems sooner, instead of burying the bad news.

» Business leaders don't need to make more jokes at work. The goal is not to be the funniest person in the room. Instead, they can let comedy inspire them to rethink ingrained mindsets, find humor in challenging situations, and seek opportunities to bring playfulness to the company's culture.

PART II

MANEUVERING FOR GROWTH

| 4 |
Leading

Chapter Overview
> » Delegation
> » Freedom to Fail
> » Innovation
> » Transparency and Emotional Availability

Management works in the system; leadership works on the system.
— STEPHEN COVEY

In chapter 5, we will examine several management skills that are essential for entrepreneurs who want to grow their business. Each day, you will put these skills into practice. However, one aspect of management is particularly critical for founders navigating the occasional chaos of high-growth phases. I'm talking about leadership. This particular aspect of management is so important that I'm devoting an entire chapter to it, before we tackle other management skills.

My favorite definition of leadership comes from Dr. John Kotter, one of the foremost leadership scholars. He called it "the creation of positive, non-incremental change, including the creation of a vision to guide that change—a strategy—the empowerment of people to make the vision happen despite obstacles, and the creation of a coalition of energy and momentum that can move that change forward." Some aspects of this definition are explored elsewhere in this book. We will discuss the importance of basing strategic decisions on a shared vision for your firm's direction in part III, and in part I we've already covered some interpersonal characteristics of a great leader, including persistence, accountability, and a growth mindset. In this chapter, we will discuss firm-level leadership topics and how they relate to the firm's growth. Those topics include the following:

- » **Delegation**, which builds accountability and persistence
- » **Innovation**, which develops a culture of creativity
- » **Transparency and emotional availability**, which build authenticity

These aspects of leadership create an organizational culture that will lead your firm to positive change in the way Kotter described. Keep in mind that your vision for these changes won't mean much unless they become a shared vision, one that inspires employees to support the organization as it transforms and reaches new levels of growth.

Delegation

If you want to do a few small things right, do them yourself. If you want to do great things and make a big impact, learn to delegate.

– JOHN C. MAXWELL

Of all the management abilities you can develop, delegation has the greatest potential to propel (or halt) your company's growth. It's also one of the things founders struggle with most.

That struggle makes sense, considering many founders started their businesses by serving in multiple roles. They spend months—or sometimes years—handling the entire value chain of the company at once, from production to marketing to customer service. You may find yourself nodding in recognition. When your company doesn't have a lot of customers or resources, it's both reasonable and necessary to juggle roles.

Unfortunately, many founders have trouble shifting away from that pattern and relinquishing control when their company starts to grow. They tell themselves, "I'm still the best person to handle this. It's the only way to do it right" or "It'll take me longer to teach them the right way than to just do it myself." Does this sound like you? It's a shortsighted way to think. You may well be the person able to do the task the best, but in the long run you're taking time, energy, and focus away from the big-picture strategic stuff that fuels growth. If your head is deep in the weeds, you won't be able to guide your company to growth.

Here's another way lack of delegation sabotages your growth plans: it stunts the next generation of leaders in your organization. As your business grows, so does your need for more leaders. The best approach to leadership development is to cultivate talent from within. This ensures that you create leaders with a common vision and work culture. Although you may need to bring in some seasoned leaders from outside your organization, you'll end up with a very strange work dynamic if you have no home-grown talent at the top levels.

All of this leads to a hard truth: if you can't delegate properly, you are holding your company back. A 2015 Gallup study supports this. It examined 143 CEOs on the Inc. 500 list and found that companies run by executives who effectively delegate authority grow faster, generate more revenue, and create more jobs.

In your Digital Assets, you'll find the Delegation Decision Matrix, which offers guidance on spotting delegation opportunities that help you spend your time and effort wisely. Download this worksheet at go.quickstartguides.com/rungrow.

When leaders can't bring themselves to delegate, they often wind up overworked and micromanaging. Leaders who micromanage hurt their business in two ways: they squander time and energy by concentrating on decisions and tasks that don't require their expertise, and they demoralize employees by not giving them responsibilities that make their jobs fulfilling. Employees' feelings are important because when you hire employees, the dynamic shifts from *your* business to *our* business—or at least it should. Getting stuck in "my company" mode shows a fundamental lack of trust in your workers, and it will undermine all other efforts to create a growth-minded culture. If you want employees to feel *passionately* about the company's mission and be strong brand ambassadors, they need to feel that they're trusted and valued by leadership.

Q: Are you willing to commit yourself to delegating effectively, so you can maximize your company's growth opportunities?

It's OK if the answer is no. Many founders can't make this adjustment. What matters is that you're honest with yourself about this issue, because if you can't delegate properly, then it's time to hire a CEO to run your company. This person can oversee day-to-day operations and allow you to focus on strategic issues such as branding and exploring new areas of potential growth.

Guidance for Delegating

We know that delegation is critical, but what steps can we take to actually put it into action? Here are a few guidelines:

INSTEAD OF DICTATING *EXACTLY* WHAT EMPLOYEES SHOULD DO:

fig. 6

Focus on what needs to get done

Provide guidelines

Warn of potential issues

» **Focus on what needs to get done, not just how it will be achieved.** In discussing work assignments with colleagues, make sure to emphasize why it's important and how it fits into the bigger picture of what you're trying to achieve. If they have this understanding, rather than a step-by-step guide for what to do, they may surprise you and find an even better way to do it.

» **Provide guidelines.** Give employees the freedom to make choices but make clear the parameters within which they should operate. Your guidelines don't have to be numerous or complicated—in fact, they usually shouldn't be—but make sure any significant restrictions are clear. Don't create a situation where employees unwittingly violate a long-standing practice that no one told them about.

» **Point out the quicksand.** If you want employees to take initiative, avoid telling them what to do. Instead, tell them what not to do, and help them learn from your mistakes and the mistakes of others. Be clear and candid about the potential paths to failure; as Covey says, "tell a person where the quicksand is and where the wild animals are."

» **Be patient.** Invest time in delegation that gives your employees the ability to make effective choices. You'll find it's one of the smartest investments you can make to help your business grow. Even if it takes them longer at first, in the long run it will save time.

How Poor Delegation Nearly Bankrupted an Entrepreneur: Some founders learn the importance of delegation the hard way. That was the case for Dan Brault, founder of a successful New York–based real estate wholesaling company. In 2021, his company had eight employees and close to $200,000 a month in revenue—but a few years earlier, he had been on the brink of bankruptcy.

At that time, Brault was doing some wholesaling and decided to simultaneously start a construction company that did custom builds. That's when he ran into trouble. "We were mid-build on a lake house," Brault explained on the podcast BiggerPockets. "The company just ran out of money. This was not like a spec house. This was for a client that had paid us to build their house." He had to lay off seven people and ended up about $400,000 in debt. As Brault's business suffered, so did his health. He barely slept and developed an ulcer. He said it was the most stressful year of his life. "I liquidated my 401(k)," he said. "I met with a bankruptcy attorney. It got pretty dark there for a little bit."

Bad delegation had helped to unleash that cascade of crises. "I was trying to maintain the ultimate control and it cost me, because I forced micromanaging," said Brault. His inability to relinquish control compelled him to work nonstop and also led to employee turnover. "It was really poor, poor leadership on my part," he said. "That's something I've been working really hard to correct."

Thanks to his business crisis, Brault learned a vital lesson about effective delegation: create a support system by surrounding yourself with capable people. "I didn't have a construction background and I didn't have the right people around me either. That was probably the biggest mistake, is that I was trying to do it all myself without the right people around me," said Brault. "The most successful people are surrounded by a lot of other successful people. They have coaches and they have mentors. They lean on the strengths of others." If he'd taken that approach, Brault said he could have avoided a year of sleepless nights and crushing debt.

The Cautionary Tale of a Delegation Train Wreck: In 2011, American Apparel had more than $500 million in revenue. By 2015, the company was in Chapter 11 bankruptcy, and in 2017 it was purchased by a competitor for less than $100 million. This is a case study for how a high-growth company can go off the rails—thanks to a founder who obsessively controlled small tasks, drove away talented managers, and positioned himself as the one and only symbol of the brand.

In addition to some bad financial deals, the company had a big leadership problem. Dov Charney, the founder and CEO, faced several sexual harassment lawsuits and was kicked off the board of American Apparel in 2014. Charney's problems became the company's problems writ large, because he considered himself an essential part of the brand. When he left, the company lacked the right management team to take over, because Charney's behavior had ensured that skilled leaders wouldn't stay for long.

In a *New York Times* article, American Apparel executives described him as "relentlessly controlling." Charney once moved into one of the company's warehouses that was having problems—and even had a shower installed—so he could monitor the work around the clock. Another time, during a traffic jam in the parking lot at the headquarters, Charney left his office to direct traffic until it cleared.

Industry analysts observed that the company had a reputation "as a place where talented people did not want to work." In his book *How I Built This*, Guy Raz sums up American Apparel's dysfunctional leadership dynamic this way: "By consistently firing or driving away talented leaders, Charney managed to yank out by the roots whatever culture there was to speak of at American Apparel, and in filling the vacuum with himself, the culture of American Apparel became the Cult of Dov. As Dov imploded, so did American Apparel."

One final word on delegation. In chapter 6, we will explore key strategies and tactics for hiring. Your hiring choices will make or break your ability to build a cohesive team culture. However, sometimes even the best hires struggle in a particular position. If you have a team member who seems to be struggling, perhaps they and their role are misaligned. Each individual brings their own set of skills, passions, and perspectives to the job. The first question to ask is not necessarily who *can* do it, but who *should*. Here are some questions effective delegators ask when attempting to create alignment between team members and their roles:

» Who needs to develop these skills?
» Who has the capacity?

» Who has shown interest?
» Who is ready for a challenge?
» Who would see this as a reward?

After answering those questions, skilled leaders don't just start rearranging roles. Instead, they explain to the team why they chose a particular person to take on a specific task or role. This provides the team with some context for their decisions.

How to Foster an Environment Where Employees Aren't Afraid to Fail

Success is the ability to go from failure to failure with no loss of enthusiasm.
– WINSTON CHURCHILL

Imagine you have a toxic fungus growing in your home. Would you want to discover it immediately, so you could eliminate it? Or would you want it hidden away in the dark, growing for weeks, months, or years while you're completely unaware, until your health starts to suffer? Business cultures filled with fear of failure are not so different. When employees have no reason to reveal mistakes and every reason to hide them, small problems will grow into big ones. Sometimes they threaten your company's very existence.

As a leader, you can show your employees that failure is not only OK but expected. What matters is how you respond to it. As we discussed in chapter 1, failure provides opportunities to learn. If you approach it with the right mindset, failure provides fertile ground for curiosity to thrive. "We want people to ask big questions," says Zander Lurie, CEO of Momentive (formerly known as SurveyMonkey). "We want them to think up experiments that haven't been done before," he said in a *Harvard Business Review* interview. "If folks aren't failing, they're not asking hard enough questions or taking big enough risks."

The Importance of Psychological Safety

To show your employees that perfection is not the goal, you need to make your workplace a safe place to fail. *Psychological safety*—not feeling threatened—is vital. "Our brains are trained to constantly scan for and avoid people who threaten our sense of well-being. When we perceive someone who is a 'threat,' we either attack or retreat, and when we retreat, we lose access to important skills such as listening, asking questions, or speaking up about our ideas," says Amy Jen Su, cofounder of executive coaching firm Paravis Partners and author of *Harvard Business Review* article "Do You Really Trust Your Team? (And Do They Trust You?)." Su says, "This is why it's so important to maintain a positive team culture. If people feel psychologically unsafe due to one bad egg, they likely won't reach their full potential."

If you discover that any of your teams lack psychological safety, Su recommends taking the following steps to build it:

» **Model healthy conflict.** When you disagree with someone else in the company, whether it's one-on-one or in a large meeting, give that person plenty of space to express their point of view. With this respectful approach, you set the tone for communication throughout the company. By welcoming other opinions, you show that opposing perspectives can lead to constructive discussions.

» **Have a zero-tolerance policy for bullying.** When blatantly rude behavior occurs, address it immediately. This includes team members who constantly talk over other people or use derogatory language about others. Don't avoid the elephant in the room and force other employees to work around a toxic team member. It doesn't matter if they're a top performer—they must be held accountable for their behavior.

» **Create a culture of appreciation.** If you focus only on things that need improvement, employees can feel defensive or discouraged. When you recognize achievements in group settings, you reinforce each person's strengths and contributions.

Google discovered the importance of psychological safety when it spent two years researching the following question: *What makes a Google team effective?* The company conducted more than 200 interviews with its employees and looked at more than 250 attributes of more than 180 active Google teams. "We were pretty confident that we'd find the perfect mix of individual traits and skills necessary for a stellar team—take one Rhodes scholar, two extroverts, one engineer who rocks at AngularJS, and a PhD," wrote Julia Rosovsky at the time (she has worked as a director at Google's People Operations, or what most companies call HR). "Voila.

Dream team assembled, right?"

Not exactly. "We were dead wrong," says Rosovsky. "Who is on a team matters less than how the team members interact, structure their work, and view their contributions. So much for that magical algorithm."

That research revealed five dynamics that distinguish successful teams from other teams at Google:

» **Psychological safety**: Can we take risks on this team without feeling insecure or embarrassed?

» **Dependability**: Can we count on each other to do high-quality work on time?

» **Structure and clarity**: Are goals, roles, and execution plans on our team clear?

» **Meaning of work**: Are we working on something that is personally important for each of us?

» **Impact of work**: Do we fundamentally believe that the work we're doing matters?

Of those five dynamics, Google found that psychological safety was the most important. "It's the underpinning of the other four," says Rosovsky. That's because people are reluctant to take risks if they're focused on how others will perceive their competence. Too much self-protection hinders teamwork. As Rosovsky notes, "The safer team members feel with one another, the more likely they are to admit mistakes, to partner, and to take on new roles."

One Founder's Three-Part Approach to Failing: As CEO and founder of mobile e-sports company Skillz, Andrew Paradise is no stranger to success. In 2017, Skillz was the fastest-growing company on the Inc. 5000 list. That accomplishment stems, in part, from the way Paradise values failure and its role in building trust. "I think the thing we try to teach at Skillz is that communication is the most important aspect of doing business," he said in an interview. "And you can't have true communication if you don't build trust and transparency around failure."

For Paradise, that means creating a culture that says failure is OK as long as you learn from it. Otherwise, a stifling culture of fear can emerge. "I think you end up in a situation where people are almost trained into hiding failure over time," he said.

That culture creation begins at the top. "It starts with me saying, 'Hey, I'm totally fine with you failing. I just want to know early and often that's happening,'" said Paradise. He summed up the communication approach at Skillz in a three-part statement: "One, if something's going wrong, you'll hear about it from me first. Two, I'm going to demonstrate to you that I care more about it than you do. And three, I'm going to demonstrate that I'm all over it." That three-part statement doesn't just influence communication between employees and their managers. "In fact, we actually run that kind of methodology across every level of the company, even in how our board works with me," said Paradise.

How IDEO Creates a Culture of Helping: To make employees feel safe, you must make them feel supported—not just by company leadership, but by each other. One organization that has fostered a culture of support and helping is design firm IDEO. "Even the most brilliant person occasionally gets 'stuck,'" said Tim Brown, executive chair of IDEO, in a blog post. "In a culture that values the lone genius, where politics and rivalries rule, no one is motivated to help that person get 'unstuck.' Projects stall and good ideas languish," said Brown, who also served for nineteen years as the firm's CEO.

One of the company's core values is "Make others successful." Those in senior leadership positions are expected to model this value, and helpfulness is a factor when employees are considered for promotion.

To make employees more inclined to accept requests for assistance, IDEO focuses on creating work schedules that aren't overloaded. If employees are constantly scrambling to finish their own tasks, it's unlikely they'll have time to share their expertise with others in the company who ask for help.

When talking with job candidates, Brown listens for a couple of specific cues that signal a person's general helpfulness, or lack thereof. "When people repeatedly say 'I,' not 'we,' when recounting their accomplishments, I get suspicious. But if they're generous with giving credit and talk about how someone else was instrumental in their progress, I know that they give help as well as receive it," he said. "It's also a good sign if they've spent time teaching. Nothing proves one's commitment to making others successful like taking a group of students under your wing."

Innovation

To stay competitive and keep up with customers' increasingly high expectations, your company will need to make innovation its lifeblood. When I say "innovation," I mean using the tools of creativity to generate ideas, then experimenting with those ideas within risk parameters that are appropriate to the potential organizational impact. In other words, don't bet the farm on an idea that might get you one more cow. Keep in mind that not all ideas will lead to radical changes in your company—but some may have a dramatic organizational effect, whether it's a product that leads to a significant new revenue stream or a new approach to customer service that causes customer satisfaction to soar. To achieve this, you'll need to develop both an organizational culture and a leadership approach that allow innovation to flourish.

Creating a Culture of Innovation

Fear of failure will compel your employees to steer clear of the uncharted territory where true innovation takes place. When you promote a culture where employees aren't afraid to fail—as we discussed earlier in this chapter—you establish an essential element of an innovation culture. Also consider fostering other cultural dynamics that will facilitate innovation.

A Culture of Curiosity: We explored curiosity's role in your development as a founder in chapter 1. Your business will suffer if you don't relentlessly seek new perspectives and question your own assumptions. These are qualities that need to be reflected throughout your entire organization. When you put your own healthy sense of curiosity on display, you can lead by example. Encouraging new ideas and allowing experimentation will develop an organizational culture of creativity.

Be aware that there's often a huge gap between how leaders perceive company culture (in other words, the reassuring story founders tell themselves about the culture they've created) and how employees actually experience it. According to one study, 83 percent of executives say they encourage curiosity, but just 52 percent of employees agree. It's your responsibility to find out what sort of culture you really have. Make sure it's not just a nice story you're telling yourself. As Pixar cofounder Ed Catmull says, "If there is more truth in the hallways than in meetings, you have a problem."

How Momentive Rewards Curiosity: Curiosity is like a muscle. That's what Zander Lurie, CEO of Momentive, has observed. "Its strength will erode if it isn't used often enough. When curiosity ebbs, people lapse into routine and complacency, which exposes a company to disruption. To prevent that, managers should continually emphasize how important curiosity is—and reward people for developing it." Let's look at some of the ways Momentive encourages curiosity across the organization:

» **Encourage good questions with public recognition**: Momentive conducts town hall meetings that include praise for a "question of the week" chosen from employee surveys. But that's not the only way the company provides encouragement. "We have a peer recognition program to reward people who dare to be especially candid," says Lurie. "In our Slack channels you'll often see remarks praised with the notation #greatquestion. At [Momentive] that's one of the highest compliments you can pay someone."

» **As the company leader, show you're open to asking and answering questions**: Lurie does this with regular "skip-level meetings" with the people one level below his direct reports. Says Lurie, "The conversation is open and nothing is off-limits." He also shows his curiosity with a monthly speaker series. "I bring in leaders from various industries and backgrounds to learn about their success—from Serena Williams on what it takes to win, to Electronic Arts' Andrew Wilson on building a culture of customer centricity. During these meetings I get real-time mentorship from people I admire while showing our team why asking questions is valuable."

» **Ask people what matters to them**: This represents the heart of curiosity, says Lurie, and leads to unexpected answers. That was the case at Momentive. "Our company spends millions of dollars a year on benefits; to make sure that spending aligns with what employees really value, we do surveys about which benefits matter most to them. In one of those surveys an interesting theme emerged. Like most other companies, we have contractors and vendors—including the people who clean our offices and those who prepare the great food in our dining area. We see them every day, but they aren't actually employees. Some of our employees expressed concern that these team members didn't have benefits comparable to ours. We began working with the companies that employ them to make their benefits packages more comparable. We wouldn't have thought to engage on this issue if not for our employees' curiosity and concern."

How Leadership Affects Innovation

You can think of leadership in terms of a metaphorical battlefield. Sometimes you will be out in front, leading the charge and urging your troops to follow. But there's another approach that's gained attention recently: servant leadership. This style of leadership emphasizes the need to help your troops on the front lines succeed—and your role is to do everything you can to support them.

Servant leadership is not a new idea. Although the concept entered Western consciousness in 1970 with Robert K. Greenleaf's essay "The Servant as Leader," its origins date back hundreds of years. "A leader is best when people barely know he exists … when his work is done, his aim fulfilled, they will say: 'we did it ourselves.'" That's a popular quote from fifth century Chinese philosopher Lao Tzu (and so is this one: "To lead people, walk behind them").

Here is the concept as Greenleaf described it: "The servant-leader is servant first … that person is sharply different from one who is leader first … the difference manifests itself in the care taken by the servant-first to make sure that other people's highest priority needs are being served. The best test, and difficult to administer, is: Do those served grow as persons? Do they, while being served, become healthier, wiser, freer, more autonomous, more likely themselves to become servants?"

If you sense a conflict between the idea of servant leadership and "strong" leaders who are always leading the charge, I have some good news for you. You don't need to pick one—and in fact, you shouldn't. It's not a question of right or wrong. Good leaders need both approaches in their arsenal and will switch between them depending on the circumstances.

Transformational Leadership

For meaningful innovation to take place—dramatic changes in the way an organization operates, whether it's a different business model or a reimagined core business—companies require transformational leaders. Transformational leaders inspire employees and unify them around a shared vision, empowering them to tackle complex problems and persist as they follow a road map for change that may take years to achieve. As employees' commitment and engagement grows, so does the organization.

This requires the ability to convey a compelling purpose that your organization can rally around during difficult times—and there will be plenty of those if you're undertaking dramatic changes. We discussed the importance of purpose as a motivating force for you as a leader in chapter 1, and the same applies to your employees. They need more than a list of tasks; they need a persuasive "why," a vision of something bigger and better.

Transformational leaders use culture and narratives to drive engagement. Recall Dr. Kotter's definition of leadership at the beginning of this chapter. You are creating a shared vision of the future and a coalition of empowered employees who will make it happen. This means setting a vision and a strategy, which is leading from the front, while at the same time constantly reminding your staff of their accomplishments and all the great things they are doing to make the vision a reality. This is servant leadership. Transformational leaders are leading from both sides simultaneously. Not an easy feat, but a necessary one.

When you combine transformational leadership with a culture that promotes new ideas and experimentation, that's your winning formula for an innovative organization. You need to have both. Your culture creates the right conditions for innovation, but it can't grow on its own. Like a garden, it needs someone to cultivate it, keep the soil fertile, and plant some seeds.

Transparency and Emotional Availability

As you've already learned in this chapter, the qualities you cultivate as a leader directly affect what happens on an organizational level. When you focus on the right qualities, they translate into building a healthy, resilient company culture that is poised for growth. One quality that can truly make a difference in your culture is vulnerability.

Vulnerability doesn't mean weakness. It can come in many forms. Curiosity is a way of showing vulnerability, because when you position yourself as a learner, you're not pretending to know everything. Leaders who display vulnerability are not positioning themselves as flawless. This makes them more approachable and more authentic. When leaders show accountability—admitting they made a significant mistake and pledging to improve—they also show vulnerability. As a result, they are better equipped to forge a culture of personal accountability among their employees.

One of the most prominent advocates of the power of vulnerability is Brené Brown, researcher and author of several best-selling books, including *Dare to Lead*. For two decades, she's studied the role of vulnerability (along with courage, shame, and empathy) in leadership. "The greatest barrier to courageous leadership is not fear—it's how we respond to our fear," says Brown. "Our armor—the thoughts, emotions, and behaviors that we use to protect ourselves when we aren't willing and able to rumble with vulnerability—move us out of alignment with our values, corrode trust with our colleagues and teams, and prevent us from being our most courageous selves."

Why do we feel more comfortable around someone who is authentic and vulnerable? "Because we are particularly sensitive to signs of trustworthiness in our leaders," says Emma Seppälä, a lecturer at the Yale School of Management and science director of Stanford University's Center for Compassion and Altruism Research and Education. "Servant leadership, for example, which is characterized by authenticity and values-based leadership, yields more positive and constructive behavior in employees and greater feelings of hope and trust in both the leader and the organization," she says in her article "What Bosses Gain by Being Vulnerable" in *Harvard Business Review*. "In turn, trust in a leader improves employee performance."

The Power of Empathy:
Treating Your Employees with Respect and Ensuring They Flourish

We talked in chapter 1 about the importance of empathy as it relates to customers; you may recall the example of the head of IKEA, one of the richest people in the world, who preferred to fly economy and use public transportation in order to stay close to the people he was serving. Similarly, empathy can help you stay close to the people who make your business growth possible: your employees. With empathy, you can find ways to serve and support them.

Some people think empathy is a "nice to have" quality but one that doesn't deserve status as an essential part of a leadership toolkit. Here's the challenge I put to those people: how can you expect to motivate others if you're unwilling to discover and appreciate the pressures of their daily lives?

Make no mistake, this requires substantial effort. You will need to focus on mindfulness, a concept we discussed in chapter 2, to listen carefully for signals. You must also remember the importance of having a learning mindset as you set out to discover the best ways to support your teams.

This includes examining current conditions even if great results are being produced. When your employees are working together like a well-oiled machine, that machine can still break if you push it too hard. That's what Pixar cofounder Ed Catmull learned when his employees were getting crushed under deadline pressures for *Toy Story 2*. By the time the movie was finished, a third of his staff had some kind of repetitive stress injury. One employee was so distracted and overworked that he left his baby in the car on a very hot day, after he had parked and gone into the office (fortunately, the baby ended up all right but was found unconscious when the employee realized his mistake and rushed out to the parking lot).

Company leaders love to say "Our employees are our greatest asset." If I had a nickel for every time I've heard that, I could build myself a mansion made of nickels. More often than not, that "greatest asset" statement has zero validity. The experience with *Toy Story 2* made Catmull realize the importance of respecting and protecting Pixar's most valuable asset. Just because your employees are willing to work ridiculously long hours doesn't mean you should let them do it for weeks or months—or years. Instead, the most effective way to encourage their best work is to foster an environment of psychological safety. As we mentioned earlier, that's the quality Google identified as the most important element of its highest-performing teams. If you want employees to take risks, you must also make them feel protected and valued.

Don't underestimate how much kindness can propel your business success. As a founder, you have the power to affect lives. That may sound like self-aggrandizing hyperbole. But presume that your sole purpose is not to make money (if it is, you need to put down this book and rethink what you're doing). You want to improve your customers' lives with useful products and services (and through interactions with your company in general). You also have the ability to create a workplace that either improves the lives of your employees or makes them a living hell. There are plenty of wildly successful leaders who have opted for the latter, but is that the kind of leader you want to be? Does the pursuit of excellence and profit give you a free pass to act like an asshole and treat your employees like crap? Here's my answer: it does not.

Think about what you're creating. What do you want your legacy to be?

Chapter Recap

» As a leader, you will need to inspire employees with a shared vision, one that propels them to overcome significant obstacles and achieve meaningful change. To execute that vision, empower your teams to address the growing challenges that accompany organizational transformation.

» Remember that the strongest leaders adapt their leadership styles for different situations. At times, you will have to metaphorically lead your troops into battle. But you'll also need to develop your capacity for servant leadership and help your company succeed by supporting the needs of your employees.

» Delegation is one of the most powerful management abilities you can develop. By giving up control over certain decisions, you gain more control over the strategic stuff that fuels growth. Leaders who don't loosen their micromanaging grip will quickly discover that their lack of delegation hurts employee morale and stunts growth.

» To expand your business, you'll need a fertile environment for experimenting with new ideas. Create a culture of innovation by rewarding and encouraging curiosity throughout your organization. By removing the stigma from failure, you give employees the freedom to explore that curiosity.

» Strong leaders don't pretend to be flawless; instead, they admit mistakes and make efforts to improve. By showing vulnerability in this way, leaders demonstrate accountability and gain employees' trust. As employees' trust in leadership improves, so does their performance.

| 5 |

Management Skills That Accelerate Growth

Pull out any textbook on principles of management, and you'll find it organized by managerial function. After you peruse several of these textbooks, you'll quickly discover that there is no magic number of functions. Are there four? Five? Seven? Depends on the book. But these books typically do have something in common: with few exceptions, they highlight three particular functions that are critical for founders who want to scale. That's why I've devoted entire chapters to them: leading (covered in the previous chapter), hiring (covered in the next chapter), and planning (the subject of chapter 9). But as you've learned repeatedly in your role as a founder, these aren't the only management functions that directly affect the health of your business. For that reason, this chapter addresses three other common managerial functions: communicating, organizing, and decision making. In addition to sharing best practices, I'll offer my take on how you should approach these three functions during a period of significant growth and change in your firm.

Communicating

As we discussed in the last chapter, narrative creation is an important leadership quality to have during times of transformational change. The ability to convey important messages to both individuals and groups in written and verbal form is always important but is even more critical during these unsettled times when change is rapid and no one is sure what's going on. Picture the guy on the horse in those old battle scenes, up front with his sword pointed ahead, yelling for his troops to follow him. That's you. Let's examine successful approaches to different forms of communication, as well as techniques to persuade and inspire. These skills will help ensure everyone in your company understands the rationale behind the critical decisions being made—especially those that affect them most, like reorganizations.

Communication Guidance for Internal Productivity Tools (Slack, Zoom, etc.)

Internal social tools like Slack and Zoom have become increasingly popular, in part because they can encourage collaboration and help your employees feel more engaged with their work. To use these tools effectively, remember to focus on three elements: define the purpose, spell out rules of conduct, and lead by example. Let's explore each of those elements in more detail:

1. **Define the purpose.** If management doesn't offer a clear explanation for why employees should use social tools, workers may be reluctant to use them. (With their workplace socializing on display online, employees may also fear that management views some interactions as frivolous.)

    Tsedal Neeley, a professor at Harvard Business School, and Paul Leonardi, a technology management professor at UC Santa Barbara, have observed five significant ways these social tools bring value to companies:

    »   **Enhancing knowledge sharing.** Social tools can offer an efficient method for internal knowledge-sharing that fosters a competitive advantage over companies with less-well-informed employees.

    »   **Improving collaboration.** Internal social tools build awareness of expertise within your organization and facilitate employees' ability to exchange ideas and problem-solve.

    »   **Preventing duplication of work.** By creating more awareness of existing projects, social tools help employees avoid wasting time on initiatives that overlap.

    »   **Increasing innovation.** Social tools create opportunities for cross-pollination because they introduce workers to other ideas throughout the organization. This can encourage them to apply success stories from other departments to their own projects.

» **Creating a connected company with a strong sense of unity.** It can be difficult to forge relationships and a shared organizational identity, particularly if many employees are working remotely. Social tools play an important role in building trust and rapport because they facilitate both personal and professional connections. For example, Slack offers unlimited channels, each with different user sets. Many companies encourage socialization on these channels and even include specific topics unrelated to work, like fantasy sports teams. It's a vital way for employees to feel connected and included.

As the leader, you set the tone for how your communication tools are used, and it's up to you and your leadership team to encourage productive use of such software. It's fine for employees to have some social channels for things like fantasy football, but is that all they use it for? Are they truly being collaborative, or are some being excluded or feeling marginalized? Are you encouraging innovation and knowledge-sharing? Finally, are you using your communication software as one of your powerful tools for creating the narratives and messages you want your employees to see and for building the culture you envision and driving the company in the direction you want it to go? Recall our discussion in the previous chapter of Momentive and their use of the hashtag #greatquestion. That's a perfect example of encouraging the behavior you want to see in Slack.

2. **Spell out rules of conduct.** One company that's benefited from this approach is Mode Analytics, which provides a platform for data analysis and collaboration. When Mode's head count exceeded one hundred employees, Slack started to feel "noisy and slow," as CEO Derek Steer described in a blog post. He led a committee to create guidelines for using Slack and shared them with all employees in January 2020. Steer reported a "profound impact on our communication," even before employees were forced to work from home due to the COVID-19 pandemic.

In a subsequent post after the pandemic began, he shared the following summary of Slack guidelines designed to make employees' communication more consistent, predictable, and effective:

» **Make your availability clear.**
   • Use status updates to let others know when you are away or when they should expect a delayed response.

- When you're not working, consider logging out or setting yourself on "Do Not Disturb" mode so that you can get out of "work mode" and recharge.

» **Assume best intent.** Sometimes tone and context are lost in text.

» **Communicate using threads.** In general, your message in Slack should be either:
  - a response to an existing message, in the thread below that message.
  - a new thread, in which case you should put the most important information or action items first, use bold text to highlight important pieces, and use line breaks or bullets to break up content.

» **Know when to go public or private.** Default to posting in public channels, but be sure to use private groups and DMs for sensitive material or for coordinating to avoid spamming public channels.

» **Abide by the conventions for @mentions,** particularly when mentioning groups or in large or reserved channels like #announcements and #general.

» **We're all responsible for our adherence to these guidelines,** so:
  - reread your message before you hit send.
  - when you think someone has strayed a bit too far from these guidelines, respond and politely let them know how they can communicate better.

These guidelines for employees go double for leaders. Publish everything in public forums. Assume anything you post will become public at some point. Triple-check your post and then have someone else read it before you hit "send." It is very easy to misunderstand anything written because we're missing the tone and nuance that we hear when people speak.

3. **Lead by example.** If you want employees to use these tools effectively, don't just create a social media manual. The best way to communicate is through your actions (including the actions of other company leaders). When leaders use these tools only for formal announcements, they're not showing employees that internal social media has enormous value for collaboration and team building.

DETOUR

Videoconferencing: With the dramatic increase in remote work triggered by the COVID-19 pandemic, you're probably well-versed in basic tips for effective videoconferencing—things like making sure your face is well lit and conducting your video call from a quiet spot (or using headphones to reduce background noise). Here are a few additional suggestions to improve your videoconferencing experience, along with tips from three CEOs given to the publication *Fast Company*. First, my thoughts after two years of daily video calling:

» Be casual, but remember that it's a business meeting, so maintain a sense of business decorum. When your cat jumps on your keyboard during a call, it humanizes you. If you stand up and everyone realizes you're in your boxer shorts? Not so much.

» Know how to use the basic functionality of the software, and make sure your team does as well. When a vote is taken, don't be that person who raises their hand on camera when everyone else is using the hand-raising function. And don't be the person who spends ten minutes trying to figure out how to share their screen. All that was very understandable back in 2020. If it's happening now, your team (or you) needs training.

» Minimize distractions for other meeting attendees by not having a garish background. Use a company-provided one, a plain office, or just blur your background. Remember that your meeting background is not the place to show off your unique personality. Better still, have an office space that's not such a junk heap that everyone chips in to give you a Marie Kondo book at the next holiday party.

Now the tips from some CEOs:

James Park, CEO of Fitbit: Build breaks into your schedule. "I think we all know that being on Zoom calls all day can be challenging, so I try to build in breaks throughout the day—even just 30 minutes—where I can step away from my computer. I've been able to squeeze in a quick workout during those breaks, too, which helps break up the day and improve both my physical and mental health."

Dan Springer, CEO of DocuSign: Keep internal meetings casual: "Working from home also brings new distractions and dynamics into the everyday work life. We're now seeing the inside of people's living spaces, meeting our coworkers' children and pets, and in general getting a glimpse into their personal life that we might not have otherwise seen. This shift has helped me to realize that it is fine to be very casual for internal calls and meetings. Setting this expectation for your internal culture helps to relieve the pressure to maintain a strict air of professionalism in an imperfect environment."

Anne Chow, CEO of AT&T Business: Stop making videoconference the default choice: "Make time for one-on-one voice calls, without video. There's a lot of video fatigue, so be conscious [of] whether all parties want to use it."

The CEO of Zoom, Eric Yuan, admitted he had Zoom fatigue and mentioned that on one day in 2020 he had nineteen Zoom meetings in a row. I have had days like that.

Make Your Team Meetings More Effective

Meetings represent one of the most important forms of communication for your growing company. As you may have noticed, they're also one of the most loathed, and for good reason. Many leaders are lazy meeting schedulers—meaning they don't bother to think about whether another meeting would help or hurt. These executives deserve a new C-suite title: CTW, or chief time waster.

If you want to avoid earning that title yourself, you'll need to reflect on the cadence of communication. The word *cadence* refers to the rhythmic sequence of sounds, whether in music or a person's voice. In a business context, cadence refers to a different kind of rhythm: the frequency of regularly scheduled stuff, like meetings. For example, in circumstances where you're operating during an intense period of immense change, daily meetings would make sense. But at times when everyone's just doing their regular work, daily meetings would be intrusive and make people less productive.

Before we explore specific strategies for effective executive team meetings, let's consider a few basic questions. If they sound obvious, think about whether you can honestly say you apply these questions to all your meetings:

» **Have you identified a specific purpose for the meeting?** Before you ask people to add an event to their calendars, you need to have clarity about what you're trying to accomplish. Once you have a purpose, spell it out clearly to the meeting invitees, so they understand what to expect.

» **Have you chosen a productive time for the meeting?** Make sure you have the information available that participants need for a useful discussion or to make a decision. If you need input from particular people at this meeting, make sure they're able to attend.

» **If the meeting was canceled—or never existed—what would happen?** This thought experiment will help you decide if the meeting is truly necessary or is merely being held out of habit. If progress on projects would continue unimpeded, why is the meeting needed?

Melanie Perkins, CEO and cofounder of Canva, said in an interview that good communication is one of the most important aspects of being an effective leader and helping the team make good decisions about achieving their goals. As the company has grown from its launch in 2013 to a business with a $40 billion valuation in September of 2021, meetings have played a key role. "At the start, there were just a few of us sitting around one table and everyone always knew what everyone else was working on. Now that we've grown to more than two hundred people across our two offices in Sydney and Manila, it's important that we have a focus on making sure everyone has as much context as possible," says Perkins. "Throughout the week, each team catches up on daily progress, and on Fridays we do a company-wide standup, which is a great opportunity to bring everyone together and share knowledge. Our structure of small, empowered teams enables everyone to be nimble and move quickly and also gives each team ownership over their work so they can be as effective and creative as they can be."

Strategies and Tactics to Fine-Tune Your Team Meetings

When your top leadership meets, is everyone focused on making decisions? If you're like most companies, the answer is no. The VC firm Bain & Company conducted research revealing that more than 65 percent of leadership team meetings aren't scheduled specifically for the purpose of making a decision. Instead, they're held for "information sharing," "group input," or "group discussion." That's not the best use of top management's time.

If you're looking for tips beyond the basics of "start on time, end on time, create an action plan," consider these techniques other companies have used to make their meetings focused, energetic, and productive:

» **Write it down beforehand**: This was one of the key aspects of a revamped approach to meetings at Superhuman, an email productivity app (in August 2021, the company had an $825 million valuation). CEO Rahul Vohra wrote about the changes in a blog post. "If somebody wants to bring something up in the team meeting, they must write it down beforehand and share it with the team by 6 p.m. on the day before," says Vohra. "The benefit: we avoid the inefficiency, inaccuracy, and impermanence of 'just bringing something up.'"

Here are three other changes that made Superhuman's meetings more effective. As Vohra says, "Our meetings are now twice as fast, with plenty of fun and banter!"

- **Read and comment in advance**: If employees want to voice their opinion on an issue during a meeting, they need to read and comment on the meeting document beforehand. The benefit: "We avoid talking about things where we did not get up to speed," says Vohra.

- **Discuss for five minutes at most**: When an issue is discussed, that conversation lasts for no more than five minutes. If consensus is not reached in that time, the conversation stops and a decision maker is identified. Then the meeting moves on. (Vohra recognizes that five minutes is ambitious and suggests that other companies could use a ten-minute limit as their starting point.) The benefit is avoiding uninformed decisions without owners. To identify the decision maker, Vohra says the company uses the Jeff Bezos rule of thumb: For reversible decisions, the decision should be made by anybody other than the CEO; for nonreversible decisions, the decision maker should always be the CEO.

- **Share one amazing thing**: "At the start of meetings we like to share one amazing thing from that week," Vohra says. The benefit is simple: "This simple practice makes everybody smile and creates wonderful positive energy."

» **Encourage honest feedback with "Wow/Nice/Who Cares?"** At Nottingham Spirk, an innovation and product design firm, index cards and pens are essential tools for effective meetings. Owners John Nottingham and John Spirk told the *New York Times* how these basic items help facilitate honest opinions:

- Lead a brainstorming session and put the ideas on a wall or whiteboard.

- Give everyone three index cards. One says "Wow," another says "Nice," and the third says "Who cares?" Everybody sits around the table with their cards face down.

- Someone gets up to pitch one of the ideas on the wall.

- The meeting attendees then hold up the card that best expresses their feelings about the idea.

"If everybody says 'Wow,' you're going to keep that idea," Nottingham told the *New York Times*. "That's easy, but it doesn't happen a lot. So another idea is presented, and everybody may hold up the cards that say, 'Who cares?' So you take that product and just shove it off the table. It's not going to work." To ensure people in the room aren't influenced by one person's response, make sure everyone holds up their card at the same time, Nottingham says.

» **Do a meeting "pre-mortem."** One of the main culprits behind ineffective meetings is the A-word: agenda. Too many companies recycle the same basic agenda for every meeting—or make one up at the last minute. "An effective agenda works like a plan for an event: it has clear goals or key questions to answer," says Steven Rogelberg, author of *The Surprising Science of Meetings*, in a *Wall Street Journal* article. To keep meetings from becoming a time suck, Rogelberg suggests conducting a pre-mortem: envision how the meeting could go wrong and devise a strategy to prevent it. "Ask attendees for agenda items and assign ownership," says Rogelberg. "Research shows that such preparation increases engagement and a sense of purpose. And if the agenda isn't coming together, that points to an obvious solution: cancel the meeting."

In an April 2018 company-wide email obtained by Jalopnik, Elon Musk had this to say about meeting attendance: "Walk out of a meeting or drop off a call as soon as it is obvious you aren't adding value. It is not rude to leave, it is rude to make someone stay and waste their time."

The Psychology of Communication: Connecting with Your Audience

Now that we've explored some strategies for structuring your communication, let's take a look at ways to make your message resonate. As your company grows, you'll need to convey your decisions in a way that makes people want to come along for the ride. Change brings risk, and you need to convince your audience—whether it's employees, investors, or customers—that the new way is better. With that in mind, let's consider ways to make your communication more nuanced.

Take Your Open-Door Policy to the Next Level

Many leaders pat themselves on the back for having an "open-door" policy, but they never actually do anything tangible to encourage candid employee feedback. To avoid being a founder with an open-door policy that exists in name only, consider how other entrepreneurs actively seek ideas and perspectives from everyone in their company:

Continually ask frontline workers for their opinions: One entrepreneur who does this is Katrina Markoff, founder and CEO of Vosges Haut-Chocolat, a chocolate company with more than $35 million in annual revenue. Speaking on the Know Your Team podcast, Markoff said she encourages candid conversations by asking, "What are your ideas? How could we make this better? You tell me, give me feedback. Please give me feedback. What do I need to be doing better?" She observes that when workers view leaders as down-to-earth and approachable, they're more likely to speak freely. Executive titles can make frontline workers "feel like they're so much further away from you than truly they are," she says. She relies on factory floor workers and other employees to offer information and observations from their daily work, providing a more complete picture of the company than what's visible from a CEO's desk. As part of her effort to encourage workers to speak their minds, Markoff says she spends time with all new hires during their first couple of weeks, even if it's just fifteen minutes. In addition to sharing her company vision, her goal is to spend that time getting to know each employee in order to create a sense of connection and trust.

Create "contrarian office hours": At mobile advertising startup URX (acquired by Pinterest in 2016), a forum for company-wide candid feedback takes place every Friday afternoon. The hour-long session is called "contrarian office hours," and, as the name suggests, it's designed to encourage arguments and constructive criticism. As CEO John Milinovich said in an interview, "It creates a safe space where people are not just allowed to mix things up, but given express permission to call things out. It also primes people to not take things personally." Before each session, the leadership team collects questions and topics. This allows them to plan how much time to devote to each question and also lets them prepare thorough responses—in other words, they budget the meeting time.

When an issue is raised during contrarian office hours, it gets logged on URX's internal wiki. This creates a system that's visible throughout the company and tracks an issue's progress. All employees can see whether actions have been taken toward a solution. The status of each issue is continually updated until it's marked as complete. "No matter who you are, you can see who is assigned to a specific action item and whether they did what they were supposed to or not," says Milinovich.

Because candid discussions can get heated, each contrarian office hours session ends on a positive note by celebrating large and small accomplishments of employees.

Schedule one-on-ones with as many people as possible in your company: As CEO of URX, John Milinovich says his most important job is to be a feedback loop between the product and the market, and also for the team. "This is how we'll build the right culture to get us where we're going as fast as possible," he said in an interview. To that end, he devotes significant time to one-on-ones—not just with managers, but with every person working at the company. When Milinovich discussed his commitment to one-on-one meetings with First Round Review, his company had about twenty employees, but he expressed determination to continue that approach as his company grew—even if head count exceeded one hundred employees.

Milinovich also meets weekly with every member of the business team. "There will always be things that people won't bring up in a community forum that are still so important to address, especially before they become bigger issues," he says.

STOP SAYING "I": One of the greatest pieces of advice I got when I was a new supervisor was to remove the word "I" from my vocabulary and replace it with "we." It is a small but critical component of building a team culture where everyone shares in team successes and takes personal responsibility for team issues. The second your team members start coming out with statements like "We missed our numbers last quarter, but I hit my sales targets," they are implicitly pointing the finger at someone else and absolving themselves of any blame. A better way of thinking would be "We missed our numbers last quarter, and we all have to go back to the drawing board to figure out why." It's even uglier for a leader to use "I," which generally makes them look egotistical and credit-mongering. The only time a leader should say "I" is when they're being accountable and taking personal responsibility for an issue. They should then immediately pivot to how "we" are going to solve it.

How Company Leaders Can Use Social Media Effectively

Some founders perceive social media as a responsibility that belongs solely to the marketing department. That's a mistake, because those leaders are overlooking an important opportunity to communicate personally with stakeholders, including customers, employees, and investors. When CEOs express themselves through social media, they speak directly to their audience, creating a personal connection that can never be achieved with a corporate social media account.

Leaders in the twenty-first century need to understand that many employees *expect* CEOs to have a social media presence. Here's some research to back that up: In its Connected Leadership survey released in 2021, global business advising firm Brunswick Group posed questions about communication expectations for corporate leaders. It gathered responses from 6,500 employees of companies with more than 1,000 employees. The results showed that the vast majority prefer to work for a CEO who uses social media (this was particularly true for workers under age twenty-five). That's because employees want their leaders to be more accessible, and they also view social media as way for leaders to provide up-to-date information.

Attracting potential talent to your company is a compelling reason to use social media, but it's not the only one. Consider other ways that a CEO's social media presence can benefit a company:

Build and protect your company's reputation. In your social media posts, you can highlight content that reinforces your company's mission. Employees aren't the only ones who will pay attention to your posts. In addition to exploring workers' attitudes, the social media survey mentioned above asked 5,200 readers of financial publications about their views. Seventy-eight percent said they would investigate the CEO's social media accounts when researching a company. Those respondents also indicated they would trust CEOs who use social media nine times more than those who don't. As your company grows and attracts more attention, you may see misinformation about your business start to increase. Misinformation can start as a spark and spread like wildfire. When that happens, you'll want every tool at your disposal to extinguish it, and that includes speaking up on social media. The people watching your company will expect this of its leadership. When a crisis hits, CEOs can't respond with silence. Social media gives them an additional way to show how the company is addressing the situation.

Respect the spirit of the 80/20 rule: You may have heard the 80/20 rule mentioned as a guideline for social media. It means that only 20 percent of your posts should be self-promotions (or, in this case, directly promoting your business), and the other 80 percent should entertain, inform, or support others. Those specific numbers aren't critical, but the intent behind them is. They underscore an important element of your social media strategy: not letting your posts become an insufferable showcase for how wonderful your company is. Adapt the 80/20 ratio as needed, but unless you want to alienate your audience, make sure most of your posts land in the "not all about me" bucket. The main reason is that this is boring. Readers will continue to follow you only if you are providing consistently interesting and insightful content. When that's the case, they don't mind if you slip in a little corporate bragging.

Listen to stakeholders and evangelize your company. Rand Fishkin, cofounder and former CEO of Moz, has said that to lead effectively he needs to both evangelize and listen to many different groups. Social media helps him do both, and he outlines the path he takes to achieve that: "I join the groups I want to influence. Experience their pain. Then participate and share to help," said Fishkin in an article. (I also shared Fishkin's observations on self-awareness in chapter 1 and his thoughts on mental health in chapter 2.) "It's exactly what entrepreneurs do when building a product, and we should apply that same logic to the social media process."

Fishkin said the communities he needs to reach as a leader include potential and current customers, potential and current employees, investors, and executives in related industries. "Social media is the most practical, scalable, and affordable way that I can interact with these communities."

Show the person behind the brand. Purchasing and investment decisions are often influenced by emotion, even for people who pride themselves on logical thinking. The way people feel about you will directly affect the way they feel about your company. With that in mind, let people see your personality and your personal values through social media. You can post about a book you loved, a TV show you just binge-watched, or a video of your failed attempt at learning to juggle. You can also spread goodwill by supporting other people and organizations in your posts.

WATCH YOUR LANGUAGE: The language we use shapes how we think. Comedian George Carlin explored this topic in depth. He urged us not to put our word choice on autopilot, because that can lead to euphemisms and jargon that (intentionally or not) conceal the truth:

I don't like euphemisms, or euphemistic language. And American English is loaded with euphemisms … Americans have trouble facing the truth, so they invent a kind of a soft language to protect themselves from it, and it gets worse with every generation … One of the reasons is because we were using that soft language. The language that takes the life out of life … I'm telling you, some of this language makes me want to vomit. Well, maybe not vomit. Makes me want to engage in an involuntary personal protein spill.

Think about Carlin's take on euphemisms and ask yourself this: when you communicate with employees, customers, or investors, do you use plain language—or do you sometimes hide behind jargon and euphemisms?

Organizing

Although the term *org structure* might not get your pulse racing with excitement, it can make or break your growth trajectory. To achieve your ambitious business goals, you'll have to navigate greater complexity as your company expands. That means creating a clear hierarchy and organizational structure and ensuring that all your employees understand the purpose of each unit and what it's responsible for. Your org structure will also need to unite those units with a common purpose and shared goals. This includes clearly articulating a meaningful mission and vision, which we will discuss in chapter 9, and KPIs to track progress, which we'll cover in detail in chapter 7. Here, we'll discuss the most common ways to approach organizing your firm, then we'll give you some tips for creating the structure that will most effectively meet its needs.

Approaches to Organizational Structure

There are three classic types of organizational structure, as well as some newer hybrid forms. Let's look at how they might apply to smaller, growing companies.

Functional: This is the most common structure, and it's grounded in the value chain (the steps taken to create a product or service and provide it to customers, through departments such as manufacturing, shipping, and customer support). In a functional structure, each link in that value chain (including secondary functions) becomes one organizational unit. Within each unit, there is some sort of employee hierarchy, often reporting to a vice president of a particular function, such as marketing, finance, or engineering (figure 7). Each of these units reports to the relevant C-level executive. For example, marketing, sales, and new product development might all report to the chief marketing officer (CMO). Typically, the C-suite executives all report to the CEO, although in larger companies the reporting structure might have a president or chief operating officer in between the CEO and other C-level execs.

For newer firms, this structure usually provides the best fit, especially when each unit consists of only a few people. Because the roles and responsibilities are clearly defined, you have a straightforward reporting structure. Particularly for a growing company, it's good to avoid unnecessary complexity. The downside of functional structures is that they can promote an attitude of "We're the sales team!" (or the accounting team, or the marketing team, and so on), and this can take the focus away from the company's overall mission and goals. It's hard enough to grow your company without infighting. When an organizational structure creates internal competition among departments and business units, you can end up with unproductive rivalries instead of the cooperation you need to overcome challenges. The best way to avoid this sort of "silo thinking" is to create a culture that rewards teamwork rather than "winning."

FUNCTIONAL ORG CHART

GRAPHIC

fig. 7

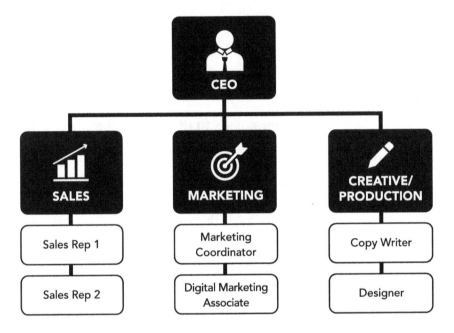

Divisional: This structure is best for more complex organizations that have multiple products in different categories and/or operate in more than one geographical location. In this type of structure, each product category or region will have its own unit, with employees reporting to a unit head who is often a VP. For very large firms, each division might be divided into subunits (for instance, a European unit could have individual countries as subunits). Each unit has its own functional heads with a team supporting them (figure 8).

Although adding divisions can be a useful way to strengthen efforts to expand product offerings or explore new markets, this structure is mostly applied in large organizations. When companies add divisions, critical expertise can get lost because it's spread out (over three sales teams instead of one, for example). For most newer firms, this structure is too complex and top-heavy.

DIVISIONAL ORG CHART

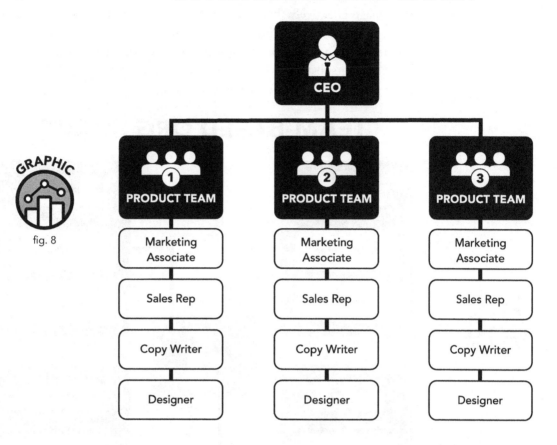

GRAPHIC

fig. 8

Team- or Project-Based: This structure organizes employees into cross-functional teams to work on individual problems or projects, based on the evolving, specific needs of the firm. Employees often work on several teams simultaneously—and in forward-thinking firms, workers have freedom to choose which teams they'd like to join (figure 9). This type of structure represents the backbone of *agile development*, a technology development methodology in which self-organized cross-functional teams work on separate tasks and iterate the development process. (You may have heard the terms "scrum" or "kanban" bandied about—these are agile techniques.) Firms using this sort of organizational structure usually still need some functional units. After all, someone has to pay the bills and handle day-to-day operations while all these cool projects are happening. The cross-functional nature of this structure does help to break down organizational silos, and it's a great reminder to harness the power of teams. When you're grappling with a complex problem, it's a best practice to create a project team to explore solutions. However, this structure requires too much time and energy for most small firms to manage effectively. It involves a great deal of ambiguity in workers' roles, and extra training is required to implement a structure focused less on hierarchy and more on self-directed teams. For organizations already experiencing substantial change, this can create a feeling of uncertainty among workers that undermines productivity.

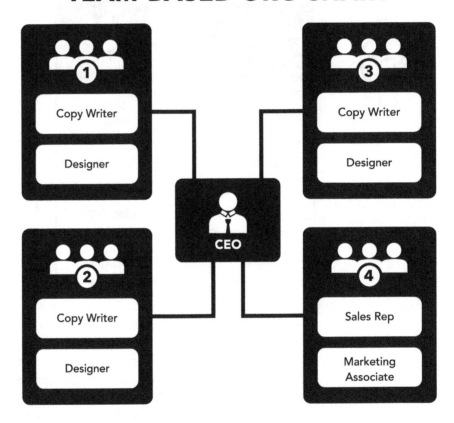

TEAM-BASED ORG CHART

fig. 9

Matrix Structure: Although there are several hybrid structures, this one is particularly common. Matrix structures are hybrids of either functional and team-based structures or divisional and functional structures. In the former case, cross-functional teams are formed around specific issues while the team members maintain their position within a functional unit. In the latter case, units are formed around specific product/geographical lines with each team member maintaining their position in a functional unit (figure 10). As you can imagine, matrix structures are very tricky to manage, as each employee maintains a normal reporting relationship to one unit head and a "dotted line" reporting relationship to another. It's good to have awareness of this structure, but growing organizations will likely want to avoid managing the complexities that accompany it.

HYBRID OF FUNCTIONAL AND PROJECT/ISSUE STRUCTURES

GRAPHIC

fig. 10

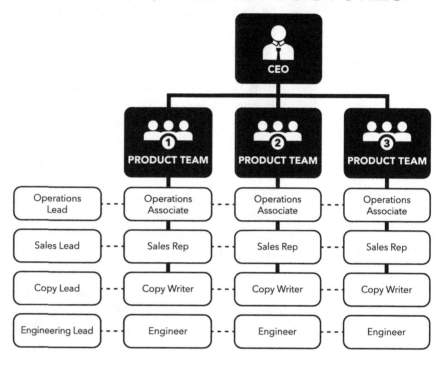

MY TAKE

Internal competition can harm morale. That's why goals and incentives for business units must align with each other as well as with the greater goals of the firm. This is really about organizational culture, which we have already covered. A highly structured organization with misguided incentives can lead to bad outcomes. If the incentives (or corporate values) you communicate encourage one unit to shine at the expense of another, look out. Your company will descend into bickering, backbiting, finger-pointing, blame, and subtle forms of sabotage. People do whatever they are motivated to do, so make sure your employees are motivated to do positive things. Build an organization that encourages collaboration, not infighting.

Create a Nimble Org Structure

When market dynamics shift, as they invariably will, how will your growing company keep up? Your org structure can either help your employees adapt and flourish or hold them back, along with the entire business. If you want to respond with agility, consider these recommendations as you shape your org structure:

» **Make it flexible.** You'll find that rapid changes affecting your business will outpace your ability to reorganize or hire quickly. That's why your company needs flexibility in roles and titles. "In addition, employees should have some latitude in choosing what work they do, and how much of it they can do," says Sharon Poczter, chair of the Strategy and Entrepreneurship Department at Yeshiva University, in an *Inc.* article. "It is essential for founders of scaling companies to continually assess the fit between the work, people, and formal and informal org structure."

» **Make it team-based and mobile.** Instead of just organizing your workers in strictly functional groups like marketing and finance, create teams around customer-, product-, or market-focused projects. If you allow workers to move between projects, their productivity will likely increase as they have the freedom to organically form groups that collaborate effectively. At Google, work employees are explicitly encouraged to change teams, notes Poczter. "Not only does this help reveal information about managers and teams, but it also ensures that high-performing individuals don't leave."

» **Make sure your reporting structure is clear and well-understood.** You may have many elements of a nimble org structure, but you'll have a hard time making them work without a clearly defined reporting structure that everyone in your company understands. This matters, because your employees can help identify threats and opportunities. Vital information can get lost in a muddy reporting structure. That reporting structure will also help your company change course quickly and effectively, because employees will have useful perspectives to share on whether a new strategy is working. You want to ensure that information reaches the right decision makers in a timely fashion.

» **Whenever possible, reduce complexity.** You may discover that a company you admire has an elaborate organizational matrix. Don't let that influence what you choose for *your* company. Your goal is to have fewer people briefing each other in meetings and more people taking action. This can be easy to forget. As your company grows, you will experience new levels of uncertainty. Uncertainty sparks fear, and fear creates a desire for control. For some leaders, adding more structure feels like more control. But if that additional structure doesn't serve an essential purpose, it will weigh your company down.

Decision Making

If the right course of action isn't clear, sometimes it's because there isn't one. Managing requires an almost constant flow of decisions that need to be made, and it's impossible to predict the specific impact of any of them. As Steve Jobs famously said, "There are downsides to everything; there are unintended consequences to everything."

When you're leading a growing company, each day will be filled with a seemingly endless flow of decisions. As you grapple with them, keep the following things in mind:

» Be thoughtful and timely in the decisions you make.

» Consult with experts and other stakeholders before making decisions. Note that "consult" is not the same thing as "pretend to listen." It means truly listening with curiosity, an open mind, and a desire to learn. It also doesn't mean you have to do what they say. At the end of the day, it's your choice, and it's you who has to live with the consequences.

» Communicate your decisions to your team along with the reasoning behind them.

» If a decision will have a significant effect, explain it on social media and other public channels so you can control the narrative as much as possible.

» Be accountable for your decisions; don't blame other people or external forces when things don't go as anticipated.

Decision making is one of those managerial topics that has filled many posts, books, and articles in the literature of both management and psychology. There is no way to do it justice here. I'd just like to add a few thoughts for you to consider as you go about making the dozens of decisions that arise in the typical founder's day.

» Make sure the time and resources you spend on a decision are proportional to its importance. If someone brings you two paint swaths for the breakroom wall, either delegate ("you decide") or pick one quickly. Don't call a meeting, take a vote, or bring in a consultant.

» On the other hand, if it is an important decision, get a variety of perspectives, not just those of your executive team, and to the extent possible, rely on data.

» Read all the articles you want about formal decision-making models, secure in the knowledge that you're not going to use any of them when the rubber hits the road.

You may be surprised at how many founders have a (hopefully symbolic) Magic 8 Ball on their desk.

As a leader, your ability to make effective decisions is critical—but your ability to communicate them in a clear, compelling fashion, be accountable for them, and deal with the ambiguity of the results is just as important.

Chapter Recap

» To motivate and inspire employees through transformational change, smart leaders continually seek ways to strengthen their communication skills.

» The content of your message is critical, but so is the mode of delivery. Take a thoughtful approach when using videoconferencing or social media, for example; otherwise, careless missteps with these communication tools can undermine your message.

» Rethink your meetings, and experiment with approaches to make them more efficient (and even fun).

» As your company expands, so will the level of complexity in your daily operations. For that reason, it's essential to have an organizational structure that supports your ambitious business goals. That can be a functional structure, a divisional structure, a team-based structure, or a hybrid structure.

» Whatever you choose, make the reporting structure clear so decision makers can receive timely updates. Allow flexibility in your structure too, so your company can stay agile when faced with market challenges and opportunities.

» Amid the uncertainty of your growing business, there's one thing you can count on: each day will bring another boatload of decisions you'll need to make. As you make those choices in a timely fashion, seek the opinions of advisors and colleagues you trust, and listen with an open mind.

» Communicate your decisions clearly, and don't make other people guess the reasons behind them. Ultimately, the choices are yours, which means you're also accountable for the outcomes. When your decision doesn't go according to plan, resist the urge to play the blame game. All leaders make business mistakes—but if you fail to take responsibility, you'll only make the situation worse.

| 6 |
Hiring

Chapter Overview
» Building Your Team
» Attraction, Selection, Attrition
» Outsourcing and Advisors

Every night, your most critical business assets walk out the door.
— UNKNOWN

I don't know who said the above quote first, but many have said it since. People keep repeating those words because they reflect a business truth. It's a truth that some founders don't fully appreciate until it's too late: your people are the key source of your competitive advantage.

In my previous book, I wrote about developing a true competitive advantage based on your firm's distinctive competencies or capabilities. Traditionally, the way to measure whether an asset confers true competitive advantage has been to ask this question: To what extent is it valuable to the customer, rare, and not easily imitated or substituted? This question leads many business owners to misattribute their competitive advantage to something like a patent. They forget that a patent is easily copied, duplicated, reverse-engineered, or just worked around entirely. The same applies to most physical assets.

The unique knowledge, culture, and talent of your employees is what will ultimately lead to your success or failure. That means hiring and retaining the right people—two of the most critical tasks you'll have as an owner.

Build a Growth-Minded Team: The Attraction-Selection-Attrition Model

So much of your company's success depends on the hiring process.

Without the right employees to help achieve business goals, your carefully constructed plans for growth will collapse like a house of cards. Founders who take a strategic, thoughtful approach to building successful teams often use a three-part model: Attraction, Selection, Attrition.

GRAPHIC

fig. 11

ATTRACTION	SELECTION	ATTRITION
Getting the best candidates to consider working for you	Choosing employees with qualities to help your company grow	Parting ways with employees who aren't supporting your company's goals

Let's look at each of those in more detail and explore the guiding principles (and concrete steps) that help in recruiting a strong team.

Attraction

To get the best employees, you first have to find them. Your network is a key asset here, but it's not the only one. By relying just on friends and friends of friends, you may not be able to build the fully diverse team that will make you grow and thrive. Cast a wide net—ZipRecruiter, Indeed, and other job boards are helpful. So are social media sites like LinkedIn and Twitter. Use them all, and start building awareness of your company as a good place to work. Follow these guidelines in your search for candidates:

Be intentional and proactive. As mentioned above, you want to cast a wide net in your search, but don't make the mistake of equating "wide net" with posting a couple of ads on Indeed or LinkedIn. A surprising number of companies take this passive—and if we're being honest, lazy—approach. What's not surprising is the lackluster results they get for their pool of candidates. If you want to choose from a top-notch group—and as noted above, you do—then meet those candidates where they are. Think about the spaces where they likely spend time, whether online or IRL, and how you can get their attention. For example, that could mean a trade show, a popular meetup, a master class, or a Facebook group, depending on where you are and what type of hire you're trying to make.

Use your network constructively. If you've read this far, you already understand the importance of building relationships with peers in your industry, as well as founders who work in businesses unrelated to yours. Time you invest in cultivating those relationships will pay off when you're hunting for top talent. Spread the word that you're seeking candidates for particular roles. There's an excellent chance that you're just a couple degrees of separation from your next great hire.

Avoid over-specificity. This is a problem I see repeatedly in job descriptions. Let's say a company is looking for a sales manager, but their ad says that they only want someone who's adept with a particular customer relationship management software. That's way too specific. Anyone who understands the sales process can learn how to use a different piece of software. Yet companies think they're being smart when they get really granular about job requirements. They convince themselves that this approach streamlines the hiring process. Instead, it leads to some bad outcomes: lack of diversity in potential candidates, missing the opportunity to hire great candidates who simply haven't been trained in that specific area, and, perhaps most important, not finding employees with growth potential. Remember that as your company grows, those job requirements will change. And in some cases, they may change rapidly. You want somebody who can say, "I have the competency to do this job right now, but I also have areas where I know I have to expand my skills. And I'm excited to work on those things." You don't need a "perfect" person who already has every single skill they could ever need.

Develop incentive structures that are fair and reward what you value. When you make your company an attractive place to work, you need to create fair incentive structures, whether it's salary, bonuses, or sales commissions. For an example of what not to do, consider this exchange from the comic strip Dilbert:

> **Dilbert's Boss:** *The best I can give you is a 2% raise.*

> **Dilbert:** *No problem. I'll just lower the quality of my work until my pay feels fair.*

> **Dilbert's Boss:** *You can't do that.*

> **Dilbert:** *I'm taking side bets that say I can.*

When it comes to compensation, too many companies benchmark the industry averages for pay and then convince themselves that top-notch employees will stick around. These are often the same companies that insist "people are our best asset." Really? Then why are you rewarding "best" with barely average pay? If you want the best people, you have to find compelling incentives that reflect how much you appreciate the value they bring.

Although compensation has to be part of that, it can't be the only part. It isn't just a matter of throwing money at top talent. Workers care about how their employment affects quality of life—and that includes the ability to work from home. The COVID-19 pandemic forced employers to conduct an abrupt, widespread experiment with telecommuting. Employees quickly became attached to the flexibility of remote work. A Gallup survey released in October 2021 showed that 91 percent of remote workers preferred to keep telecommuting as an option; 37 percent wanted to work from home exclusively, and 54 percent preferred a hybrid work arrangement that included some in-person collaboration. The survey also showed that 31 percent of remote workers said they would be extremely likely to seek another job if their current employer removed the option to work from home.

Now that so many employees have experienced the joy of a work wardrobe consisting of sweatpants (or no pants), they have no interest in going back to the way things were. Unless the position is one that absolutely requires the employee to fulfill their role in person, your company will be at a huge disadvantage if you don't offer work-at-home options. If you want to attract the best people, assume that they are not going to be interested in coming to the office every day.

As younger generations enter the workforce, they're introducing additional priorities that may be unfamiliar to those who have been around longer. Wellness is one example. Although most companies now have wellness programs, they often fail to meet employees' expectations because their focus is too narrow. Wellness isn't just about physical health. This is something younger workers pay close attention to—they prioritize a broader range of wellness aspects, including mental, emotional, and social health. Younger workers also value ethical behavior in company leaders and want to be able to align their personal values with those of their employer. This can include seeking out employers who have a diversity, equity, and inclusion (DEI) officer on staff or who emphasize corporate social responsibility (CSR) initiatives such as reducing environmental impacts and developing more ethical supply chains.

Pay close attention to what younger workers want: Gen Zers and millennials now make up nearly half (46 percent) of the US full-time workforce, according to Gallup research, which also showed that flexible work arrangements are the top priority for those groups, much more so than for baby boomers. To assess whether recruiting strategies are aligned with the expectations of young job seekers, as mentioned above, Gallup suggests considering the following questions:

- Does my talent attraction strategy include an emphasis on employee well-being?
- Does my onboarding program address ethics in a meaningful way?
- How transparent and open are our leaders when they communicate downstream?
- How does my system for advancement and promotion address diversity and inclusion?

At the risk of sounding like Captain Obvious, I will say that younger workers are probably going to make up the majority of your hires. If you happen to be in one of the older demographics, resist the urge to grumble about their "unreasonable" demands, and accept that making your company a welcoming, hospitable place for them to work, grow, and thrive is imperative. This is a business decision, not a political one.

Selection

Thanks to your proactive search process and your company's reputation as a great place to work, you have a pool of well-qualified, high-potential applicants. Well done! Now comes the hard part: picking the one who's the best fit for your company's particular needs at this particular time. To help with this phase of the process, let's examine two of the most common methods used by employers to assess candidates: interviews and personality tests.

The Interview Process: Behavioral Questions and STAR Responses

When you talk with potential candidates, pay careful attention to what they know about your business. Have they done their homework? If not, how can you expect them to be industrious self-starters at your growing company? Gauge their interest in your firm and the industry by noting whether they ask relevant questions that demonstrate they've actually spent time researching your company and thinking about it. And pay attention to thoughtful questions in general, even if they don't relate specifically to your business.

Of course, good responses are enabled by strong interview questions. Over the years, employers have evolved in their thinking about what that actually means. Many have realized there's little value in overly complicated questions, aside from giving the interviewer a momentary thrill of cleverness. But there's nothing clever about ridiculous questions designed to stump interviewees. Google finally came to that conclusion after years of asking questions like "How many golf balls can you fit into an airplane? and How many gas stations are in Manhattan?" By 2013 they had stopped; Laszlo Bock, senior vice president of people operations, called brainteaser questions a "complete waste of time" and said that they "don't predict anything."

Instead, Google emphasizes the sort of questions that have helped many companies strengthen their interview process: behavioral interview questions. These are designed to reveal how candidates have navigated specific workplace challenges in the past, and they can highlight an individual's skills and how they think about problems. This benefits your hiring process because the past informs the future. For example, when you ask, "Tell me about a time when you had a really tough deadline to meet," you get a glimpse into how a candidate might perform if a similar situation occurred at your company. Google's Bock sees the response to these types of questions as revealing on two levels: "One is you get to see how they actually interacted in a real-world situation, and the valuable 'meta' information you get about the candidate is a sense of what they consider to be difficult."

When you ask a behavioral interview question, listen carefully not only for the content of the candidate's answer but for the way they structure their response. The ideal candidate will provide an answer that follows what's known as the STAR framework—Situation, Task, Action, Results—in which the speaker presents information in a specific order (figure 12).

Candidates don't need to know the name of this framework or even realize that they're using it. What matters is that they understand it intuitively. Look for people who use this approach effectively to convey how they addressed a challenge and what outcome it yielded. When candidates give responses that adhere to the STAR framework, you learn two important things: the person cares enough about the position to prepare thoroughly, and they have the ability to clearly communicate important information in a logical, organized way.

GRAPHIC

fig. 12

S T A R

SITUATION	TASK	ACTION	RESULT
Set the scene. What happened, and why was it relevant to the question asked?	Describe the work that needed to be done to resolve the situation.	Explain the specific steps you took to resolve it.	Share the outcomes your actions achieved. Be as specific as possible. Numbers are much better than generalizations.

Open-Ended Questions

Another very revealing type of question is an open-ended one without any expectation of a specific answer. These sorts of questions do a good job of revealing the candidate's personality, ability to think on their feet, and conversational dexterity. Consider these questions:

» "Tell me about yourself."
» "Why are you interested in this position?"
» "Why are you interested in working at Firm X?"

Although you're not expecting any specific answer, you should be expecting a logical, well-formed, and honest-sounding one.

CREATE A GOOD IMPRESSION AS THE INTERVIEWER: Some interviewers think that just because they ask most of the questions, they also hold most—or all—of the power. Someone with this perspective lacks a clear-eyed understanding of the interview dynamic. Remember, the interview evaluation cuts both ways. As you're talking with candidates and wondering if they could be valuable employees, those individuals are wondering whether doing this job is how they want to spend most of their waking hours. With that in mind, here are a couple of steps you can take to make a good impression with candidates:

IMPORTANT

- **BE POSITIVE AND PROUD OF YOUR FIRM**. Entrepreneurs are constantly in problem-solving mode, thinking about the company's weaknesses and how to improve them. That's useful, but don't put that inner monologue on display with potential employees. For instance, when you're interviewing candidates for a head-of-sales position, it's not the time to talk about how hard it is to reach your target audience or how the sales process is a real pain in your industry. Unless your goal is to scare off great candidates, avoid describing the company crisis you're facing that week and focus instead on the benefits of working at your company.

- **PUT YOURSELF IN THE CANDIDATE'S SHOES AND MINIMIZE THE STRESS**. Don't show up late and keep the interviewee waiting, and make sure you create a process that respects the candidate's time overall. That means you need to avoid having many rounds of interviews that drag on for months. Another important way to show respect for your candidates is to clearly communicate what the process entails (we have three rounds of interviews before making a job offer, for example). Give them clear expectations about when they should expect to hear from you after each interview.

Radio silence is not an acceptable way to respond to candidates who didn't make the next round.

Personality Tests: An Imperfect Tool for Your Hiring Process

In recent years, personality tests have gained popularity as a way to assess job candidates. Can these tests help you find the best employees for your company? The short answer is, kind of. These tools have pros and cons you must weigh carefully. On the positive side, personality tests might help you determine whether or not someone has characteristics that would be a good cultural fit with your organization. But there's a complicating factor: the free versions of those tests (which many companies use) won't necessarily capture every facet of the candidate's personality type. Even if they did, I would argue that there's not a "bad" personality type. As you vet potential candidates, you'll want to focus on how people relate to situations and particular work environments. If you take a rigid approach and say, "This type of personality is going to fit here, and this one isn't," you will likely miss out on some excellent employees.

Before you incorporate a personality test into your process, consider this: do you have evidence that the assessment can predict job performance? Remember, the fact that a bunch of other companies use the tests is not the same thing as evidence. If your company is going through transformation, like rapid growth, it might not be a great idea to use them at all. When Integra LifeSciences was experiencing a transformation, the company deliberately put a halt to personality tests. "We're very careful about not putting people in a box with personality tests because we need people who can transform the company and then succeed beyond," said Padma Thiruvengadam, chief human resources officer, in an interview. "Sometimes personality tests give you data that could narrow down the talent pool to something very specific and … that might actually inhibit a company [going] through transformation," Thiruvengadam said, noting that once Integra achieved operational stability, she planned to use personality assessments again as part of the hiring process.

To truly achieve transformational change, your company will need diversity of thought, experience, and background. It's a theme you'll notice throughout this book. Personality matters, because it's yet another area where different types can bring fresh, valuable perspectives.

Here's something else to keep in mind: using personality tests could make you run afoul of federal regulators. That was the case with Best Buy and CVS. In 2018, both companies agreed to stop using personality tests as part of the job application process, after a US Equal Employment Opportunity Commission probe investigated whether the tests were discriminatory (neither company admitted liability).

If you want to explore personality tests as an option, here are three of the most popular assessments used by employers:

» **Myers-Briggs Type Indicator**: Also referred to as the MBTI or simply Myers-Briggs, this is the most well-known test. Although The Myers-Briggs Company notes that 88 percent of Fortune 500 companies use the test, it doesn't specify what percentage of those use it specifically in the hiring process (some companies use it only for team or personal development with existing employees, for example). Inspired by the theory of psychological types described by C. G. Jung, the Myers-Briggs test has ninety-three questions and measures people across four spectrums.

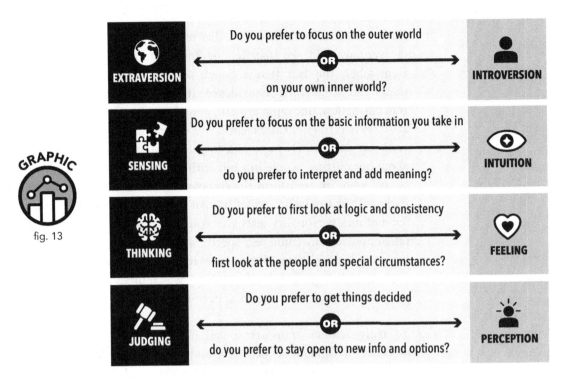

GRAPHIC

fig. 13

The four personality categories (also referred to as the four dichotomies) of the Myers-Briggs Type Indicator (MBTI)

This yields a total of sixteen personality types. When you take the test, you'll end up with a four-letter identifier from the Myers-Briggs alphabet soup. In case you're wondering, INFJ is the rarest personality type, with about 1.5 percent of the (US) population fitting in that category. I'm an INTP, or a "logician."

FUN FACT

Myers-Briggs was developed by Katharine Briggs and her daughter, Isabel Myers. Neither had training in psychology or psychiatry or any clinical experience, but they were both well-educated. Myers graduated from Swarthmore, and Briggs, born in 1875, graduated top of her class from Michigan Agricultural College (now Michigan State). By the mid-1950s, the Myers-Briggs test had taken hold in the corporate world. At one point, General Electric asked Myers to classify personality types for their top executives. She concluded that there was no "perfect" executive type, because each one offered different strengths.

» **The Big Five**: This assessment is based on the five-factor model (used by most psychologists to test personality), which measures the following five traits (figure 14):

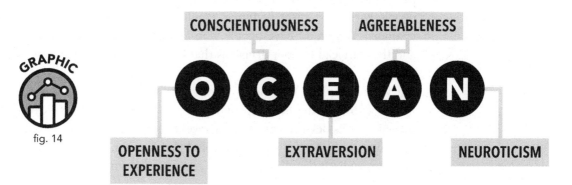

fig. 14

This method also goes by the acronym OCEAN or CANOE, depending on your preference for scrambling letters.

There are different versions of this test with a varying number of statements. Often there are about fifty statements such as "I am respectful and treat others with respect," and "I am full of energy." The test taker responds with one of five options that range from "strongly disagree" to "strongly agree." The final score is on a scale from 0 to 100, based on how strongly the individual associates with each personality trait.

» **The Caliper test (also known as the Caliper Profile)**: This test has been used by more than 65,000 companies and measures twenty-one personality traits. According to Caliper (now called Talogy), it "measures an individual's personality characteristics and individual motivations in order to predict on-the-job behaviors and potential." In an example on the company's website, the candidate for sales manager could be evaluated for "critical competencies" (such as coaching others), "important competencies" (such as composure and resiliency), and "supporting competencies" (such as relationship building).

The Value of Diversity

As you vet job candidates, remember that fostering diversity means much more than fulfilling a legal requirement or applying a "feel-good" label to your business. Diverse workplaces bring different points of view—which lead to better decisions, more innovative problem solving, and better outcomes. Of course, for that to happen you need to include those diverse perspectives in the decision-making process. If you simply hire more people with your exact pedigree, you'll end up shouting into an echo chamber. You won't have people who challenge your way of thinking, and that can lead to poor decisions that harm your company's growth.

The venture capital (VC) industry is a great example of how homogeneity fosters a "follow the herd" mentality. To get a sense of VC's dearth of diversity, consider the results of a recent report on the VC workforce compiled by National Venture Capital Association, Venture Forward, and Deloitte. Of the VC investment professionals surveyed:

» Women represented 23 percent, up from 21 percent in 2018.
» Black workers represented 4 percent, up from 3 percent in 2018.
» Latinx workers represented 4 percent, down from 5 percent in 2018.

Keep in mind that according to some research, about three quarters of venture-backed firms in the US don't return investors' capital. That can't necessarily be always attributed to poor decision making and groupthink, but I do believe strongly that having diverse perspectives and points of view on your team is a strong competitive advantage and leads to better decisions and better outcomes.

That lack of diversity has real implications for who gets funding. Crunchbase found that, by the end of August 2020, Black and Latinx founders had raised $2.3 billion in funding, representing 2.6 percent of the total $87.3 billion in funding given to all founders by that point in the year.

So it's no wonder Tristan Walker ran into trouble when he sought funding. You might remember reading about that in chapter 1. He founded Walker & Company Brands in 2013 to provide health and beauty products to people of color and created the product line Bevel focused on the shaving needs of Black men. Walker met with sixty investors to ask for funding, and all but three said no. His company grew nonetheless, and in 2017 it was purchased by Proctor & Gamble, which reportedly paid somewhere between $20 million and $40 million.

PUSH BACK AGAINST "NOT A GOOD CULTURAL FIT": A common criticism you'll hear of potential candidates is that they're "not a good cultural fit." That objection has a big problem. "Cultural fit" is a vague term that's often based on gut instinct, says Wharton management professor Katherine Klein, vice dean of the Wharton Social Impact Initiative. "The biggest problem is that while we invoke cultural fit as a reason to hire someone, it is far more common to use it to not hire someone. People can't tell you what aspect of the culture they are worried about."

When this phrase pops up, make sure you nail down exactly what the person meant. The "cultural fit" criticism can be shorthand for "I don't feel comfortable around this person because they're different from me," and that is not a valid reason to reject a candidate. "Sometimes I hear feedback like 'She isn't a good cultural fit,'" said Dawn Smith, formerly the chief legal officer at VMware, the Palo Alto–based maker of virtualization software, in an interview. "So I say, 'Tell me exactly what you mean. Why don't you think she's a good fit?' And if they say, 'I can't put my finger on it,' I ignore it. But if they say something like, 'She sees things as black-or-white' or 'She jumps to conclusions,' then I consider it."

Attrition

No matter how thorough you are with the hiring process, people are going to leave your company at some point. Sometimes it will be their choice, but there are also situations in which you realize an employee isn't going to work out. This is why it's so important to have strong HR processes and procedures in place (an issue we will cover in chapter 7). Even if your company isn't large enough yet to have a head of HR, you still need to ensure that procedures are not only followed but documented. You'll quickly discover how much that matters if someone files a complaint that you lacked sufficient reason to fire them.

I've never met anyone who enjoys firing people (I know they exist, but I wouldn't want to hang out with them). It's not fun. You know what's even less fun? Delaying the inevitable. When you do that, the situation doesn't go away. Instead, it becomes increasingly unpleasant for you and everyone else on your team.

Sometimes you'll have a good employee who's just in the wrong position, and you can find another role for them on a different team. But if an employee truly isn't working out at your company, they likely know it and feel it. If you wait for weeks or months and let the situation fester, you're not benefiting anyone.

Here's how you can help the person you're about to fire: be kind. Don't be a jerk. And unless you're Michael Corleone in *The Godfather*, don't try to tell them "it's strictly business." That line is for execs trying to reassure themselves when they act like jerks.

Remember that when you terminate somebody, you're taking away their livelihood. You're also telling them that on some level their work is not good enough, and it always hurts when we feel like we've failed. Even though you'll reassure them, the voice inside their head will likely say, "You're a failure." It's a very emotional, vulnerable moment for most people. Try to make that moment a little less painful by showing kindness.

Being decent to others should be your main motivation here. It's always the right thing to do. But since this is a business book, I'll throw in a couple of pragmatic reasons too. If you act like a jerk when you're firing someone, you could be inviting a lawsuit. Even if that doesn't happen, think about this: imagine that everyone who gets fired from your company receives a megaphone on the way out the door. What message would you like them to shout in the streets? Think about how many times people will retell the story of how they got fired—in private and on social media. Now think about all the top-tier talent you'd love to have working at your company and how they'll react when they hear someone was treated like crap when fired. Be kind or be a jerk. It's your choice, and one that can make or break your company's ability to attract the best candidates.

Outsourcing: How to Decide What to Keep In-House

The team that supports your company extends beyond your employees. It also includes outsourced workers—a topic I covered in my first book because outsourcing decisions play a critical role in the early days of a business. As your company grows, you'll need to make even more choices about outsourcing. Fortunately, there is an abundance of resources to help you select contract workers. In recent years, it's become much easier to find contractors, freelancers, and virtual assistants—as well as more traditional companies that you can outsource entire functions to, via apps and online marketplaces. In fact, with services such as Shopify or Fulfillment by Amazon (FBA), you can run an entire e-commerce empire with practically no employees. But don't get swept up in an outsourcing frenzy. To maintain a serious competitive advantage, you'll need to be judicious.

Your Value Chain and Competencies

As I describe in my first book, *Starting a Business QuickStart Guide*, your **value chain** includes all the steps involved in creating your product or service and providing it to customers—for example, receiving raw materials, manufacturing the product, selling it, shipping it, and providing customer service (figure 15). To clarify where the real value resides in your company's activities, I have an incredibly useful exercise for you to do: map out the major pieces of your value chain. If you haven't done this exercise yet, don't wait any longer. Set aside time for it this week.

fig. 15

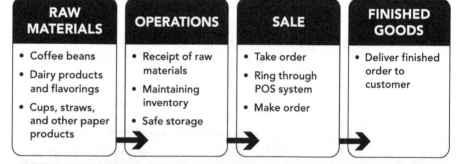

RAW MATERIALS	OPERATIONS	SALE	FINISHED GOODS
• Coffee beans • Dairy products and flavorings • Cups, straws, and other paper products	• Receipt of raw materials • Maintaining inventory • Safe storage	• Take order • Ring through POS system • Make order	• Deliver finished order to customer

SECONDARY ACTIVITIES

1. Marketing to bring customers into store
2. Upkeep, maintenance, and regular updates to retail space
3. IT to maintain POS system, accept payments, and support an order-ahead app

By mapping out your value chain—as shown here with a coffee shop example—you'll have a visual tool to help assess each step of your value-creation process.

The value-chain exercise will help you determine if there's a redundant step in your process, or one that doesn't provide any benefit as an in-house activity. This will allow you to pinpoint your distinctive competencies. When you thoroughly analyze your value chain, you assess the areas where you are irreplaceable. If the answer is "nowhere," then you have a real problem, because you're going to lose in the marketplace.

Once you've identified your competencies, you need to determine how various functions within your company support them. When part of your value chain isn't creating real value, you should explore the possibility of outsourcing. If your strength is R&D, consider outsourcing manufacturing. Perhaps marketing is a strong skill set at your firm; if so, you could think about outsourcing part of your product development. If a function isn't supporting your real distinctive competencies—the things that give you a true competitive advantage—then it may not make sense to keep it in-house.

As you contemplate shifting your business into an even higher growth phase, consider whether your outsourced services can scale with your company. You need stable, reliable vendors with the capacity to ramp up quickly, whether or not they're part of your primary value chain. For example, if your web services group consists of a teenager living in his parents' basement in Eastern Europe, what will happen when your site hits increase by one thousand?

Options for Outsourcing

After you've decided what you want to outsource, you need to identify who you can trust to do the work. Here are three approaches to help guide your search:

» **Hire contractors through Upwork or Fiverr.** If you need assistance with a discrete function or a specific project, you can explore websites like Upwork, Fiverr, or Toptal that connect businesses with contractors. These sites feature contractors for a range of work, including sales and marketing, IT, customer service, and admin tasks. You'll find that the quality of contractors on these sites varies widely, so pay close attention to the ratings for each individual, and look for contractors with a long record of positive feedback from previous clients.

» **Use social media.** Twitter is a popular tool for finding contractors, particularly in the tech startup space. If you're active on Twitter and have a decent following, start tweeting about what you'd like to outsource and ask your followers for recommendations. LinkedIn is useful for this purpose as well. If your need is great enough, consider joining LinkedIn Premium and using its recruiting services.

» **Use your network**. If you've followed the advice in this book, you likely belong to more than one professional group, whether it's local entrepreneurs, a mastermind group, or a Facebook group related to your industry. You should use them to recruit contractors. That's why these groups exist. They allow members to help each other reach business goals. Inform the people in your groups about your search for a web designer, and let them know if you have certain requirements in mind (like you're hoping to keep your budget below a certain amount). You'll likely end up with plenty of recommendations from people who can provide detailed descriptions of their experiences with contractors.

Advisors: An Indispensable Part of Your Team

As you look for professional advisors who can work with you and support your goals, seek out individuals who can grow with you. This is not a collection of people you want to swap out every year or two. Ideally, you will maintain long-term relationships that give them a deep understanding of the inner workings of your business. When you assemble your team, here are some of the professional advisors you will want to include:

» **Attorney**: You might not have a legal department yet, but you absolutely need an attorney to help you sort out contracts and navigate potential legal minefields. If you don't have one, ask your network for recommendations.

» **Accountant**: Could you do your own taxes? Sure, but should you? Here's my answer: you'd be crazy to do that on your own. Accounting is an area where you need to rely on an expert. And even if you happen to be brilliant at accounting, it's not a smart way to spend your time as a founder. (However, that does not excuse you from understanding your financials!)

» **Board of advisors**: Your *board of advisors* is a group of industry experts who meet periodically to review your progress, go over any issues you're having, and act as a sounding board for you to bounce ideas off of. Boards range from very informal groups to formal, compensated structures similar to the fiduciary board of directors required of a C corporation. If you have investors, they will want a seat on your board, and they may bring others with them. Seek people who have strong networks in your industry. This will help you attract talent, and it could even help you attract financing. Your board of advisors may also connect you with high-quality vendors. As part of your criteria, you'll want people who will challenge your ideas. You won't be able to achieve that if most of your advisors are just a reflection of you, whether in gender, race, or education. It's critical to have people who bring different perspectives and aren't shy about expressing them. Think of your board as your last line of defense against potentially stupid decisions. You don't want a group of disinterested people who will simply give your ideas a rubber stamp of "Sure, sounds good."

If you've been using the same advisors since your startup days, now is a good time to take a fresh look at them. Are they able to help you take your firm to the next level? As with your employees, a little attrition among your advisors is not only expected, it's healthy.

Although your business may have started with one great idea and one person (namely, you), its continued success and expansion will depend on the team you build. As we emphasized in this chapter, that team extends beyond employees—it includes contractors and advisors. When you select all of these individuals with care, you'll find diverse opinions to challenge your own and skill sets that strengthen your organization's weak spots.

Chapter Recap

» If you can hire and retain the right people, you will create a significant competitive advantage for your company. One strategic approach to building a growth-minded team is the Attraction-Selection-Attrition model.

» Attraction means getting the best candidates to consider working for you. Design a proactive search that targets the places where your ideal candidates spend time, and enlist your network in the hunt. After you hire talented workers, show how much you value their contributions by creating attractive incentive structures.

» Selection involves choosing employees with qualities that will help your company grow. Ditch the overly complicated interview questions. Instead, focus on behavioral interview questions, and pay close attention to the way candidates structure their responses. The information they provide should follow the STAR framework (Situation, Task, Action, Results).

» Attrition requires you to part ways with employees who aren't supporting your company's goals. When you determine a worker isn't a good fit at your company, don't delay in taking action. The longer you wait, the more difficult it becomes for all parties involved. It's painful to fire someone, but it hurts a lot more for the person losing their livelihood. When you need to terminate an employee, kindness is key.

» To maximize growth potential, include contractors on your team. The goal isn't to outsource as much as possible. Instead, take a strategic and selective approach by assessing your value chain. Look for functions that don't support a true competitive advantage and consider whether they really belong in-house.

| 7 |

Create Scalable Systems and Processes

Chapter Overview
» Policies vs. Processes/Procedures
» Your SOP Manual
» KPIs and How to Develop Them

Standard operating procedures (SOPs) and key performance indicators (KPIs) are terms you've doubtless heard used over and over again in business media. But do you know how they are used, why they are important, and how to develop them? The crux of this chapter is about creating and using these fundamental operational tools. I then dive into the rough waters of essential software for your organization (rough because it changes so quickly that the sections may be obsolete by the time this is published!). I finish with a few other operational issues that may not have occurred to you but will become more important as your firm grows.

Standardizing Policies and Procedures

When people aren't immersed in the world of management, they sometimes confuse *policies* with *procedures* and vice versa. You might be one of those people, and that's OK—because this chapter is where the confusion ends and clarity begins. Before we go any further, let's define the two terms. As you'll see, they play fundamentally different roles in your organization:

» **Procedures** are sets of steps designed to achieve an outcome; they specify how you do things. Be aware that I'll use this term interchangeably with *processes*. (Although they actually mean slightly different things, the difference isn't relevant for our purposes here.)

» **Policies** are sets of rules for specific decisions that organizations need to make periodically. They explain why you do things, or why you do them a certain way. If you construct your policies carefully, they should reflect your company's culture and overall mission.

To make this more concrete, here's an example of the distinction between procedures and policies. Let's say you need to add someone to your marketing team. To achieve that, you follow the procedure of your hiring process. You go through basic steps like placing ads and vetting candidates through interviews (and possibly background checks). But you will likely have policies that shape the way you take those procedural steps. You may have a policy on diversity, which underscores your organization's preference for a diverse workforce. That policy informs your hiring procedures—by providing a "why," it influences the specific steps you'll take. That could mean advertising the job opening on certain sites and online forums that are more likely to attract a diverse pool of candidates.

Although policies and procedures aren't the same thing, they do complement each other. Make sure they're closely linked when you document them. For example, if you have a chapter on hiring in your manual, include all your policies and procedures for hiring in that section.

Tacit vs. Explicit Knowledge:
What's the Difference, and Why Does It Matter?

You've heard the phrase "knowledge is power." But that's only true if you have access to the right knowledge at the right time. When it comes to the availability of knowledge, you want a system that's reliable. To that end, we must distinguish between two categories of knowledge: explicit and tacit.

Explicit knowledge is codified in a ***knowledge management system***, which is software that collects and organizes essential information for your company so all employees can easily access what they need. *Tacit knowledge* resides only in the heads of one or a few of your workers. You want your organizational knowledge to be durable like granite rather than like sand that can easily slip between your fingers and be lost forever. That's the difference between explicit knowledge and tacit knowledge.

To illustrate this distinction, let's use a hypothetical Bob the HR Guy. Bob knows his CEO wants a diverse workforce, so he follows specific steps to ensure the company can attract and select diverse candidates. And that's great, except those steps only exist within Bob's head. Thus, those steps are—you guessed it—tacit knowledge.

An organization that runs on tacit knowledge will do just fine if there are no staff changes. But as you know by now, that's a fantasy scenario. Those changes occur throughout the year, every year. What happens when Bob the HR Guy resigns, or gets fired, or suddenly needs to take medical leave for weeks or months? His replacement doesn't know any of the stuff that resides in Bob's head. That means Bob's replacement has to start from scratch. Not only is this inefficient, it also practically guarantees that the replacement will make some significant mistakes that could have been avoided if only he'd had access to explicit knowledge about HR's processes and policies for diversity. That's why you have to write it down. Take the tacit knowledge in Bob's head and make it explicit.

It may seem obvious that explicit knowledge plays an essential role in your company's health. Still, it's worth considering the specific reasons why this is true. As you know from the HR Bob scenario discussed above, having a repository of explicit knowledge prevents information and expertise from residing solely in individuals who might leave your company, forget important steps, or make changes of their own accord that foul up a process. Documenting knowledge in your company may feel tedious, but it will be worth the effort. Here are other ways that explicit knowledge matters in your organization:

1. It creates a common understanding of how and why your company does things in certain ways.

2. It helps build company culture by establishing a unified approach to important issues.

3. It makes decision making transparent. This removes questions of bias or capriciousness.

4. Everyone does things the same way, which helps your organization operate with consistency.

5. Everyone can be fairly held accountable for their actions because they understand what's expected.

6. It helps in training new employees, allowing them to get up to speed more quickly—as opposed to having them learn from key employees and hoping they take good notes (or even figure out the right questions to ask).

Standard Operating Procedures (SOPs)

When you have specialized knowledge that's readily available, it can also help you make better decisions faster. This information—including your policies and procedures—should be gathered in one place. Specifically, that place is a document called a *standard operating procedure manual*, or SOP manual. It is your organization's bible. It should be the go-to reference for everything, and you should have policies and procedures in place for—you guessed it—updating and modifying your SOPs. Next, we'll take a look at the basic steps you'll take to develop one.

Steps for Developing an SOP Manual

1. Download a standard SOP manual template. You can find an SOP Template in your Digital Asset Vault to get started. You can also find others available online. If you decide to pay a few bucks for one, consider it money well spent, because you will avoid starting from scratch and potentially missing important areas that should be covered.

2. Collect all existing policies and procedures and place them in the appropriate sections of the template.

3. Evaluate your current policies and procedures, and look for obvious gaps. For example, are you missing procedures related to operations or customer service? If you identify gaps, assign teams in the relevant areas to draft what's missing, based on their understanding of the correct way to do things. Do not hire consultants to do this, except as potential facilitators if you're really stuck.

4. Set up a committee of key managers and unit owners to review and amend. Make sure to include consequences for noncompliance. Rules don't mean much unless they're enforced, and they're not fair unless workers have a clear understanding of the repercussions. For example, let's say someone doesn't follow the safety procedures for handling hazardous materials. Will they get a warning? Will they get suspended with pay? Or will you just ask them nicely not to do it again?

5. Post the policies and procedures, which will allow for comments from your employees, and make changes as necessary. This step is critical because, to get buy-in, you need to get everyone involved. And by giving all your employees the chance to voice their opinions, you'll have a better final product. Frontline workers may

have suggestions for policies or procedures that never would have occurred to management.

6. Publish the resulting manual.

7. Provide training for complex issues, such as bias or harassment, and offer ongoing refresher training on key policies and procedures such as hazardous materials handling and accounting fraud.

8. Stay open to feedback and continue to modify as needed. Remember, this a living document, just like your strategic plan. It's not something you put on a shelf and never look at again.

Key Areas to Include in Your SOPs

Although no two SOP manuals will be exactly the same, there are some basic areas that all should cover. Keep in mind that SOPs serve a purpose beyond helping you run your business. If you decide to sell the company, a detailed SOP manual will be critical. This documentation gives potential buyers (and investors) the confidence that a hand-off to new owners will go more smoothly. At the bare minimum, be sure your SOP manual includes the following:

Human Resources

As your company grows, you will need to formalize your approach to HR. The system (or lack thereof) you used when your company had five employees won't work as your head count reaches fifty and beyond. When a founder is focused on growing their company, it's easy to put this on the "someday" list. Don't make that mistake, because if you lack essential HR documentation, you could quickly find yourself in legal trouble. When you hire and fire workers, you don't want to be accused of violating labor laws. If you aren't documenting your HR processes (like hiring and employee evaluation), make it a top priority. Not doing so can be costly: look at Riot Games, a video game publisher recently ordered to pay $100 million in damages and legal fees to female employees past and present as a result of discrimination, harassment, and misconduct. A clear employee handbook will show how to address violations well before they become bigger legal problems.

Remember that your employee handbook should be a living document, so update it regularly. Your HR documentation might include the following areas:

fig. 16

DEPARTMENT: **HUMAN RESOURCES**
• **HIRING AND FIRING**: creating job descriptions and placing ads; evaluating applications; interviewing; parameters for benefits and compensation, onboarding, and termination procedures (including ongoing feedback and documentation of substandard performance) • **MANAGING WORKERS**: training, disciplinary actions, wellness programs, annual reviews, etc.

Sales

To increase revenue and take advantage of new markets, you'll need documentation that helps new salespeople contribute sooner to your organization's success. When you formalize your sales process, the expansion of your sales team will require less effort. As with the rest of your SOPs, you'll want to do more than outline tasks. Your documentation should give employees a sense of why these things matter and how they guide the business toward critical objectives. For example, managers and sales representatives can forecast revenue by using the sales pipeline—it lets them know where prospects are in the sales process and can help them estimate the likelihood of closing a deal. Areas to cover in sales SOPs include the following:

fig. 17

DEPARTMENT: **SALES**
• **CREATING A SALES PIPELINE**: hopefully with robust customer relationship management (CRM) software • **LEAD NURTURING**: what are the steps involved in building relationships with qualified leads throughout stages of the sales funnel? • **TRACKING CUSTOMER SATISFACTION** • **PRODUCT RETURNS OR REQUESTS FOR REFUNDS**

Accounting

Accounting is responsible for keeping a complete, accurate record of every financial transaction. Unless you have a reliable system in place, you'll have a hard time fulfilling that basic role. If you don't have a handle on the numbers that matter, it will be difficult to assess the true health of your business. A powerful accounting system will help you spot trends and anomalies—and guide your decisions to change course—as you run daily reports with relevant metrics. Below are some areas to document:

GRAPHIC

fig. 18

DEPARTMENT: ACCOUNTING

- **PAYROLL:** policies and procedures

- **BUDGETING AND FINANCIAL MANAGEMENT**

- **FINANCIAL REPORTING**

- **TAX READINESS** (although I always advise my clients to use a CPA to actually file taxes)

MY TAKE

FINANCIAL FRIDAYS: Many founders dread looking at their numbers, usually because they don't understand them as well as they should. This has led an increasing number of firms to adopt "Financial Fridays." As the name suggests, it's a set day, either weekly or monthly, when the founder or founding team looks at their financials in detail. Having Financial Fridays enforces the discipline needed to monitor this critical part of running a business. My advice is to keep it lighthearted and fun, and reward yourself afterward with a happy hour or other relaxing team activity. However, the event's main purpose should be taken very seriously. Your financials are the health diagnostics of your firm, and Financial Fridays are your "checkups." You need to know if everything is going well—and if not, you need answers. For example, let's say sales are coming in according to plan, but inventory is still piling up. You need to investigate why. Or perhaps sales are lagging, and all your salespeople are making their quotas except one. What are the challenges faced by this employee? How can you help? You need to be proactive and resolve issues before they escalate into major problems. Financial Fridays can serve as your early-warning system.

Procurement/Purchasing

When done effectively, procurement serves as a strategic function that can help improve your company's profitability. It allows you to streamline processes, reduce costs, and identify better suppliers. When you document effective procurement strategies at your company, it equips your employees to make smarter purchasing choices. Here are some areas to include:

fig. 19

DEPARTMENT:
PROCUREMENT/PURCHASING

- **DEFINING THE NEED:** outline the specifications and scope of work

- **IDENTIFYING POTENTIAL SUPPLIERS**

- **SOLICITING BIDS AND EVALUATING PROPOSALS**

- **ETHICAL CONDUCT:** avoiding conflicts of interest, etc.

Quality Management

If companies aren't careful, rapid growth can ruin the quality of the products they provide. This happens for a variety of reasons: teams grow too large and the focus on product excellence gets diluted, or a surge in new customers leaves the organization scrambling to fill orders. That's why quality management becomes even more critical as your business grows. It can prevent problems with your products, address problems quickly when they do occur, and enable continuous improvement. As you grow, you may want to adopt industry certifications like LEED (the gold standard for green buildings) or Six Sigma (which requires workers to demonstrate vital skills for identifying and eliminating business process errors). Trust me, nothing will stunt your growth like product quality issues. Keep these areas in mind when you create documentation for quality management:

fig. 20

DEPARTMENT:
QUALITY MANAGEMENT

- **QUALITY OBJECTIVES:** what are the stated goals of your product and what purpose does it serve for customers?

- **ORGANIZATION:** define how the entire product life cycle links to clearly defined roles in your org chart

- **DATA MANAGEMENT:** track customer satisfaction and supplier performance

- **CONTINUOUS IMPROVEMENT PROCESSES**

The **Entrepreneurial Operating System**™: Gino Wickman, best-selling author of *Traction: Get a Grip on Your Business*, is the creator of the Entrepreneurial Operating System, or EOS. It's designed to help entrepreneurs focus on the right outcomes for their businesses. EOS includes a trademarked approach to running meetings called Level 10 Meetings. This ninety-minute meeting agenda is broken into several sections, most of which last only five minutes. For example, the five-minute Rock Review is meant to identify any issues standing in the way of completing your company's quarterly priorities. As EOS Worldwide (the company founded by Wickman) explains: "Rocks are the three to seven most important objectives for the company and each person for the quarter. Reporting on the Rocks keeps everyone apprised of your progress toward achieving your quarterly priorities. It also helps people focus on the ultimate purpose of the meeting: to work toward achieving those priorities. Go through the list of Rocks and ask each Rock owner to simply state if they are on track or off track."

The EOS model focuses on six components of a business that must be strengthened. Here they are, as described on the EOS Worldwide site:

» **Vision:** Strengthening this component means getting everyone in the organization 100 percent on the same page with where you're going and how you're going to get there.

» **People:** This means surrounding yourself with great people, top to bottom, because you can't achieve a great vision without a great team.

» **Data:** This means cutting through all the feelings, personalities, opinions, and egos and boiling your organization down to a handful of objective numbers that give you an absolute pulse on where things are.

When those components are strong, this leads to a transparent, open and honest organization where challenges become more visible. According to the EOS model, this allows your business to focus effectively on the remaining three components, as described on the EOS Worldwide site:

» **Issues:** Strengthening this component means becoming great at solving problems throughout the organization—setting them up, knocking them down, and making them go away forever.

» **Process**: This is the secret ingredient in your organization. This means "systemizing" your business by identifying and documenting the core processes that define the way to run your business. You'll need to get everyone on the same page with what the essential procedural steps are, and then get everyone to follow them to create consistency and scalability in your organization.

» **Traction®**: This means bringing discipline and accountability into the organization—becoming great at execution—taking the vision down to the ground and making it real.

Key Performance Indicators (KPIs)

Key performance indicators, or KPIs, are more than just numbers in a report. They help you analyze your company's performance and health so you can make adjustments to your execution. Like any metric we've discussed, KPIs must be specific, measurable, achievable, relevant, and time-bound to be effective. For example, "improve our average customer satisfaction score" isn't an effective KPI metric. The intent to improve it isn't enough. If you decide you'll aim to improve that score by 10 percent within twelve months, now you've made it concrete and given it a sense of urgency. KPIs allow you to see if you're on target and enable you to implement company goals. By measuring the appropriate KPIs, you can achieve faster results.

KPIs play an important role in strategic planning (as we will explore in chapter 9) because they support business objectives. They also serve as a useful management tool, allowing teams to see how they are contributing to (or hindering) the organization's success. Let's explore the need to develop KPIs for each unit in your company. Here's what KPIs enable you to do:

1. **Break down large-scale organizational strategic goals into specific tasks for each organizational unit**. For example, to acquire more customers, one of the steps your sales team might take is to respond more quickly to customer leads. As it turns out, many companies could improve in that area. A study from a few years ago measured how long it took 2,241 US companies to respond to a web-generated test lead. The results: among companies that responded within thirty days, the average response time was forty-two hours—and 23 percent of the companies never responded at all.

2. **Measure progress on each major task and assign it a goal value**. If you track sales team response time, you might also want to track

sales close ratio, for example (the number of deals closed compared to the number of formal quotes given to potential customers). But don't go overboard with KPIs—limit them to five per unit at most. You want to motivate your teams to improve, not make them feel overwhelmed from the start. Also, some KPIs will relate to more than one unit. For example, the MQL to SQL conversion rate looks at cooperation between marketing and sales, because it's the percentage of marketing qualified leads that get converted into sales qualified leads.

3. **Empower unit heads to run their day-to-day operations without interference**. Give them the flexibility to problem-solve and remove obstacles that impede progress.

4. **Monitor unit progress by tracking KPIs.** Look for trends as you compare each month's data set with those of previous months. In manufacturing, for example, patterns in unscheduled downtime (the result of operator error or equipment malfunction) could highlight ways to improve processes and assess overall equipment effectiveness. Keep in mind that the frequency for monitoring KPIs will vary widely. Although some KPIs may be viewed in real time (such as defect tracking, so manufacturers avoid running defective lines for several days), most KPIs can be tracked weekly, monthly, quarterly, or even yearly.

NOTE

KPIs are not a measure of individual performance. If you're a salesperson, you can be held accountable to a sales quota, but you can't be held accountable for the sales of the firm. KPIs track group performance. But they must focus on quantifiable activity that's within the control of the relevant unit. Here's what I mean: you can't take a new product development group and make them responsible for sales. Sure, that group has some control over the quality of products, but that's not the same thing as influencing sales volume. If you hold someone responsible for things they can't control, that's not a reasonable goal. You can go crazy with these metrics, trying to make everything measurable. When you choose what to measure, remember to make it meaningful. Something may be quantifiable, but that doesn't mean it's worth tracking.

Legal and Government Compliance

Compliance obligations will inform your KPIs if your business has many regulations to follow; a waste management company will be much more concerned about compliance-related KPIs than a jewelry store. Even if your industry isn't a highly regulated one, you'll likely still have some basic regulations to follow regarding employment and marketing, for example. When you meet compliance obligations, you are not only reducing the risk of fines or lawsuits, you are also demonstrating that your organization cares about the health and well-being of its employees and customers. Some regulations do cover a broad swath of organizations—the examples below aren't comprehensive, but they serve as reminders of rules that likely apply to your company:

Use email marketing responsibly, or face tough penalties
The CAN-SPAM Act established rules of conduct for all commercial email, which the law defines as "any electronic mail message the primary purpose of which is the commercial advertisement or promotion of a commercial product or service," including email that promotes content on commercial websites. Companies that choose not to comply will quickly find that it's expensive to flout this law. According to the FTC, each separate email in violation of the CAN-SPAM Act is subject to penalties of up to $46,517. This is how the FTC's website describes the main requirements of the CAN-SPAM Act:

1. **Don't use false or misleading header information.** Your "From," "To," "Reply-To," and routing information—including the originating domain name and email address—must be accurate and identify the person or business who initiated the message.

2. **Don't use deceptive subject lines**. The subject line must accurately reflect the content of the message.

3. **Identify the message as an ad**. The law gives you a lot of leeway in how to do this, but you must disclose clearly and conspicuously that your message is an advertisement.

4. **Tell recipients where you're located**. Your message must include your valid physical postal address. This can be your current street address, a post office box you've registered with the U.S. Postal Service, or a private mailbox you've registered with a commercial mail receiving agency established under Postal Service regulations.

5. **Tell recipients how to opt out of receiving future email from you.** Your message must include a clear and conspicuous explanation of how the recipient can opt out of getting email from you in the future. Craft the notice in a way that's easy for an ordinary person to recognize, read, and understand. Creative use of type size, color, and location can improve clarity. Give a return email address or another easy internet-based way to allow people to communicate their choice to you. You may create a menu to allow a recipient to opt out of certain types of messages, but you must include the option to stop all commercial messages from you. Make sure your spam filter doesn't block these opt-out requests.

6. **Honor opt-out requests promptly.** Any opt-out mechanism you offer must be able to process opt-out requests for at least 30 days after you send your message. You must honor a recipient's opt-out request within 10 business days. You can't charge a fee, require the recipient to give you any personally identifying information beyond an email address, or make the recipient take any step other than sending a reply email or visiting a single page on an Internet website as a condition for honoring an opt-out request. Once people have told you they don't want to receive more messages from you, you can't sell or transfer their email addresses, even in the form of a mailing list. The only exception is that you may transfer the addresses to a company you've hired to help you comply with the CAN-SPAM Act.

7. **Monitor what others are doing on your behalf.** The law makes clear that even if you hire another company to handle your email marketing, you can't contract away your legal responsibility to comply with the law. Both the company whose product is promoted in the message and the company that actually sends the message may be held legally responsible.

Report workforce data if you have one hundred or more employees. Companies with one hundred or more employees (federal contractors with at least fifty employees and at least $50,000 in government contracts) must submit an EEO-1 Report to the EEOC and the US Department of Labor every year. This is a government form that requests data about the ethnicity, race, and gender of your employees.

Comply with federal employment antidiscrimination laws

As your head count increases, make sure you continue to comply with federal employment antidiscrimination laws. These laws vary depending on the number of employees your business has. Here's how the EEOC website describes that breakdown. (Remember that state and/or local employment discrimination laws may also apply to your company.)

» **If you have at least one employee:** You are covered by the law that requires employers to provide equal pay for equal work to male and female employees.

» **If you have 15 to 19 employees:** You are covered by the laws that prohibit discrimination based on race, color, religion, sex (including pregnancy, sexual orientation, or gender identity), national origin, disability, and genetic information (including family medical history). You are also covered by the law that requires employers to provide equal pay for equal work.

» **If you have 20 or more employees:** You are covered by the laws that prohibit discrimination based on race, color, religion, sex (including pregnancy, sexual orientation, or gender identity), national origin, age (40 or older), disability, and genetic information (including family medical history). You are also covered by the law that requires employers to provide equal pay for equal work.

Stay up to date with licenses and certifications for your industry.

Renewal requirements vary for different states, cities, and counties. For some professional services, you may need to obtain certification with a third-party board; otherwise, you won't be able to keep your license.

Choosing the Right Digital Tools

To help support policies, procedures, and all your efforts to manage and scale your business, you'll need to choose appropriate digital tools. This is commonly referred to as your tech stack—meaning the software, platforms, apps, and other tech tools used to run your operations.

With the right tech stack, you can perform essential day-to-day operations more efficiently and allow your employees to focus their efforts on fueling growth while minimizing time-wasting tasks. You'll have many tech tools to choose from. Unfortunately, that's also the bad news—because you may quickly find you have too many options, and new contenders emerge with remarkable speed. This dynamic has really taken hold during the past five years. We now live in a world where, instead of "there's an app for that," you'll likely find more than a dozen apps for that.

With so many options, you'll face a basic dilemma: should you cherry-pick the pieces of your tech stack or focus instead on using an all-in-one option? An all-in-one option would be something like Microsoft 365 or Google Workspace. They don't do everything, but they pull a lot of functionality into their fully integrated applications. If you decide to cherry-pick, you have the benefit of selecting the products that exactly fit your needs. But with this approach, there's a significant trade-off: you have to find a way to integrate those pieces so they talk with each other seamlessly. Here are the basic elements you'll want in the tech stack for your growing company:

» **Dashboard**: A dashboard is a central hub where you can quickly and easily view reports from the various apps and software you use to run your business. There are any number of potential dashboard categories, such as Sales, Financials, and Operations. CRM software companies like HubSpot and Salesforce provide templates with their services, and there are many free templates available on the web as well, if you want to integrate your own software. They are essential if you want to use KPIs effectively. They help with Financial Fridays too!

» **Communications**: You'll need to decide what email system works best for your employees (whether it's Outlook, Gmail, or another option), as well as choosing a videoconferencing service. Keep in mind that many services have options that are free but come with limitations. As of this writing, the free version of Zoom allows up to one hundred participants, and meetings can run for a maximum of forty minutes (after that, participants get booted from the call). Many companies also opt for an internal communication system that offers chat and video calls; Slack and Microsoft Teams are two examples.

» **Productivity**: This includes the tools you'll need to perform basic daily tasks, such as creating documents and spreadsheets. For example, Microsoft Office includes Word and Excel for these tasks, and Google offers Google Docs and Google Sheets.

» **CRM**: Using a customer relationship management (CRM) system, you can collect, organize, and manage the information that relates to every customer you interact with, so that you can streamline communication, improve customer service, and better manage your marketing funnel. Salesforce and HubSpot are two examples.

- » **HR**: Your growing business will need software to handle hiring, payroll, training, benefits, and compliance issues. You may also outsource this function, but, as discussed earlier, don't ignore it!

- » **Project management**: With this type of software, your teams can collaborate by keeping track of tasks and milestones. Examples include Asana, Trello, and Basecamp.

- » **Analytics**: The goal is to gather relevant business intelligence to identify trends and guide decisions with data. Two examples of data analytics platforms are Tableau and Looker.

- » **Finance**: As we have discussed, this software needs to be up to date and monitored closely. QuickBooks is the gold standard, but many easier-to-use competitors such as Zoho and Xero are emerging.

This list could go on and on. You may need a payment system (such as Square), an inventory management system, an integrated marketing system, etc. Tailor your stack to your company's specific needs, growth stage, and budget.

Other Operations Issues

When you pay careful attention to operations, you can discover ways to improve effectiveness, cut costs, and reduce risk. Three domains that will help you achieve those goals are supply chain management, compliance, and Lean Six Sigma (a combination of two methodologies—Lean and Six Sigma—designed to boost efficiency). Supply chain management and Lean Six Sigma can help your company improve customer satisfaction, and legal and government compliance supports another very important goal: avoiding lawsuits. Let's take a closer look at these critical operations issues.

Supply Chain Management

If your supply chain is managed well, your operating expenses can be reduced. But cost isn't the only reason to develop effective systems for supply chain management. It's a critical component of your growth strategy, and one that's often underappreciated by entrepreneurs.

Your supply chain can affect your ability to scale new product launches. It will also affect whether your customers are pleased or extremely frustrated when they have an immediate need for your product. This is true not only for companies that sell tangible items, but for service organizations as well.

Smart entrepreneurs continually reevaluate their supply chain approach. Remember, just because a system is popular doesn't necessarily mean it makes sense for *your* business. Consider that for several decades, the just-in-time (JIT) supply chain method was considered a savvy way for businesses to operate "leanly" and save money. That's because with JIT (popularized by Toyota in the '70s), material is only shipped right before it's needed. That approach can offer significant advantages—as long as supply chain disruptions don't occur. With the ongoing COVID-19 pandemic, businesses around the globe are experiencing widespread supply chain disruptions and have begun to question the wisdom of relying on JIT. The degree and duration of this disruption has been unprecedented and as of this writing shows no signs of resolution.

Supply chain management has always represented a fundamental trade-off between costs and risks. The pandemic was a wake-up call for many companies that have now decided to invest more in supply chain resilience. Years ago, a smart approach might have involved choosing the cheapest vendor and allowing that single source to handle all your needs for part of the supply chain. But after experiencing severe pandemic-related disruptions, many businesses are now viewing that tactic as too risky. To establish a more reliable supply chain, companies are taking steps that include the following:

» Boosting inventories to increase the safety stock on hand. It may be time to rethink your company's inventory buffer. If you only have enough safety stock for five business days, you might consider increasing that buffer.

» Ensuring that distribution channels include sufficient infrastructure for online sales. If your business doesn't already have the capability for online sales, now is a good time to invest in that. You'll want to have the pieces in place before the need becomes urgent (as it did overnight for many businesses during the pandemic).

» Hedging bets by enlisting more alternative suppliers, in case key suppliers suddenly aren't available to fill demand.

» Sourcing more with local suppliers—or at the very least, a more diverse collection of supplier locales.

Lean Six Sigma

As your company seeks to optimize efficiency and maximize quality, keep these three words in mind: Lean Six Sigma. If you're already familiar with this term, you might think it only applies to engineering or manufacturing. That's a common misconception. But Lean Six Sigma is relevant for any business that wants to fine-tune its operations. It's actually a combination of two concepts, Lean and Six Sigma.

Lean is a methodology focused on eliminating waste and increasing value for the customer. It targets eight wastes, which are summed up with the acronym DOWNTIME (figure 21).

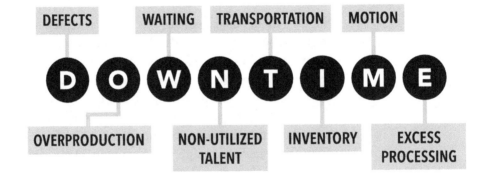

fig. 21

Six Sigma is an approach designed to reduce defects and promote consistency throughout the process. It uses two main methodologies—one for existing processes and the other for new processes—typically executed with five steps each.

DMAIC is meant for existing processes, and it stands for define, measure, analyze, improve, control (figure 22).

DMADV is meant for new processes, and it stands for define, measure, analyze, design, validate (figure 23).

D M A I C

DEFINE	MEASURE	ANALYZE	IMPROVE	CONTROL
the problem or goal.	process performance.	the process to find the causes of defects.	the process's performance by eliminating the causes.	the improved process.

fig. 22

D M A D V

DEFINE	MEASURE	ANALYZE	DESIGN	VALIDATE/ VERIFY
the process and goals.	characteristics that are critical for quality of the product, service, or process.	the data to identify the best design.	and test the process or product (whether physical object or service).	that the end result meets customers' requirements.

fig. 23

By blending the methods above, Lean Six Sigma can create an organizational mind shift. Process optimization becomes a source of continuous improvement and business growth, as workers seek ways to reduce waste and defects. Teams become more efficient because they are focused on avoiding costly, unnecessary mistakes. Being trained in the language and tools of Lean Six Sigma equips them with a shared approach for problem-solving with quality improvement efforts. As a result, employees feel empowered to make changes that contribute to efficiency. With each improvement—whether it's decreased waste, a faster process, or fewer defects—your ability to satisfy customers increases.

Individuals are certified in Lean Six Sigma based on their experience level and knowledge of Lean Six Sigma principles. The six official certification levels are named after the colored belts in martial arts: white belt, yellow belt, and so on, with a black belt indicating full mastery.

Operations can make or break a growing company. Hopefully, the examples I've given in this chapter have shown you that systematizing and routinizing your operation will ensure that issues are addressed consistently, efficiently, and effectively. Even better, you and the rest of the founding team won't have to get involved in putting out every little fire that pops up. If you invest time and effort in systems that cultivate continuous improvement for all areas of your operations, your company will have an advantage over those that concentrate on sales and revenue and tend to forget about everything else. Documenting processes and procedures—the driving forces of "how" and "why" in your company—will compel you to evaluate how HR, accounting, and other departments can contribute to your company's growth. You can then better support those departments by providing them with digital tools to do their jobs better. And methodologies like Lean Six Sigma can help guide your efforts to seek areas for improvement. To track the progress of those improvement efforts, KPIs (key performance indicators) will make useful analysis possible, with metrics that allow you to adjust your approach. They will also help you with strategic planning, as we'll see in part III.

Chapter Recap

» Policies and procedures are not the same thing. They serve different purposes within your company. Policies explain the "why" behind your organization's decisions, and procedures describe the "how" by providing steps to achieve specific outcomes.

» Record your policies, procedures, and other specialized knowledge in a standard operating procedure (SOP) manual. As your growing organization faces more challenges, this vital document—which should cover areas such as sales, HR, and accounting—will help you respond more efficiently. Remember to continually revise and improve this document to reflect changes at your company.

» Use key performance indicators (KPIs) to reach company goals faster and to track your progress. If your KPIs are vague, they won't be effective. Make them specific, measurable, achievable, relevant, and time-bound. Although KPIs are valuable for strategic planning and managing teams, don't get caught up in a metrics frenzy. Be selective and measure the meaningful stuff.

| 8 |

Growing and Scaling

Chapter Overview
» New Product Development
» Acquisitions
» Related vs. Unrelated Diversification
» Vertical Integration
» Overexpansion and Underexpansion

Finally, we get to the good part—I'm actually going to talk about growing your business! You may feel I've taken an unnecessarily long path to get here, but there's a method to my madness. Think of your company as a building: before you add more floors, you'd better have a strong foundation. That means taking personal inventory to ensure you're ready to take your business to the next level and then determining whether your organization is well-equipped for the significant change to come. This is why we covered these topics in earlier chapters. They are essential precursors for the successful growth of your company.

As the founder of an established company, you will continually evaluate opportunities to expand your operations. Expansion can take many forms but fundamentally boils down to two decisions:

1. If you want to add products, should you design them or buy products that already exist?

2. Should you remain focused on a specific sector or broaden into new product categories?

(A quick note about terminology for this chapter: when I say "products," I'm basically referring to stuff for sale, and that includes services as well as physical items.)

In this chapter, we will discuss the advantages and disadvantages of designing and acquiring products, and of focusing on a specific sector or broadening into new categories. We will also examine ways to avoid the common pitfalls of overexpansion and underexpansion. By the end of this chapter, you'll have guidance on how to apply the strategic logic that needs to drive all your expansion decisions.

Product Extension and Product Expansion

Growth can be understood strategically in several ways, but for the purposes of this book we will look at two possible variations: *product extension* and *product expansion*. Which of these you might be interested in employing can affect the decisions you make when deciding how you'll diversify, whether through in-house development, acquisition, or other means.

Product Extension

Product extension involves creating new variations in an existing product line. A classic example is the Oreo cookie, launched in 1912 by Nabisco. For nearly six decades, Oreo existed as a single product. Then in 1974 the Double Stuf Oreo hit grocery store shelves, and after the turn of the millennium the flavor floodgates opened. As of this writing, there are about thirty Oreo varieties, and several limited-edition flavors are rolled out every year.

Another great example of product extension is the iPhone. Apple doesn't see any need to add entirely new products to its existing lines very often, when advances in technology and their own design improvements mean they can launch a new version of the iPhone every year or so and people will literally line up outside their doors to buy it. Though they're superficially dissimilar, Oreos and iPhones are both cash cows for their respective corporations—that is, products with a large market share in a mature industry. These sorts of products are good candidates for extension, because they can be developed and launched at a low cost relative to the revenue they generate.

Product Expansion

Product expansion involves your company creating new products or services in different categories than those of your existing product lines. The purpose is to grow by diversifying your offerings. The diversification can be either related or unrelated. *Related diversification* involves products or services similar to what you already offer. *Unrelated diversification* involves products or services that are significantly different from your existing line, often appealing to a new customer segment.

While understanding related diversification is pretty straightforward, the strategic logic behind unrelated diversification is much trickier. If the "S-word" of business strategy (synergy) creeps into your thought process, beware—these are dangerous waters filled with rocky shoals. Synergy, as you may know, is the attempt to combine businesses in a way that benefits two (or more) businesses under the same umbrella. Synergies are often sought but rarely fully achieved. However, if your goal is to diversify your income stream, and especially if you intend to diversify by acquisition and hire operators to run the new units, this can be an attractive option. Owners who go this route frequently use a system like the Entrepreneurial Operating System (described in chapter 7) to manage their time.

Related or Unrelated Diversification? HubSpot Buys *The Hustle*: In February 2021, HubSpot, a popular maker of customer relationship management (CRM) software, purchased *The Hustle*, an online newsletter for budding entrepreneurs that included a podcast and a premium product trends research line. An SaaS company buying a newsletter? Seems pretty unrelated. But as it turns out, HubSpot was already offering training and other online content via its blog and YouTube. That content gave HubSpot a steady source of new customers. By purchasing *The Hustle* (with 1.5 million readers), HubSpot not only gained a highly profitable new business line but also the attention and goodwill of many potential buyers of its core product. Pretty savvy strategic move!

Jimmy Buffett Moves from Rock Star to Business Tycoon: Jimmy Buffett's business methods are an interesting example of both related and unrelated diversification. He's a musician who became an incredibly successful entrepreneur. In 1977, his song "Margaritaville" hit No. 1 on Billboard's Easy Listening chart. In the 1970s and 1980s, his products were basically albums, concerts, and merch—the typical interrelated products of a musician. Today, I think of Buffett less as a maker of music and more as an extremely lucrative brand. He's built a marketing empire on his brand, one that reportedly generated more than $1 billion in revenue in 2020. Consider what his business encompasses and you'll see how it exemplifies the concept of unrelated diversification. Buffett's product mix includes retirement communities, luxury resorts (including a $370 million location in Times Square), salad dressing, casinos, a line of cannabis products, and LandShark Beer. He's even the popular author of books for both adults and children. That's just a partial list of the businesses under the umbrella of Margaritaville Enterprises LLC, which manages his brand and intellectual property.

fig. 24

BRAND GROWTH ↖↗↙↘	DESCRIPTION	STRATEGIC OBJECTIVE	ACTIONS
PRODUCT EXTENSION	Extend existing product or service using similar benefits	Refresh the core value proposition with new options	Extend existing brand with new variations, including different formats, flavors, or sizes
PRODUCT EXPANSION	Offer new product to reach different categories, consumers, or markets	Enhance competitive advantage with new products in a different area	Launch new product or service addressing a different consumer need

Your strategic objective will inform whether extension or expansion makes sense for your company.

Growth by Acquisition

When companies take the most straightforward path of growth, they develop new products and product categories in-house. (Remember, "products" means both goods and services.) This approach works best if you have an innovative new-product development team, along with workers who have enough availability for building and testing new products. You can also hire team members for these tasks, but keep in mind that new hires will struggle to build on your product line before they know it intimately.

On the other hand, the desire to add new products to your business could represent an opportune time to make an acquisition and get all the expertise you need in one fell swoop. In other words, you diversify your product line through buying, not making. However, as I discussed above, it takes work to identify the right expansion option. You need to carefully weigh available human and financial resources before choosing a path.

MY TAKE

Here's one stock answer to the "make versus buy" question: creating new products internally is cheaper, but acquiring companies is faster. This conventional wisdom is not necessarily true. As noted above, it is cheaper to make when you have team members with the ability (and schedule availability) to succeed in a new product development role. If you have to hire new staff and onboard them, the costs get pretty high pretty quickly. On the other hand, if you have enough capital to at least make a down payment on an acquisition, buying can be the cheaper option.

Related Diversification vs. Unrelated Diversification

Expansion by acquisition can involve related diversification or unrelated diversification, and several well-known businesses offer examples of each practice. Most people know Honda Motor Company as a manufacturer of cars and trucks, but many don't realize that Honda started out as a motorcycle business. As the company developed expertise in building small, reliable engines, it expanded using related diversification and added new products in categories such as lawn mowers and boat motors.

The strategic logic behind related diversification is obvious: you have already developed the competencies and capabilities to produce and sell this sort of product. All you need to do is validate that there is a market for it and you can commence with planning. Often that involves acquisitions: buying competitors with products similar to yours. Facebook provides many examples of this, including its acquisition of Instagram and WhatsApp.

Lately, however, Facebook has made unrelated acquisitions, such as GIPHY, the GIF database company, and several artificial intelligence (AI) companies. This has been underlined by Facebook's recent decision to rebrand its corporate name to Meta and operate Facebook and its many other businesses under that umbrella. Amazon has also expanded into very different product categories; to cite just one major example, it acquired the grocery chain Whole Foods in 2017. This is unrelated diversification—branching into areas that aren't similar to what your company already does. Amazon did not have any grocery stores before their Whole Foods acquisition.

For behemoths like Meta and Amazon with overflowing coffers, multimillion-dollar acquisitions hardly make a dent in their resources. But very few companies are like those. For most businesses, an acquisition takes up a lot of resources. It forces them to carefully consider this question: will we have adequate resources not only to integrate this acquisition, but to improve it and manage the larger resulting enterprise?

Where Do You Find a Business to Buy?

Although you run the risk of draining resources when you buy companies, a strategic acquisition can provide an efficient way to grow. If you stick with the same type of product or service through related diversification, you can use your core capabilities—or even strengthen them if the acquiree has highly skilled employees. This approach makes sense if your own resources aren't under too much strain and there is continued demand for the increased size of your operation. Taking out loans to fund acquisitions can also make a lot of sense, as long as the debt service isn't too onerous. We'll cover funding options in chapter 10.

If you do decide to buy rather than build, you need to find a business to acquire. There are several ways to find existing businesses for sale. The first is through your network. And yes, I know I sound like a broken record that keeps playing a song called "The Importance of Your Network." All those groups you've joined, people you've met, and Twitter followers you've acquired should be the first place you turn to find a target company. Here's the one downside to this approach: it essentially tells the world that you plan to buy a certain type of business. You have to decide if that is a good strategic move on your part.

The second possibility is to kick it old-school and do cold calling. If you decide a particular company would be a good acquisition target, contact the owner and ask if they're interested in discussing a sale. Even if they say no, it's worth following up occasionally to see if they've changed their mind. Sometimes an owner who has never considered a sale will warm up to it over time when the option is presented to them.

Or you can use a business broker. Like many industries, this one has largely gone online. Numerous sites list businesses for sale and let you filter your results to fit your unique criteria. Some of these sites are general, and others are industry-specific. Two of the most well-known are Flippa.com and BizBuySell.com. Check them out. It's easy to go down a rabbit hole when searching for businesses, so stay focused when you do these searches.

I've curated a list of several business brokers for you to peruse at your pleasure. Check out Ken's Business Broker's List included with your Digital Assets at go.quickstartguides.com/rungrow.

SHOULD YOU HIRE AN OPERATOR? When a company makes an acquisition, it's common for the owner of the buying firm to hire someone else to run the acquisition—this avoids doubling the acquirer's workload. Although it can be a good idea, this approach still has strategic and financial ramifications to consider.

Strategically, you have to decide if you want to integrate the new firm closely with yours. If the company is in a related industry, it could make sense to combine operations and eliminate redundancies. If it's in a new area that you want to learn about, you may want to keep it close, because that helps you and your team learn from your new coworkers. In this case, you may want to make an agreement specifying that the previous owner stays on for a while to show you the ropes.

On the other hand, if the new business is just meant as passive income—or if it's in an unrelated field that would not contribute relevant knowledge to you and your team—then you might consider hiring an operator to run it for you. This could be the previous owner or a new hire with the experience and ability to run the acquisition independently. Remember, "independently" is critical. You don't want to pay someone to run the business only to end up being heavily involved in it anyway. Make sure you agree on a set of KPIs, and meet with the operator occasionally to go over them. Now the concern becomes financial. You need to review your projected P&Ls with the operator's compensation figured in and make sure you're still hitting the desired margins. Some operators will want an equity position in the combined firm as well, so be prepared to factor that in. Conduct your due diligence carefully; there is no point in buying a company and hiring an operator to run it if that acquisition turns into a poorly performing investment.

Acquire for Culture, Not Just Finances

When it comes to acquisitions, too many entrepreneurs focus exclusively on financial information. They're busy examining P&L statements, revenue projections, and tax returns. Meanwhile, they neglect a critical element that can quickly derail a merger: cultural factors. A company's culture is its unique way of operating, how it solves problems, and how employees interact with each other. Anyone who's worked in more than one company knows that each one feels distinctly different, even if they're in the same industry. Corporate culture is subtle, yet critical. It's often the source of a company's competitive advantage, because culture is not easily imitated. When considering an acquisition, be aware of these culture factors:

» What is the founder's role in the firm? Does their personality dominate everything? Do all important decisions have to go through them?

» What is the mission and vision of the firm? Does it align with yours? Is it generic or specific? Do employees feel a kinship with that mission? Are they used as guidance for important decisions?

» What is the management's approach to strategic planning? Do they set goals and work toward them, or do they chase after every shiny object (new opportunity) that they find?

» What is their approach to operations? Does each unit have KPIs? Are they tracked? Are unit leaders free to operate when they are meeting their KPIs, or does senior management often interfere to "help"?

» Does the staff seem happy? Are they free to offer opinions, both positive and negative, or are they guarded in what they will say?

» How do staff communicate with each other? Do they seem to get along well? Do they use informal communication methods such as Slack throughout the day, or are communications generally through formal emails and meetings?

» How formal is the hierarchy? Are staff treated as valued colleagues? Are they empowered to make decisions and suggest changes?

This is a far-from-exhaustive list of cultural elements within a firm, but it gives you some idea of what to look for when considering an acquisition. Huge companies like Apple and Cisco have well-established processes for integrating their acquisitions, but that's rarely the case for smaller companies. An acquisition with poor cultural fit can mire a growing company in conflict and distraction, or maybe even doom the whole enterprise, regardless of how positive the financial metrics appear.

Growth by Vertical Integration

One unique type of expansion is a form of unrelated diversification called *vertical integration*. Vertical integration is closely related to a more fundamental concept: the industry value chain, or supply chain. This is the series of steps taken to produce, sell, and deliver a product or service.

Vertical integration involves adding capabilities and products up and down your company's supply chain, either by acquiring companies or developing new capabilities/products internally. The goal usually isn't to own the entire supply chain. Instead, your company obtains pieces of it, either to increase profitability or to reduce supply-chain logistics issues.

A classic example of this is the auto industry. Many automakers used to own their steel-processing plants. Though that approach has fallen out of favor, some companies still continue this practice, like Hyundai, which has its own processing plant that produces some of the raw material used for its products. And like other automakers, Hyundai exercises another form of vertical integration by owning the distribution channels for those products, in the form of car dealerships.

Although vertical integration was fairly common in the late twentieth century, it's no longer favored by most companies. Entrepreneurs have found that the flexibility and cost efficiency of outsourcing provides more advantages than owning the means for producing raw materials for their products. Companies now think of distinctive competencies or capabilities (rather than scope) as key to their strategic advantages. (For a visual refresher of this value chain, refer to figure 14 in chapter 6.)

The idea of having control over more pieces of the supply chain *sounds* great. More control is a good thing, right? Not necessarily. When you're considering vertical expansion, here are three useful questions to ask:

» From a potential growth/profit viewpoint, how attractive is each new market/product category that I am considering entering?

» How much will it cost to enter each new market/category? Will the expense be worth it?

» The better off test: Will the firm be better off when the dust settles on the new acquisition or internal development process?

Instead of spreading limited resources across a bunch of capabilities, you can use outsourcing to give your company more freedom to excel at one thing. With this approach, you rely on third parties that already excel in certain areas, instead of attempting to ramp up those capabilities yourself. For example, if I can buy any products I want directly from the manufacturer on Alibaba and have them shipped straight to one of Amazon's warehouses where they will fulfill all my customers' orders for me, I am free to spend my time learning how to pick the best products and market them on Amazon. I have just outsourced manufacturing, supply chain logistics, inventory management, order fulfillment, and customer service by using two service providers. Alibaba is free, and Fulfillment by Amazon (FBA) is about $30 a month to start. Not bad.

Not every company prefers this approach for every situation. Apple relied on Intel to produce processor chips for its full line of products. However, Apple became dissatisfied with Intel's rate of innovation and quality assurance. They could have switched to rival chipmaker AMD. Instead, they took microprocessor production in-house, convinced they could create faster, more energy-efficient SoCs (systems on a chip) themselves.

Tesla is another company that's moving toward vertical integration. In 2020, it announced plans to produce its car batteries in-house. The company had been sourcing batteries from Panasonic, and Elon Musk said that Panasonic's delays had slowed production of some Tesla vehicles.

One of the most active proponents of vertical integration is Amazon (ironic, since it also provides outsourced services to hundreds of thousands of small businesses). The company's investments demonstrate a strong belief in the competitive advantage of controlling the entire value chain. For example, Amazon continues to control logistics and reduce reliance on UPS, FedEx, and the USPS by expanding its private fleet of long-haul and last-mile delivery trucks. It even had seventy planes by mid-2020, with plans to add more. Amazon built Amazon Web Services (AWS) because it was dissatisfied with the cloud-computing services it was receiving from its vendors. AWS now represents over 40 percent of the cloud-computing market and hit a $54 billion annual sales run rate in April 2021. It is one of Amazon's fastest growing and most profitable divisions.

Shopify, a Company that Eliminates the Need for Vertical Integration and Also Embraces It: There's a compelling logic behind many B2B web services—they're designed to take a component of your value chain and do it better, faster, and cheaper than you could. For example, the company Stripe launched in 2010 and reached a $95 billion valuation by April 2021 by handling payment processing, which used to be a nightmare for small businesses. Shopify is another great example of a booming business that's designed to outsource huge chunks of your value chain, specifically for e-commerce stores. Shopify's message to online retailers is this: you take care of marketing your product, and we'll do the rest. You can build your website, source products, and hire drop shippers (with their partner Oberlo), all on their platform. You don't even need have any inventory—or payment services, which means you don't have to collect any money from your customers.

This creates a situation in which merchants need only one competency: provide a product or service that people actually want, and know how to market it. You don't have to be a web guru or understand logistics or worry about channels of distribution. Companies like Shopify allow you to focus on your competitive advantage, which is the distinctive capability that you have and your competitors don't—otherwise, they would just reproduce exactly what you do. (Shopify and other B2B web services companies allowed many businesses to adapt quickly and shift their sales online during the 2020 pandemic.)

While Shopify facilitates a shift away from vertical integration, the company itself is vertically integrated. It has a web creation system, integration with other sellers like Amazon, and a payment system rivaling that of Stripe. Instead of contracting with multiple vendors for different capabilities, Shopify invites retailers to outsource all those capabilities to one place.

Expansion-Related Pitfalls

Suppose you are starting a company that makes widgets. You anticipate initial demand to be X. Which would you prefer: for demand to be higher or lower than X?

This is a question I've asked many of my MBA classes. The first hand to shoot up will usually respond with "Higher." The answer seems so clear: more demand is always better! But the truth is more nuanced and complex, and it reflects a miscalculation entrepreneurs commonly make. Regarding whether demand is higher or lower than expected, neither outcome is particularly great for a startup.

Here's why. If real demand exceeds the number of widgets you produced based on demand projections, you will have stockouts. Your customers will have to wait until supply catches up with demand. That is not a recipe for success. Rather, it's a recipe for highly dissatisfied customers. They probably won't wait until you restock. They will move on to a competing product. This has long-term implications for your business, because people—your customers included—are creatures of habit. When they switch their purchasing behavior, it's unlikely they will return.

On the flip side, overproduction also has its pitfalls. Unsold stock sits in inventory and ties up capital that could be deployed elsewhere. This might not be a big deal if it's a short-term situation. But if you have fundamentally overestimated demand for your product, you will be forced to discount it and eat the resulting losses.

Overexpansion

"The undisciplined pursuit of more." That's how author Jim Collins described the relentless pursuit of greater success that leads to a company's downfall. When you focus only on growth, you lose the focus that matters more: the distinct mission and vision of your company. In other words, its reason for existence. This is what I referred to earlier as "chasing shiny objects."

Continual improvement is essential, but don't confuse that with continual expansion. Some entrepreneurs believe that "you have to keep growing or you'll die." That's a dangerous misconception, because if you grow in an undisciplined fashion, with a false sense of urgency, your business will die anyway. Don't pursue growth to the point of myopia. Do you need to keep looking for improved products and better ways to serve your customers? Absolutely. But that's not the same thing as increasing your head count, product lines, or branches in a haphazard way.

When you expand, you must carefully consider your company's mission and goals and the financial cushion you'll want to help you weather unexpected developments. If you overexpand, you'll quickly find yourself without the resources or capabilities to manage your bloated enterprise.

Many entrepreneurs think their goal should be growth, full stop. That's where they spend their time, energy, and resources. What should you be pursuing instead? Profitable, sustainable growth. "Growth at all costs" is a lot easier—it looks good short term, and it doesn't require discipline or hard choices. But if you head down that path, just know that you're racing toward a dead end.

How Can Overexpansion Harm Your Business?

When you expand without a disciplined strategy, your company can suffer in myriad ways. Let's examine a few:

» **You won't have systems and processes in place to handle growth.** If you find that your enterprise is growing and evolving faster than your systems are, that will lead to problems. It will quickly overwhelm your ability to run your business effectively. Take an example from HR. The hiring process you used when you launched your company will no longer serve you well, and when you start hiring the wrong people, it will trigger a cascade of bad outcomes. You'll have low morale because new hires clash with company culture and create unnecessary tension. With the wrong hires, your customers' experience may decline due to subpar service. This can cause lasting harm to your business's reputation. As your company becomes more complex, it's easier to lose track of critical information. Growing companies can find themselves unable to efficiently track essential data, because the right systems aren't in place.

If a company grows too fast, decision-making processes won't adapt to keep pace. Company leadership becomes overwhelmed, and their strategic default mode is no longer a deliberate, useful response. Instead, it resembles a Whac-A-Mole game of frenetically reacting. Important details get overlooked and important questions are never asked.

» **You'll lose the cushion that allows you to weather unexpected shifts in the economy or your industry.** When you overexpand, you may end up taking a loss month after month. As you draw down on your capital reserves, you lose the contingency plan that could have allowed you to survive a crisis. When you're losing money, that's the opposite of everything you're trying to achieve.

» **Your culture will turn toxic.** As mentioned earlier, your competitive advantage comes from the distinct competencies and capabilities that your firm possesses. They can't be easily replicated by another firm. When you have truly distinctive competencies and capabilities, they don't reside with a handful of employees but are embedded in the culture of the company. If you acquire another firm that has a separate (and not necessarily bad) culture, and you don't have a way of integrating them successfully, that can lead to ongoing clashes and a toxic atmosphere. Even without a merger, overexpansion can harm your culture in other ways. Morale can take a nosedive if your staff is overworked, or if you use up all your capital reserves and employees know you are in financial distress.

Telltale Signs of Overexpansion

When entrepreneurs become immersed in the pursuit of growth, they can miss the warning signals that they're losing control of their organization. To help you avoid that fate, let's consider some red flags that indicate you may have veered into overexpansion territory, along with some tips to keep you on a sustainable growth path:

You're expanding because that's what some competitors are doing.

» **Why it's a problem:** "Oh, hey, the competition is doing it, I should do it too!" Plenty of mismanaged businesses fall into this trap. It's reactive, and that's never good for your business. Do not plan your strategies based on what competitors do. Take competition into account and compete successfully by building the internal competencies and capabilities that serve your customers best.

» **How you can avoid that trap:** Focus on being a mission-driven organization. Here's what that means: there has to be some reason why you're doing what you're doing, beyond trying to earn every dollar you possibly can. Ironically, the "earn every dollar" path will lead you to less money. That's because your decisions won't be grounded in a logical strategy, and you'll make mistakes that do lasting damage. Think about what your company does, and why. Now think about this: Does the expansion area you're considering represent something your company excels at? Is it something that will allow you to add value?

NOTE

TO DO MORE WITH FEWER PRODUCTS/SERVICES, TRY CULLING.
When entrepreneurs have aggressive growth goals, they can confuse "more" with "better." They think an ever-widening selection of products and services will help guarantee exponential sales growth. In fact, the opposite is often true. Although it's important to continually experiment with new ways to serve your customers, a vast array of products and services can be counterproductive if they drain too many resources. An antidote to that problem is culling, which means cutting the products/services with lackluster profitability so you can focus time, energy, and money on stuff with the most potential. Steve Jobs helped to revive Apple with this approach. When he returned to the company in 1997 as CEO, he cut 70 percent of its product line. Jobs and his team examined the future product road map and found that 30 percent of the products were "incredibly good," and about 70 percent were either "pretty good" or represented businesses the company didn't need to be in. As Jobs said in an interview, that allowed Apple to "focus the same amount of original resources even more on what was remaining—and add a few new things in ... So, the resources that we're investing are equal or greater than we have been, but it's on fewer things so we're going to do a better job at them."

Every growth strategy looks like it's worth pursuing.

» **Why it's a problem:** This shows a basic lack of focus. It's never a good idea to pursue every customer or every potential market. You will quickly find yourself biting off more than you can chew. You will end up unintentionally changing your organization in undesirable ways. Here's how that will end: you'll be outside your realm of competency, which creates a big problem for the management team. The more you expand the operation and the more you depart from your main competencies, the harder it is to manage the expanded operation.

» **How you can avoid that trap:** You need to have a strategic plan and keep to it in a disciplined way. When I say "disciplined," I don't mean rigid. If your strategic plan is carved in stone, your business will sink like one. Flexibility and focus are the key here. Every year, have your team look at your strategic priorities. If you have more than four or five, you're probably stretched too thin. Within those four or five strategic areas, consider up to five goals you can achieve during the upcoming period (as part of this, you'll want to set SMART goals, which we'll cover in the next chapter). Sometimes an unexpected opportunity will come up, and you can evaluate it accordingly. And when you do, apply a disciplined strategic process to decide whether it makes sense for you.

YouTube's first head of marketing and communications, Julie Supan, has advised Airbnb, Dropbox, and other companies on their positioning prior to launch. She urges companies to focus their efforts rather than pursuing every possible customer. "Think about the customer who'll get the most out of your product, so you can speak directly to them—and bet on their emotion," she says. Here are the five questions Supan asks when working with founders:

1. Who is the customer that needs/wants your service or product most?
2. Why does your product or service matter to them?
3. How do they feel about your product or service?
4. What is its true benefit to them?
5. Will your product exceed their expectations?

Your company's culture is watered down and no longer focused on a handful of specific core values.

» **Why it's a problem:** Remember that if you're making an acquisition, you're inheriting people, so you're inheriting their culture too. You may end up with a different sort of company than you had before.

» **How you can avoid that trap:** In terms of acquisition, due diligence plays a critical role. Make sure you share a common set of values, a common perspective that is going to endure when the new entity is formed. When entrepreneurs give that the short shrift, it rarely ends well. Due diligence is more than reviewing tax filings for the past five years or chitchatting with the other company's CEO. You have to really dig into that issue of culture. Talk to employees, not just the CEO, and figure out if they're going to fit in well with your goals. Also keep in mind that culture problems can emerge with other forms of expansion apart from acquisitions. That was the case with restaurant chain Sweetgreen. "Like many startups, we started off with a few core values, but it quickly ballooned from there. I think at one point we got up to twenty values and we couldn't even memorize all of them," CEO and cofounder Nathaniel Ru told First Round Review. "That was definitely a reflection of us trying to do too much in our early years. Over time we learned the power of saying no and slowing down."

You're rushing through the hiring process.

» **Why it's a problem:** All the things about your company that look good on paper—your repeat customers, your intellectual property, your brilliant strategic plan—are due to people you trust paying attention to details, using creative problem solving, and, most important, having a strong desire to make your customers happy. I'll return to a point made earlier in this chapter, because it's so critical: you can't grow effectively without systems and processes to support that growth. And HR is part of that.

» **How you can avoid that trap:** This ties into a recurring theme you'll notice in this book—the need for inherent discipline, as an owner and in the way you approach business operations. Although you're not going to be able to anticipate everything, you have to ensure that you're thinking things through and following the entire strategic plan that you have set out. If the plan is tenfold growth over the course of a year, that's fine. There's a part of the growth curve where you are growing exponentially; that's what this book is about. You can set that as a goal, but then you have to ask, How am I actually going to do that? You need to make that plan carefully, and then you've got to follow it. Start with the end in mind and think backward about how you will get there. If you typically hire two people a year and all of a sudden you need to hire twenty, do you have a system in place to do that? If not, who are you going to outsource it to?

Want an example of the damage a growth-at-all-costs approach will do, particularly with a capital-intensive business? Look no further than WeWork. By 2019, WeWork had become the biggest tenant in the "flexible office space" sector. It held leases on about 11 million square feet of real estate. With a failed *IPO* attempt later that year and investors who were growing increasingly concerned about the company's ability to turn a profit, WeWork reminded us that bigger doesn't mean better. At one point, the company reportedly had to delay plans to lay off workers because it couldn't afford to pay their severance. It had spent heavily as it attempted to go public. Within three years, WeWork purchased four hundred locations. Along the way, CEO Adam Neumann earned a reputation for questionable financial choices, which included purchasing a $60 million jet for the company and using company money for investments that seemed to be pet projects, like $32 million in surfer Laird Hamilton's startup, Laird Superfood, and $14 million in a company that makes surfing wave pools. Repercussions from that lack of fiscal discipline continued to mount, and by November 2019, quarterly losses at WeWork had reached $1.25 billion, compared to a loss of $497 million in the same quarter a year earlier.

Underexpansion

With a combination of hard work and luck, your business will arrive at an opportunity to enter into an exponential growth phase. This level is often referred to as the knee of the curve—if you track your growth on a chart, this is the point right before the line angles up sharply to the right, following your revenue as it takes off like a rocket.

It's a big moment of truth for your business: you're either going to do it or you're not. There's no in-between. And if you don't do it—or if you don't commit to doing it fully—your opportunities to attract investors will dry up. Also, your competition will move in and claim market share. I've heard some entrepreneurs say, "I don't have competition." Here's one thing I know about those people: they're idiots. Everyone has competition.

Even if that competition is hypothetical today, you can easily get blindsided by a brand-new rival that launches tomorrow. If somebody sees room in your market for a more aggressive company to grow, believe me, somebody will do it. Look at the social media site Clubhouse. They had no competition for online audio gatherings until they proved that their concept was successful. Then Facebook (Live Audio Rooms), Twitter (Space), and Spotify (Greenroom, now called Spotify Live) suddenly entered the market. Can your business survive as a smaller organization, without exponential growth? Absolutely. But if your goal is to create something much larger, you must seize critical opportunities when they emerge.

How to Avoid Underexpansion

As with the pitfalls of overexpansion, there are concrete steps you can take to avoid underexpansion. Let's explore two of them:

Plan Ahead

"Failing to plan is planning to fail." If more entrepreneurs used that quote as their business mantra, they could put some bankruptcy lawyers out of business. Think ahead to the changes and processes you will need, rather than letting a lack of those things hold you back. This will help you avoid coming to work every day and just reacting to what happens. You need to have a plan and execute it in a disciplined way. There's a reason I keep emphasizing that point. You might think the need for a plan is obvious. But here's the thing: when entrepreneurs immerse themselves in the pursuit of growth, "obvious" stuff easily gets overlooked and forgotten. By reemphasizing key points, my goal is to help you avoid that fate.

Cultivate Opportunity Awareness

Some entrepreneurs fall into the underexpansion trap because they fail to recognize the right timing for growth. You need to have a keen eye for that moment. It's a combination of factors such as having market traction and operating in an industry or product category that has plenty of room to grow or, even better, is surrounded by plenty of buzz. When you have proof of concept and the right customer demand, those factors catch investors' attention. But you have to recognize when you're in that position, and hopefully it's something you've planned for. (For a detailed exploration of systems and processes necessary for sustainable growth, take a look at chapter 9.) If you're reading this book, you probably started the company with the intention of cultivating opportunity awareness. When everything is aligned, you'll see what's keeping you from growing exponentially and how to fix it, whether it means making an acquisition, ramping up marketing to sell more products, or expanding your R&D budget to develop new and better products.

The Fallacy of "First-Mover Advantage"

Founders can trick themselves into a false sense of security because they believe "first-mover advantage" is a widespread phenomenon that they are well-positioned to harness. Here's the reality: *first-mover advantage*—having an edge over your competition by being the first to offer a product or service—is very difficult to pull off. Any advantage will be fleeting. It will disappear the moment your potential competitors see you demonstrate that a strong market exists for your product or service.

There are always exceptions. Here's a recent example: Around 2019 or 2020, email newsletters became a popular way for writers to make money from their work. Soon, lots of people started thinking about creating their own newsletters to generate revenue. Useful tools emerged to help them distribute their newsletters. Guess what happened next? The market got saturated. However, the founders who had jumped on the trend early had an advantage. That's because, over many months, they'd built up their lists with hundreds of thousands of subscribers. Other newsletter writers covering a similar topic had to start from zero. For the newsletter trend, there was a brief window of opportunity to get in before the market was flooded.

Sometimes the early bird gets the worm. But there's a related adage that describes a much more common business dynamic: the second mouse gets the cheese. You probably understand the value of learning from your own mistakes, but entrepreneurs often overlook opportunities to learn from the mistakes of others. That type of education can save you enormous amounts of time and money. You should also seek ways to learn from competitors' successes. That's the idea behind being a "fast follower"—quickly adopting ideas that have worked well for other companies.

While first-mover advantage is rare, first-mover *disadvantage* is common. One example is the Apple Newton, the first personal digital assistant (PDA). When it was introduced in 1993, the technology hadn't yet caught up with the vision. The Newton was clunky, hard to use, and had limited functionality. It bombed, and smartphones soon took over the basic functions that PDAs had tried to introduce.

On the other hand, the iPod was a fast follower—it was by no means the first MP3 player, but it learned from the limitations of others and made something consumers loved. This is what happens when entrepreneurs enter a market before it's fully mature and then get pushed aside by companies (like Apple) that learn faster and adapt more quickly. First movers can jumpstart a "hype cycle," which doesn't always favor the first product out of the gate. As explained by the Gartner organization, a research and consulting firm, the hype cycle starts when some kind of breakthrough generates press and industry interest, which builds buzz—and raises expectations. Inevitably, impatience for results begins to replace the original excitement about potential value. Problems with performance, slower-than-expected adoption, or a failure to deliver financial returns in the time anticipated all lead to missed expectations. Disillusionment sets in. But then early adopters overcome those initial hurdles and begin to experience benefits, which allows organizations to learn from them. Eventually, more organizations feel comfortable with the product, and its use rises sharply.

As you can see, there is no one-size-fits-all expansion plan. So instead of aiming for "disruption"—a buzzword that's overused and often a meaningless, self-important badge of honor—focus on creating a defendable and sustainable competitive advantage, solving a real customer problem. It will likely take some trial and error, but if you carefully examine the nature of your business and the needs of your customers, you'll find the right path on which to expand your company.

Chapter Recap

» Product extension and product expansion represent the two main paths to growth.

» With product extension, you develop new versions of existing products (think Oreo: Nabisco launched that cookie with one flavor and eventually created about thirty varieties).

» Product expansion involves more than tweaking what you already have. Instead, you diversify by entering product categories that are new for your company. The new products you develop can be similar to your current offerings (related diversification) or they can be notably different and able to target new customer segments (unrelated diversification).

» To fuel growth with new products, founders have an important decision to make: should they rely on an in-house team or acquire a company that already has the right expertise and aim for vertical integration? If you're looking for the cheapest option, don't assume that in-house is always the way to go; your costs will increase rapidly if you need to keep making new hires to support the development of your new product. In some situations, it will be more cost-effective to acquire a company or division with the skills you need (but only if you have sufficient capital for a down payment).

» Expansion should be done carefully, not continuously. If you pursue every opportunity for growth, you will fall into the trap of overexpansion.

» Stay focused on your company's mission and goals, and avoid the mentality of "growth at all costs." Instead, pursue long-term growth that's built on a profitable, sustainable business.

» Don't create a false sense of security by convincing yourself that you lack competitors. If you don't have a sense of urgency, you will miss the opportunities that can propel your business toward exponential growth. You don't need this type of growth to survive as a company, but you do need it if your goal is attracting investors.

| 9 |
Planning

GRAPHIC

fig. 25

FAILING TO PLAN = PLANNING TO FAIL

Hopefully, the last chapter got you thinking about the logical possibilities for growing your business. Now let's start planning for it. As I've said before in this book, failing to plan is planning to fail. A great shift has occurred in strategic planning since I entered the field over twenty years ago. Corporate strategic planning was once a bureaucratic endeavor, with a top-down approach that relied heavily on the executive team and their consultant advisors. They created large, complex planning documents that typically covered five or ten years, and they often emphasized tactics over strategy. Each hefty strategic plan followed a predictable life cycle: after team members celebrated its completion, the document would be placed on a shelf to collect dust for many years, until it was time to dust off the old version and repeat the whole process again.

This approach doesn't serve modern firms, because they can't afford to waste time. With today's rapid changes in markets and technology, the old approach would lead to a planning document that was so out-of-date you could almost smell its mustiness. Modern managers understand that they can't make reliable predictions about industry and economic developments for the next five years or more. They need to plan one year ahead—at most—and consider what they can accomplish to advance their strategic priorities.

Although the evolution of technology creates challenges for strategic planning, it has also ushered in advantages. Modern systems and processes allow for much more automated data collection; now managers can measure results and monitor them on a real-time basis, which makes progress (and red flags) more visible. In this chapter, we'll explore ways to approach strategic planning with the necessary flexibility to fuel your growth.

Review Your Business Plan

To keep your company's growth on track, you may want to start by reviewing your initial business plan. As you go through that process, consider these questions:

Is it Still Relevant?

Examine your initial business plan and determine whether it still serves your goals. A business plan is essentially a strategic planning document, and although it may have worked just fine for launching your business, that doesn't mean it's designed to take your company to the next level. You may find that your business has evolved beyond the point where your business plan makes sense. You might need to start from scratch with a new strategic plan, or you may find that elements of your business plan still have relevance for the strategic plan you're developing for the coming year.

Have I Checked My Assumptions?

When you create your first business plan, you must make a range of assumptions, including who your customers will be and what products or services will best serve their needs. Even when you can support some of those numbers with information gathered from surveys, focus groups, or industry research, many aspects of that initial business plan are educated guesses at best. Once you have a solid track record for sales and serving customers, you move beyond the realm of educated guesses. Instead of making stabs in the dark, you have some real data to illuminate your business decisions. Recognize that some of your assumptions have proved to be wrong. Correct them by continually seeking new information and perspectives.

As you reflect on those questions, remember to do so with the mindset we discussed in chapter 1: curiosity. This will ensure that you're well-equipped to detect any external influences—like changes in customer needs or the competitive landscape—that could help or hinder your growth.

Keep These Growth Factors in Mind

Throughout your planning process, it's useful to revisit the many factors that affect your company's growth. These factors are the same as when you started the business: industry factors, market factors, and management factors. To help set the stage for your growth plan, review these questions:

Industry Factors to Consider

» How has your industry changed overall since you entered it? Are volatility, product innovation, and barriers to entry the same, or have they shifted?

» How has the competitive landscape changed? Do you have new competitors (which is likely if you've been successful)? How have you responded to them, and vice versa?

Market Factors to Consider

» What is the size of your target market(s), and what are its characteristics?

» Are you still solving the same problems for your customers, or has your value proposition shifted?

» Did you initially define your target market correctly? Do you need to redefine it to prepare for your next phase of growth?

» Does your current marketing plan reach your target market effectively? Does it need to be adjusted?

Management Factors to Consider

» Were you able to execute your business plan? If not, why?

» Did you need to pivot on your initial business model?

» Are you flexible enough to make the necessary role transitions as the business grows?

» Are you motivating your team effectively? If not, why not?

A Workable, Actionable Strategic Business Plan

To create a strategic plan that fuels your growth, it's essential to begin with the end in mind, and then think about what's required to actually achieve it. Without a clear vision of your destination, you may feel like you're making progress, only to discover you're heading off course. Later in this chapter, we'll look at specific steps to create an effective strategic plan. But if you don't start the process with the end in mind, you'll build your strategy on shaky ground. This includes careful consideration of the human, financial, and other resources needed to execute each strategic goal.

Once you have clarity about what your business should ultimately achieve, you need concrete goals to get you there. Think about it this way: let's say you want to run a marathon, and it's not something you've done before. You need to establish a training plan to build up your stamina, and then stick to it. Otherwise, your marathon will get added to the list of things you'd like to achieve someday. As it turns out, "someday" is not included on most calendars. It's a hazy, wishful vision of a future that never arrives.

I'll share more detail on the topic of goal setting when we look at the specific steps for strategic planning, but here's a guiding principle to keep in mind: focus on setting "stretch" goals, those that make you feel a little uncomfortable about your ability to execute. Feeling pretty confident about your capacity to double revenue in the next twelve months? Then consider setting a stretch goal to quadruple in size during that time. It's OK if you don't hit that mark, because you will have pushed yourself to reach new limits you wouldn't have considered otherwise.

Most entrepreneurs perform better when they're a bit outside their comfort zone. What's more, if you never leave your comfort zone, you'll never enter the high-growth zone. If all aspects of your business are running smoothly all the time, that's not necessarily a good thing. It could suggest a lack of experimentation. That's a common dynamic for entrepreneurs. Because running a business is hard, it's easy to fall into complacency. But if you're looking for explosive growth, the "knee of the curve" that will take you to the next level, then complacency will prevent your business from gaining the momentum it needs (figure 26).

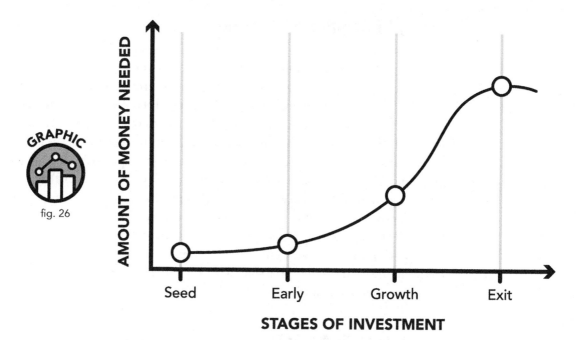

AMOUNT OF MONEY NEEDED

Seed   Early   Growth   Exit

STAGES OF INVESTMENT

TO BEGIN WITH THE END IN MIND, INCLUDE AN EXIT STRATEGY: Even if you plan to stay with your business until retirement and then turn it over to your kids, you should operate as if you have an exit strategy to sell your company or take it public in the foreseeable future. There are two major reasons for doing so:

- **It enforces management discipline**. If you run your business like a family operation, you may find yourself making decisions that are more about your lifestyle than about what's good for the firm. Always act as if you have investors and bankers scrutinizing your every move, even if you don't. Better still, assemble a board of advisors (a topic we covered in chapter 6) who will provide that level of scrutiny and won't be afraid to hold you accountable.

- **Things don't always work out as planned**. If you do need to sell at some point, you need to make sure that your company looks attractive to buyers and that the books are clean. This means not overleveraging, having clear equity tiers, and having systems and processes in place (which we explored in chapter 7).

Steps to Strategic Planning

Now that we've gone over some preliminary guidelines for strategic planning, let's drill down into the specific steps you'll take as you go through this process. Here's the highly condensed version: refine your mission and identify a handful of broad strategic directions, then set supporting goals and determine what's needed to achieve them and to track progress. If you're wondering how long the resulting document needs to be, the answer is "not very." Remember, we are rejecting the old-fashioned approach to strategic planning, when executives convinced themselves that the document's length was proportionate to its usefulness. You'll find that brevity yields quality. For example, my strategic plan for the business school I run is about six pages. A plan of this length, properly constructed, will be a living document that you can use as a management tool, as opposed to a spiral-bound tome gathering dust on a bookshelf somewhere. Here are four essential steps to creating that document (figure 27).

THE STRATEGIC PLANNING PROCESS

fig. 27

1

REVIEW YOUR MISSION

Be sure to plan from the perspective of a mission-driven organization

2

DEVELOP STRATEGIC PRIORITIES

A maximum of five broad strategic directions

3

REVIEW PROGRESS

Celebrate success and debrief on goals that were not met after one year

4

UPDATE STRATEGIC GOALS

Set new goals and assign or update KPIs for the year ahead

Step One

Review your mission and vision, and update if necessary. Some entrepreneurs dismiss this mission stuff as a feel-good exercise designed to elevate their image in the eyes of customers and investors. They entirely miss the point. They don't understand that long-term sustainable growth will be elusive unless you have a mission-driven organization. Your mission is a guiding force that will help you make tough choices as you pursue growth. It will keep you from falling into the trap we mentioned in chapter 8, the *undisciplined pursuit of more*. To ensure a successful review process, remember these guiding principles:

» **Keep it short and convey your firm's uniqueness**. You need to express what the company does and how it does it. This means having a reason for being. "Make as much money as possible" doesn't qualify. Making money is not a reason—it's a by-product of managing the enterprise correctly.

If your mission and vision are too general, they will lack meaning. They won't provide guidance for how to run your company and will likely just set you up for ridicule. Google gave us a good example of what not to do with its motto "Don't be evil" (which the company wisely dropped from its code of conduct in 2018). When a mission is vague and banal, it creates flimsy guardrails for running your business. How are you going to differentiate yourself from your competitors? What markets will you explore? How are you going to grow? All of that starts with the mission and requires a company vision with something concrete and specific. (And that does not mean changing the Google motto to "Don't be evil unless absolutely necessary.")

Your mission and vision will resonate more with customers and employees if you can keep them simple. It's OK if your workers can't recite them verbatim, but it's pointless to create them if you can't make them compelling for the workers you rely on every day. Although it will be necessary to update your mission at times, it shouldn't change drastically every year. That in itself would suggest an underlying problem and lack of focus.

» **Include all stakeholders in the process**. This means ensuring that your employees, customers, and investors all have a say in discussions about the company's mission. For employees, this could take the form of a short company retreat, at an off-site location if possible. A change of scene can help prompt new perspectives. An in-person customer gathering could also be a good way to collect opinions on company mission, but if it would be inconvenient for your customers, a different approach might be required. You can still gain useful insights from customers without gathering them together in a room. For example, if you have a few clients who represent the bulk of your revenue, have private calls or meetings with them. This will show them how much you value their opinions.

MISSION VS. VISION – WHAT'S THE DIFFERENCE?: The terms "mission" and "vision" are often used interchangeably, but while they are related, they're ultimately very distinct from each other. Simply put, the vision is a specific, single-sentence statement of how the world will be different as a result of your company's success, and the mission is a slightly longer statement (three or four sentences) of the guiding principles the firm will use to move toward its vision. The vision is an idealized state that is never fully achieved. The mission is more specific. Both should be used to guide your strategic planning.

For example, Charles Schwab & Co.'s vision is "Charles Schwab exists to help people achieve better financial outcomes." Their mission is "We offer investors a contemporary, full-service approach to build and manage their investments, providing investment-related products, services, and sophisticated financial planning that combine the best of what people and technology have to offer."

Notice how the vision is something that will never be achieved but can always be strived for. The mission provides specific guidelines for how they will move toward their goal. Both inform their strategic planning by framing Schwab as a financial services company that leverages people and technology to help its clients achieve better financial outcomes. It is unlikely that you will see Schwab start to invest in, say, oil rigs, regardless of how attractive an investment they may be. Oil is not part of their mission or vision.

Think about your company's purpose. What are the specific ways you make customers' lives easier? Think beyond the function of your product or service, even beyond the problem it solves. How does it make customers feel to have that problem solved, and how might that affect more than one aspect of their lives? If you're a B2B company, how does your product or service affect your customers' customers? You should exist for some larger purpose than enriching your shareholders.

Q: How is your business making the world better?

Step Two

Based on your company's mission, develop no more than five broad strategic directions for your firm over the next few years. At the beginning of this chapter, we emphasized the value of starting with the end in mind. That's what you'll be doing as you narrow your focus to determine your company's overarching goals. They are your strategic priorities. The following steps will help you develop them:

» **To support your strategic priorities, create goals at the company level and also at the team or division level.** If you want to turn a priority into a reality, you'll need to have goals that position you to make progress and also provide a way to monitor it. Remember, these are company-level goals. Each unit (team or division) should have goals in support of the company's strategic plan. The unit-level goals take the form of key performance indicators, which we covered in chapter 7. They make the execution of company goals possible and allow you to see if you're on target.

SMART GOALS: Whether they're company-level or unit-level, all your goals must have one thing in common: they should be SMART goals. The SMART goals method is a key framework for setting detailed, meaningful goals for business growth. The acronym stands for Specific, Measurable, Achievable, Relevant, and Time-Bound (figure 28). Here's what each one represents:

- **SPECIFIC**. This is the mission statement for your goal. Spell out exactly what you want to accomplish.

- **MEASURABLE**. You need to establish a way to measure progress. Think about the metrics you can use to determine if your goal has been completed.

- **ACHIEVABLE**. Consider what skills you might need to develop in order to make this goal a reality.

- **RELEVANT**. Does this make sense within your broader business goals? How is it aligned with other objectives?

- **TIME-BOUND**. Is your target date too ambitious? What needs to have been achieved halfway through the process? It's important to create a sense of urgency, but consider what can realistically be accomplished during that time period. Don't set your employees up for burnout.

fig. 28

SPECIFIC	MEASURABLE	ACHIEVABLE	RELEVANT	TIME-BOUND
Describe exactly what you plan to accomplish.	Choose metrics to measure progress.	Ensure that available skills can support your goal.	Align your goal with business objectives.	Set a deadline that creates urgency, not burnout.

» **Assign responsibility for your KPIs, and make sure these responsibilities are well-understood.** Remember, you can set the loftiest of goals, but if no one thinks it's their job to help meet those goals, they will remain nothing more than a wish list. As previously discussed in chapter 7, KPIs need to be assigned to specific team members to help guide their efforts, but this doesn't mean that you'll use those KPIs to measure individual performance. KPIs track a group's progress, so don't hold specific workers accountable for things beyond their control. Check in with the responsible unit head frequently to ensure that adequate progress is being made, and remove roadblocks as needed. Remember, too, that if KPIs are developed for a specific department, that department leader should have a say in the process. Otherwise, they may feel as if unreasonable demands have just been dumped in their lap.

Step Three

At the end of the year, reconvene the strategic planning team. Celebrate successes and carefully debrief on goals that were not met. This is not a time to blame anyone for underperformance. If you have SMART KPIs and you're tracking progress throughout the year, then you won't have any surprises when the team reconvenes. You'll already have some idea of why goals were missed. Take time at this strategic planning meeting to consider problems that need to be addressed. Were insufficient resources provided? Or are the goals no longer relevant? For example, maybe you planned to develop a new product or service, but you reevaluated demand and found it wasn't strong enough, so you decided not to pursue it. That's a perfectly good reason not to achieve a goal. There can also be external factors beyond your control—like a pandemic—that prevent you from achieving goals. That doesn't mean you failed. It just means that unexpected changes compelled you to adapt.

This is why I never advocate for strategic planning documents to be rigid things carved in stone. If it's going to be useful, your strategic plan has to be a living document. If it doesn't have flexibility, it will break your company. If a goal becomes irrelevant, then you either replace it or shift resources to other areas of importance. Or perhaps a temporary obstacle prevented you from achieving it; you could still revisit it in the next period. Perhaps a goal is simply going to take longer than you originally anticipated. Maybe that's because there's a system or process that isn't effective and needs to be changed. See what you can learn from what's happened with that goal so far.

Step Four

Set new SMART goals (including KPIs) for the next year. You can also change your strategic priorities, but they should be much less fluid than your specific goals. Unless you're doing a complete pivot, your priorities, which are informed by your mission and vision, should be relatively stable. Also, set aside time each year to go through these steps. The discipline of reviewing your strategic goals and priorities, celebrating successes and carefully examining things that did not go so well, will put you one step ahead of your less organized competition.

Twilio CEO on the Advantages of Small Bets: As CEO and cofounder of Twilio, Jeff Lawson understands growing pains—and the importance of learning from them. Twilio provides a technology platform that lets developers build communication capabilities within apps. Uber and Lyft are two examples of businesses that use Twilio's technology to communicate with their customers. Launched in 2008, the company had a successful initial public offering in 2016, and by 2020 it had reached a valuation of $1.76 billion, up 55 percent year-over-year.

The company didn't arrive at those impressive numbers without a few stumbles. In an interview with First Round Review, Lawson admitted he initially lacked disciplined planning. "In the early days of Twilio, the notion of resource allocation would have been such an academic concept for us," he said. The company's leadership often took a follow-your-gut approach, "and we made a lot of mistakes." That doesn't mean leaders should always ignore gut instincts. "It's good in terms of, we listen to customers," Lawson explained. "We had an instinct that said, 'Hey, there's something here. We should go follow it.'" Entrepreneurs do need to find balance with that approach, because it carries risks. Lawson said the company would neglect to invest enough in core products that were already succeeding. "We got distracted by the next shiny thing."

During the company's early days, someone suggested it would be a good idea to have an annual planning process to develop budgets. At the time, Lawson's response was, "Really? That's a thing?" Over the years, a thoughtful approach to planning has definitely become a thing at Twilio. To help other entrepreneurs learn from his experience, Lawson shared his approach to investing for growth:

» **Put some resources into the next big bet.** This is the thing that might make you money five years from now. Although it's important to have a framework that ensures that you're investing in your core business to keep it healthy and growing, "clearly that can suck all the resources of the company," Lawson said. "There's no shortage of wisdom that will say, 'Hey, you've got this core business. That's the cash cow of the company. It makes all the money. And so therefore you need to keep investing in growing it.'"

» **Don't focus everything on that safe bet.** Instead, set aside some resources to invest in your next big bet; Lawson said conventional wisdom suggests the amount could be approximately 5 percent or 10 percent of your budget. Invest in the things that might make you money but will take a while to pay off. If you don't set aside resources for that, "then you're probably running the company for too short-term of an outcome," he said.

» **Instead of one big "next thing," have several small bets.** That could be five small bets or twenty, depending on the size and scale of the company. "You need to have more than one potential bet that you're working on," said Lawson, noting that new companies often get married to one "great new idea." He recommended adopting this mindset: *There are many things that could potentially be the next great thing, but we need to run experiments to figure out if indeed customers want those things.* As Twilio grew, the company started to think more about this question: How do we run a number of those experiments at any one time? "There's a certain wisdom and discipline in being able to run multiple of those experiments, and to be patient and to not expect those things to become giant businesses overnight," Lawson said.

» **You can't experiment with multiple bets if you allocate all your budget at the start of the year.** When one of your experiments with small bets starts to pay off—when you learn the market does want and need something new—you must be ready give that spark the fuel it needs. "One of the common mistakes that we, and I'm sure other companies have made, is you fully allocate your budget at the beginning of the year," said Lawson. What happens when one of those ideas takes off and you need more people to work on it? As Lawson observed, you're told, "Well, you know, it's March and you know, your budget gets done in December. So we'll talk to you in December." That's a great way to starve an idea because of an arbitrary budget cycle on your calendar, he said. "One of the key things you need to do is to hold back and to be prepared to invest when you see the signs of success and the idea merits that investment … Make sure you've got the ability to double down in real time."

DELEGATION IS A STRATEGIC SUPERPOWER: We talked about the importance of delegation in chapter 4, and it's important to think about this within the context of strategic planning. You'll be very involved in making the plan itself, but that should not be the case with executing actual goals. The idea is not for you to make a plan and then micromanage the execution. But it is a common mistake that entrepreneurs make. They forget that what worked with five employees won't work when you have fifty. It may feel uncomfortable at first, but you'll need to rely on delegation to execute your goals. If you insist on being involved in everything, you'll quickly find that nothing gets done.

Chapter Recap

» Review your initial business plan to see if it needs a refresh. Take a hard look at that document to see if it will support your growth goals. Examine your initial assumptions too, because they may no longer be relevant. You had to rely on educated guesses when you launched the company, but now you have data about your customers and related business decisions.

» As you plan for your business, reflect on these three growth factors: industry factors, market factors, and management factors. Consider how your industry has changed since you launched your business and whether you should adjust your response to shifts in competition. Think about whether it's time to redefine your target market or reconsider your value proposition. Ask yourself if you have the right team in place to execute your business plan and adapt as your business grows.

» When creating a strategic plan, make sure you have a clear, well-defined mission to guide your direction.

» The most effective way to support your strategic priorities—and track progress—is the creation of goals that are specific, measurable, achievable, relevant, and time-bound (known as SMART goals).

| 10 |
Funding

Chapter Overview
- » Raising Money to Fuel Growth
- » Debt vs. Equity
- » Sources of Debt and Equity Funding
- » New Funding Sources
- » Stages of Startup Funding

Readers of my previous book, *Starting a Business QuickStart Guide*, may recall that most startup funding comes from either bootstrapping (self-funding) or an investor category with a colorful name: friends, family, and fools (FFF). The one thing these FFF investors have in common is that they're willing to back a company with no product, no sales, and no track record. Self-funding and FFFs are still the major funding options for startups, but considering how the current startup ecosystem is awash with cash, someone with successful previous startup experience and/or good networking skills might find other pathways for raising money.

However, we're no longer talking about startups. If you're reading this, you probably have a successful product or service with real sales and real growth. This means bankers and private equity have become real possibilities for you. They can be important ones, too. Sticking with the familiar approaches that served you well in the early days will limit your growth. With that in mind, let's take a look at other types of funding available to you and how to determine which options make sense for your business.

Raising Money to Fuel Growth

Whenever I am asked when a company should raise money, I always give the same simple answer: "When you need it." Those four simple words matter, because entrepreneurs can lose sight of the risks that come with new funding sources. Raising money before you have a legitimate use for it is foolish. You'll have to give up equity in your firm or start payments for interest and principal immediately (as we will discuss below). Don't venture into this territory without a compelling business need.

How do you decide when you need it? Here's the overarching answer to that question: when the lack of capital limits your growth. You raise money to grow your firm. If this isn't the rationale behind your pursuit of outside funding, then you will dilute and devalue your business. Think of the funds as rocket fuel that allows your company to take off with explosive growth.

So what should you spend the money on? Anything that will help take the business to the next level. Conducting R&D for a new product line, hiring high-value employees, expanding into new sales territories, developing new marketing channels—these are all great uses of funds. Moving into a shiny new HQ, giving everyone a much-deserved raise, or bringing in consultants to help you reorganize? Not so much.

When fueling growth, one of the most critical decisions you'll make is whether to pursue funding in the form of debt or equity. You may end up with a combination of both for your *capital structure*, meaning the combination of debt and equity that finances your operations. It's also possible that your choices will ultimately be limited to one or the other. Let's take a look at how debt and equity can affect your business.

Debt

In the simplest terms, *debt financing* means you are borrowing money and promising to pay the lender back, including some rate of interest. Those payments will typically be made monthly, and you may need to make a down payment or provide some other form of collateral.

fig. 29

DEBT ADVANTAGES	<ul><li>With debt, you retain full ownership and control.</li><li>Because you'll receive a lump sum, the money can be used immediately to work toward your business goals.</li></ul>
DEBT DISADVANTAGES	<ul><li>Cash flow will be important for your growing business. Your debt payments will cut into that immediately, because scheduled payments generally begin when the funds are disbursed to you.</li><li>If for some reason you can't pay back your debt, a bank could seize your assets or your company.</li><li>Failure to make scheduled payments will negatively affect your credit score and that of your business, which may make it harder to obtain loans in the future.</li></ul>

Over the past few years, businesses have increasingly used debt because interest rates have been low (though of course that may not always be the case). The rate you get will depend on both your creditworthiness and the bank's perception of your risk of default. Your lenders will care very much about receiving payments in full, on time, but they usually won't tell you how to run your business unless a problem occurs with payment.

Sources of Debt Funding

If you want to keep your ownership and control of the company intact, and your business enjoys healthy, reliable cash flow, a loan may be the best route to financing your growth. Some major options available for entrepreneurs who want to borrow money include banks, SBA-backed loans, and peer-to-peer online lenders. Let's take a closer look at all three.

Banks

Banks focus on mitigating or eliminating risk, and new companies take risks as part of their standard operating procedure. As a result, banks and new companies are not a natural fit. It's uncommon to see a fast-growth tech startup that's financed with a bank loan. Instead, bank loans are better suited for a business with a solid track record that feels predictable. This allows loan officers to look at returns, see revenue patterns over the years, and understand how a business has grown. If you're an established, practicing dentist with a steady patient base who wants to buy new equipment, a bank would happily give you a loan in the low six figures. They would probably assume, based on the steadiness of your dental practice, that you could pay it back without a problem. If you're a fast-growing startup, on the other hand, it will take plenty of effort to convince a bank to take a chance on you. However, for a profitable business that wants to expand, bank loans can be a good option, particularly when interest rates are low and the loan feels like free money that's not a burden to pay back.

If you want to pursue a bank loan, Small Business Development Centers, or SBDCs, can help. Although they don't provide financing, SBDCs do offer training and technical assistance to small business owners. Each center is made possible through the collaborative efforts of the Small Business Administration (SBA), a university or college, and sometimes other private or public partners. There are more than one thousand locations operating throughout the United States where entrepreneurs can receive guidance on how to properly package their business information when applying for a loan. You can find a location near you by visiting www.sbdcnet.org/find-your-local-sbdc-office.

SBA-Backed Loans

There's a common misunderstanding about Small Business Administration loans. People sometimes wonder where they should go to get one and then are surprised by the answer: their bank. SBA-backed loans aren't actually from a different source. The SBA doesn't give loans; they *back* loans, working through local lenders across the country to help entrepreneurs access financing. The same basic loan criteria I just discussed also apply here: they're looking for ventures that aren't risky, that have a solid track record, and that want to expand. When you apply for a loan through the SBA, you'll need to meet specific requirements, including operating as a US for-profit business. Typically, these loans are intended for entrepreneurs who have found it challenging to get a traditional loan.

Thousands of SBA lending-approved banks exist in the United States. Whatever bank you're using, it probably offers SBA loans. Although the SBA oversees a range of funding, its most common loan program is the 7(a) loan, with a maximum loan amount of $5 million. According to the SBA, the basic uses for 7(a) loans include the following:

» Long- and short-term working capital
» Revolving funds based on the value of existing inventory and receivables
» The purchase of equipment, machinery, furniture, fixtures, supplies, or materials
» The purchase of real estate, including land and buildings
» Construction of a new building or renovation of an existing building
» Establishing a new business or assisting in the acquisition, operation, or expansion of an existing business
» Refinancing existing business debt, under certain conditions

With its loan programs, the SBA supports longer-term small business financing. The maximum maturities for its loans are twenty-five years for real estate, ten years for equipment, and ten years for working capital or inventory loans. Your business must meet the following criteria to be eligible for a 7(a) loan:

- » Operate for profit
- » Be considered a small business, as defined by the SBA
- » Be engaged in or propose to do business in the United States or its possessions
- » Have reasonable invested equity
- » Use alternative financial resources, including personal assets, before seeking financial assistance
- » Be able to demonstrate a need for a loan
- » Use the funds for a sound business purpose
- » Not be delinquent on any existing debt obligations to the US government

The SBA website has a checklist of all the information you'll need to apply for a loan. This includes a profit-and-loss statement that's current within 180 days of your application (along with supplementary schedules from the last three fiscal years) and a detailed, one-year projection of income and finances that explains how you expect to achieve those numbers.

The 7(a) loan program includes several types of loans:

- » The 7(a) Small Loan, with a maximum loan amount of $350,000 and a turnaround time of 5-10 business days

- » The SBA Express program (also with a maximum loan amount of $350,000), which has a quick turnaround—after you submit your application, the SBA will respond within 36 hours

- » Loans to veteran-owned small businesses (and businesses owned by spouses of veterans), with reduced fees. To be eligible through the Veterans Advantage program, a small business must be at least 51 percent owned and controlled by someone in one of the following groups:

  - Honorably discharged veterans
  - Active-duty military service members eligible for the military's Transition Assistance Program (TAP)
  - Service-disabled veterans
  - Reservists and/or active National Guard members
  - Current spouse of any veteran, active-duty service member, Reservist, National Guard member, or the widowed spouse of a service member who died while in service or as a result of a service-connected disability

Peer-to-Peer Online Lenders

Peer-to-peer (or P2P) online lenders aren't banks. Instead, they connect loan-seekers with investors willing to help with financing. Although the amount can be smaller than a typical bank loan, the application process is usually much faster. Because peer-to-peer lending has only existed since 2005, there are fewer regulations—which means you'll want to be extremely thorough about vetting these lending platforms before you decide to work with one. Although the money can be used for your business, it comes in the form of a personal loan. You'll need to provide personal financial information, including access to credit reports.

One of these lenders is Funding Circle. Launched in 2010, this P2P lending platform connects businesses in the United States, the United Kingdom, Germany, and the Netherlands with accredited and institutional investors (it's also been listed on the London Stock Exchange since September 2018). According to the company's site, Funding Circle investors have loaned $15.2 billion to 100,000 businesses. The loan amounts range from $25,000 to a maximum of $500,000, with repayment periods from six months to nine months.

Funding Circle says the loan application review process typically takes no more than twenty-four hours. To get approved, here are the minimum qualifications you'll need to meet:

1. Two years in business
2. A personal FICO credit score of at least 660 for business owners
3. No personal bankruptcies among the business owners within the last seven years
4. Not located in Nevada, due to state lending regulations
5. Operates in an industry other than select industries that include speculative real estate, nonprofit organizations, weapons manufacturers, gambling businesses, marijuana dispensaries, and pornography

In summary, debt has its place as part of a founder's growth-funding portfolio, especially if interest rates remain low. However, keep in mind the drawbacks of taking on debt and be careful, just like with your personal finances, not to borrow more than you can comfortably pay back.

Equity

Going with equity rather than debt can seem more exciting than simply seeking a loan, but it's also a less straightforward funding process. With *equity capital*, you're not promising to repay money; rather, you're giving away part of your company in return for funding. This means you're diluting your ownership stake in your company. Although that's a downside entrepreneurs should carefully consider, equity capital can bring significant competitive advantages to your company if the investors are *smart money* investors. This means they are trusted in your industry and have a good network of connections they can tap into to help you. As a result, these expert investors can expose you to more potential clients, negotiate better terms with suppliers, and find well-qualified key employees. Many people associate equity investments with flashy tech companies, but it's important to note that investment firms have wide-ranging preferences for the types of deals they target for their portfolio. For example, the firm Permanent Equity invests specifically in family-owned businesses in non-sexy industries (as the firm's website says, "we love 'boring' businesses," meaning less flashy but perpetually needed industries like swimming pool installation, glass manufacturing, and airplane parts).

How to Value Your Business

If you're considering equity financing, valuation is an important first step in that process. Your investors will have a good idea of what they think your company is worth, and so should you. Any money you accept implicitly values your firm. Let's say you give up 10 percent of your business in exchange for $1 million. That means you're valuing your business at $10 million. But you don't want an impressive-sounding, aspirational number; you need to have a solid rationale to support that figure.

Another thing to keep in mind is to treat equity as a scarce resource and be extra judicious about giving away slices of ownership. Entrepreneurs are often too relaxed about this and get in trouble when they seemingly hand out shares to pretty much anyone. I know of at least one startup that paid the people who painted their offices in equity shares because they didn't have any cash (the startup went on to become very successful, so that arrangement worked out well for the painters). When startups have a hodgepodge of owners, it's a red flag for investors. If you have a collection of random shareholders who own small slices of your company, it will be particularly challenging to get funding. In private equity lingo, this messes up your cap table. The *cap (capitalization) table* is a list of who owns what equity in the company, and the more complex it is, the more potential investors worry.

Valuations can be a funny thing, particularly for tech unicorns—that is, privately held companies valued at more than $1 billion when they go public. When Uber went public in 2019, a decade after it was founded, the company had a valuation of $82.4 billion. That year, it suffered $8.51 billion in losses. That number improved in 2020, but still reached a whopping $6.77 billion in losses.

For companies with fairly stable revenue, the valuation process is pretty straightforward. If I have a laundromat, then I have a certain number of washing machines that take a certain number of quarters. This allows me to make simple spreadsheet calculations about what my revenue is likely to be, assuming I have estimates for the percentage of machines in use during certain hours. Then I can use an industry-standard formula of X times sales or X times profit to get a reasonable ballpark valuation. But if you're poised for significant growth, you probably don't run a laundromat, and the valuation process won't be so straightforward. Unfortunately, if you're valuing your business based on potential future growth, there's no clear-cut formula or rule of thumb.

You can start with a well-known industry standard, such as 1x to 5x the company's annual profit. The multiplier depends on the industry you're in; faster growth requires a higher multiplier. This gives you a baseline, but it's just an average. If your company is winning in its category and growing quickly, its valuation can be many times that average. Here are some questions to get you started and help establish guidelines:

» What is your market share of the niche you serve? How fast can you capture more of it? How fast can the niche itself grow (particularly if it's a new niche you created)?

» Can you expand outside your current niche by expanding your product/service lines?

» How strongly differentiated is your product from those of your competitors? How easily can that differentiation be maintained? How strong is your brand and your customers' perception of it?

» Look at your key employees. Is your team world-class? How tightly are they bound to your company? Are they truly dedicated to seeing it through this difficult period? (Some companies, such as Apple, use an *aquihire* strategy. They look at target companies as a way to acquire talent and they value companies by how many technical staff they employ.)

» What do others in the startup community, such as other investors, lawyers, or accountants, think your valuation should be? A few meetings with some unbiased observers can give you invaluable information.

» Have any of your competitors been sold lately? What were their valuations? Can you make an argument that changes in the market or your unique product should earn you a higher valuation?

In other words, you're constructing a narrative about your valuation and why it should be much higher than industry averages; but remember, that narrative must be based on facts. Just as with your initial business plan, document your assumptions carefully.

If you like math, you'll love the Business Valuation Workbook I've provided for you with your Digital Assets. It shows how private equity investors use discounted cash flow modeling to arrive at valuations. It ignores current cash flows and profitability and instead uses profitability, or earnings, at the time the investor would like to exit (i.e., sell out of) the investment. Check it out at go.quickstartguides.com/rungrow.

Pitching to an Equity Investor

We'll discuss the different types of equity investors shortly. But almost any equity investor will probably want you to make a pitch to them with some sort of a "deck" (PowerPoint or other presentation software). The formal presentation should briefly address the same topics as the Executive Summary of your business plan. Many of these topics are covered in greater detail in my previous book, *Starting a Business QuickStart Guide*. To review, a summary of your business plan should answer these questions:

» What exactly is your product/service?

» What is the addressable market?

» Who are your customers?

» What is your value proposition? Why will your customers buy from you and not your competitors?

» How big can this venture grow? (You need to get them excited about the investment potential.)

» What is your business model? How will you make money?

» Who is on your team? (The investors need to understand that you have a team in place that can execute on your ambitious growth plan. If you have gaps on the team that you need to fill using the funding, you can discuss that here.)

Prepare no more than one or two slides for each of these topics. Rehearse your presentation so you can deliver it smoothly, without notes. Although you shouldn't worry about delivering the "perfect" pitch, I do have a few words of advice to set you up for success:

» **Soon after you start your presentation, you'll probably get interrupted with questions**. Don't let this throw you. Just answer them as completely as possible. Bring members of your team as necessary to answer questions that are outside of your expertise, such as technology or the financials.

» **Make a big first impression**. They see tons of pitches and will get bored easily. Organize your presentation to hit them with the "wow" factor of your deal right away, whether it's the cool new technology, the potential to "disrupt" an industry, high profitability or growth potential, etc.

PRO TIP: Have your standard deck, but anticipate what questions they may have and prepare extra slides that you can use to answer those questions as they arise. Nothing is more impressive than when the potential investor asks a question and you immediately pull up a slide that directly addresses it.

Plan for about an hour, but know it could take more or less time. More is good—that means they're interested. Less is probably a bad sign. Do not expect to get an offer during the first pitch. This isn't *Shark Tank*. It's the real world. As noted above, the investor will generally have a due diligence process that this meeting will trigger if they are interested. Although pitching can feel stressful, it doesn't have to be. Recognize that if they pass on your deal, it's not the end of the world. Have fun with it. Treat it like dating, and imagine how supportive friends would cheer you on: *You're a great catch and there's someone out there for you!*

UNDERSTAND WHAT "NO" MEANS: No matter how great your deal is, chances are you will have to deal with a lot of rejection before you find the right fit. It's easier said than done, but try to see this as feedback and fit, instead of feeling down about it. Always be polite and always ask for feedback, but take it with a grain of salt. Continuing with our dating analogy, a lot of potential investors don't want to be confrontational or offend you, so they'll give you some version of "it's not you, it's me." Nonetheless, if you read between the lines and really listen to what they're telling you, you can glean valuable information:

- **Feedback**: Are your assumptions reasonable? Are you making a strong enough case? Is your presentation clear, or are you repeatedly getting the same questions? Are there common objections you're hearing that you should directly address? Are your terms and valuation reasonable, or are you so far out of the box that they won't even try to negotiate?

- **Fit**: Do the investors you're targeting typically work in your industry? Do they work with deals of the size you're going after? Are you looking for debt when you should be thinking equity, or vice versa? Reread this chapter and think about the various kinds of investors, their characteristics, and what they're looking for.

One Founder's Perspective on Staying Focused While Fundraising: Launched in 2013 with a Kickstarter campaign, nondairy creamer company Nutpods reached No. 2 in *Inc.* magazine's list of the 5,000 fastest-growing food and beverage companies after just a few years. During that time, founder Madeline Haydon spent plenty of time raising money to fuel growth. She shares her perspective about staying focused on business operations while pitching investors:

It seems like somehow the goals of starting a business have gotten conflated with being able to raise millions of dollars when you're pre-revenue or before your first million-dollar validation of whether you have a market. I think there's never been this much access to capital, but keep laser-focused on your unit, economics, your cash flow, and make sure that you're building a healthy business that has a route to profitability just as quick as you can because at the end of the day, raising money is not the goal when you're building a business, it is a way for you to get to your goals, which is namely profitability and growth.

After your initial presentation, potential investors will need to conduct their **due diligence** process before they make a deal. This process, which we discussed in chapter 8 with respect to growth by acquisition, involves a detailed investigation of your company, because investors want a clear picture of the potential risks and rewards before they make any funding commitments. Equity investors can (and do) contact customers, suppliers, key employees, competitors, and their own set of experts in your field to test the validity of your claims.

One Investor's Framework for Vetting Founders: Angel investor Shaan Puri has backed more than twenty-five startups. When vetting founders, these are the questions he considers.

1. Are they committed?
2. Are they relentless?
3. Do they know what the hell they are talking about?
4. Do they learn quickly?
5. Have they done anything before?
6. Do I want to spend time with them?
7. Are they rational about the problem?
8. Are they irrational and ambitious about the solution?

Although lenders have a due diligence process as well, it is usually more mechanical and involves the borrower filling out forms and providing documents such as prior tax returns. The due diligence process for an equity investor can take a lot more time than meeting with a commercial loan officer and completing some forms, but not every equity investment deal is a lengthy waiting game. Investors can and do move very quickly if they fully agree with your vision of the future of your company and are well-versed in your industry. They don't want to lose out on a great investment prospect!

Need some help with due diligence? Check out my comprehensive, category-by-category listing of due diligence checkpoints in the Due Diligence Checklist included with your Digital Assets at go.quickstartguides.com/rungrow.

fig. 30

EQUITY ADVANTAGES	<ul><li>You're not promising to pay anyone back. The investor only makes money if your company grows beyond their initial appraisal of your firm and they can sell their shares at some future date.</li><li>Your cash flow isn't lowered by your having to make debt payments.</li><li>"Smart money" investors will provide a competitive advantage with a far-reaching network and advice that can help you run your business more efficiently.</li></ul>
EQUITY DISADVANTAGES	<ul><li>It can include an intense due diligence process that can become all-consuming and a major distraction from growing your business.</li><li>You no longer have full control of your business. That's a big problem if your investors insist on changes that you don't like, which can include replacing you as an employee if they believe someone else can do a better job (more on that below).</li><li>The investor will need to get their funds back at some point in the future, so they will require an exit strategy. This will usually involve either the sale of your firm or an initial public offering (IPO).</li></ul>

WATCH OUT FOR TERM SHEET TRAPS: A term sheet is a nonbinding agreement that outlines the broad terms and conditions of an investment. These documents tend to be relatively short, but don't let the size fool you. Term sheets are very complex and need to be reviewed carefully by an attorney who specializes in startups, private equity, and business valuation. Even parts of the document that appear to be boilerplate need scrutiny by an expert. There are numerous term sheet traps to be wary of, but I am going to highlight two—equity clawback provisions and anti-dilution clauses—to show how seemingly innocuous terms can have a huge impact on founders.

Equity clawbacks give the investor the right to take ("claw back") equity shares that have already been awarded to founders or key employees under certain circumstances, generally if they leave the company. To a founder, that can seem incredibly unfair. This is their baby! No one can take it from them! But there is a compelling counterargument, made passionately by the excellent blog/podcast *Startups.com*. Their point is that employees who have left the firm have no right to keep enjoying the fruits of the labor of those who remain, and that any contribution to the success of the firm is finite. The combined equity in the company of people who no longer work there adds another complexity to your cap table, so-called "dead equity." My point here isn't to say there is an absolute right or wrong answer to this issue, just that it is negotiable and needs your attention. The clawback doesn't have to happen immediately and doesn't necessarily apply to all of your equity.

Anti-dilution is even more technical, so I'll try my best to describe it in layman's terms. Every round of financing your firm undergoes involves the issuance of new shares to the new investors. This dilutes the percentage of ownership of previous investors. As a simple example, let's say you issued one million shares of your company at $1 each to an investor in exchange for 50 percent ownership in the firm. This values your firm at $2 million (if a 50 percent stake in the firm is worth $1 million, the entire firm is worth $2 million). Now let's say that after a period of time, you need another round of funding. The company has grown, so you issue one million new shares at $1 to a new investor. The first investor now has a $1 million stake in a $3 million firm. Their valuation has been diluted to 33.3 percent of the firm (figure 31).

DILUTION OF A COMPANY

fig. 31

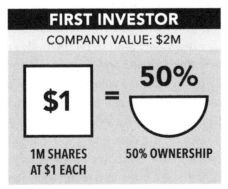

FIRST INVESTOR
COMPANY VALUE: $2M

$1 = 50%

1M SHARES AT $1 EACH   50% OWNERSHIP

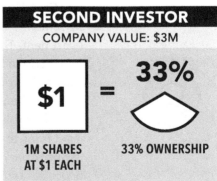

SECOND INVESTOR
COMPANY VALUE: $3M

$1 = 33%

1M SHARES AT $1 EACH   33% OWNERSHIP

Private equity firms often invest in a company using ***convertible preferred*** shares. With a full anti-dilution provision, their conversion price would be adjusted to $1.50, so their stake would be worth $1.5 million, or 50 percent of the now $3 million firm (figure 32). The person who bears the brunt of this is you, the founder, as your stake in the company has been reduced to $500,000 of the $3 million firm, or 16.6 percent. Obviously, this gets pretty complicated pretty quickly. Another reason to get expert help with your term sheet!

ANTI-DILUTION OF A COMPANY

fig. 32

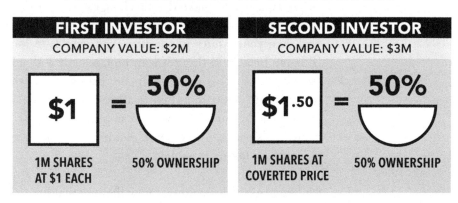

FIRST INVESTOR	SECOND INVESTOR
COMPANY VALUE: $2M	COMPANY VALUE: $3M
$1 = 50%	$1.⁵⁰ = 50%
1M SHARES AT $1 EACH — 50% OWNERSHIP	1M SHARES AT COVERTED PRICE — 50% OWNERSHIP

NOTE

HYBRID DEBT AND EQUITY FUNDING: Although a full discussion is beyond the scope of this book, there are many ways to structure investments that involve debt that can be converted to equity under certain circumstances. So-called mezzanine financing is very common and has advantages for both investors and investees.

Sources of Equity Funding

If you work with experienced equity investors, you're getting a lot more than just money. But that doesn't mean that all options under the "smart money" umbrella will serve you well. When determining which source is right for your business, the answer depends in part on your company's stage of development and how much money you actually need.

Private Equity

Private equity is funds invested into businesses outside of the normal capital markets (the stock exchanges). This can be either an individual making a personal investment in your firm (an ***angel investor***) or a firm that raises a fund of other people's money (OPM) and invests that money (a *venture capitalist*, or VC). They do so in exchange for a percentage ownership stake in the firm, which is determined by their valuation of the firm. As described above, this is more of an art than a science for fast-growing firms. Assuming they make a significant investment, the private equity firms will want to establish some control over what you are doing, typically by taking a seat or seats on your board of directors and by funding only to specific milestones. You receive only the funds needed to get to the first milestone, then enough for the next milestone, and so on. If you have a problem reaching a milestone, they can cut off your funding or pressure you to make drastic changes. This can include replacing the firm's founder with a more experienced executive. Although you would still own your equity in the firm, you would no longer be running it. This can be a good thing if your replacement does a better job than you (that possibility is one of the many reasons founders need to cultivate accountability and humility, qualities we explored in chapter 1). And again, whether or not things go as planned, the PE investor will need their funds back at some point, requiring an exit strategy like selling the company or taking it public.

Unlike banks, PE investors know they are making risky investments and that most of them won't pay off. Some will completely fail, and some will just break even or make a small profit. To justify that risk, a small percentage of their investment portfolio must do exceptionally well to compensate. If a PE investor can stay somewhere in the range of 20-60-20, where 20 percent of the portfolio fails entirely, 60 percent either breaks even or makes a small profit, and 20 percent does exceptionally well, they will be very successful indeed. It only takes one unicorn to make the investor look like a star. For example, when Facebook acquired WhatsApp for $19 billion in 2014, Sequoia Capital's approximately $60 million investment in WhatsApp was worth $3 billion, a return on investment of 50x.

Angel Investors

Angel investors are individuals who invest their own funds into startup firms. They may be an entrepreneur who's had a successful exit or two, a retired executive from a related industry, or just a wealthy person who enjoys working with startups and is attracted by the potentially high returns (and high risk) that accompany this sort of investment. They often work in clubs or syndicates where their funds are pooled with those of other investors. Because angels aren't investing from massive funds of OPM (other people's money), they are often more willing than VCs to make smaller investments earlier in the firm's life cycle and tend to be more flexible on terms.

They will have their own due diligence process, which may or may not be less formalized than a VC's. They definitely have the ability to make quick decisions. Numerous online directories can help you identify angel investors and angel investing clubs/syndicates. But as I write this, there's so much cash floating around the entrepreneurial ecosystem that if you are well-networked, an individual you know or meet could quite possibly offer to invest in your firm in a less formal way.

Venture Capital

Venture capitalists raise funds from a variety of sources—institutional investors, high-net-worth individuals, family offices—and then invest that collective pool of money in startups. VC investments have increased significantly in recent years; during the first half of 2021, VCs invested $288 billion, an all-time record (according to Crunchbase). If you receive a check from a venture capitalist, it will be for millions of dollars. These VC funds have gotten so large that they're mainly interested in companies that need $10 million or more. Otherwise, it's just not worth their time.

Thanks to their large network, VCs can help professionalize your business by recommending process improvements and helping you identify the right executives or other key employees to fill roles at your growing business. When VC firm Kleiner Perkins invested in a young company called Google in 1999, it introduced cofounders Larry Page and Sergey Brin to some tech luminaries—like Bill Gates, Andy Grove, and Steve Jobs—to get advice on hiring a CEO. That helped inform the cofounders' executive search process, which led to their hiring Eric Schmidt to run the company.

Keep in mind that because VCs are managing other people's money, they have extra incentive to invest in high performers. They usually have great expectations for the companies in their portfolios. You may experience significant pressure to get big and do it quickly. Often, they are seeking returns of 10x or more.

New Sources of Funding

During the past decade, funding options available for entrepreneurs have expanded dramatically. Now you can choose from some unorthodox options that didn't even exist twenty years ago. Three of the most prominent of these options are family offices, crowdfunding, and mini funds.

Family Offices

When a family has a total net worth of $100 million or more, it's common for them to handle investments and wealth management through a privately held company known as a family office. An interesting trend has emerged among family offices in recent years: instead of putting their money in private equity funds, many family offices are choosing to invest directly in companies. They're looking for lower fees, more control over their investments, and greater transparency. This trend is underscored by a 2020 study from research firm FINTRX, which found that, of the approximately 3,500 to 5,000 family offices around the world, more than half invest directly. The ability for family offices to invest directly is nothing new, but this approach didn't take off until 2010 (according to the FINTRX study). Between 2010 and 2015, direct investing jumped 206 percent and has kept rising. These are professional investors and represent the type of "smart money" we discussed earlier in this chapter.

One example is DNS Capital, one of the family offices for the Pritzkers (heirs to the Hyatt Hotel chain fortunes and ranked by Bloomberg in the top twenty-five wealthiest families in the world). DNS targets middle-market companies with $10 million to $50 million in EBITDA (which stands for earnings before interest, taxes, depreciation, and amortization), with a typical initial equity investment of $25 million to $100 million. In 2017, DNS assessed 450 potential deals and ultimately made fifteen investments (that includes brand-new investments and incremental investments in existing holdings). Its portfolio covers a wide swath of industries and business types, including health care, IT, steel-mill services, vegan burger-maker Beyond Meat, salad kiosk company Farmer's Fridge, and Atlanta-based New Realm Brewing Company. Like most family offices, DNS focuses on long-term investing, with a preferred time horizon that can extend well beyond ten years.

Crowdfunding

Many people think of crowdfunding simply as a vehicle for launching businesses. But it doesn't have to be used only on shiny new startups. Growing companies have discovered that crowdfunding sites like

Kickstarter can work to their advantage too. With crowdfunding, anyone can contribute money to your project. You don't give these backers any ownership in your company, but you do need to give them regular updates on your product's development. If you run into challenges and need to make changes, always keep your backers informed. In addition, you'll want to provide incentives for people to pledge money at different levels. That incentive can take a variety of forms, such as an extra discount when your product launches or a limited-edition version of it.

The benefits of crowdfunding extend beyond the financing of new projects. There's a reason why big brands with deep pockets, including Lego, Gillette, and Coca-Cola, have used crowdfunding. It provides an effective way to gain valuable feedback on new products under development, from people who are much more engaged than a typical focus group. That's because with crowdfunding, people are basically pre-buying the product from you, paying you to develop it. More likely than not, they have some emotional investment in your success. They're signing up to come along for the ride as you send out periodic updates to let them know what challenges you've faced with the design or manufacturing process and how you're solving those problems. As crowdfunding campaigns generate buzz, they can also help you reach new potential customers.

KICKSTARTER NUMBERS YOU SHOULD KNOW: Launched in 2009, Kickstarter had received pledges worth more than $6 billion by August 2020, according to the company, with more than 200,000 successfully funded projects. Most of its projects raise less than $10,000, but a growing number have reached six, seven, and even eight figures.

The company uses an "all-or-nothing" model, meaning that you set a funding goal and receive the donations only if you reach that goal. Although 11 percent of projects have ended without getting a single pledge, the overall rate of fully funded projects is just under 39 percent, according to Statista.

One of the most successful products to raise money on Kickstarter was the card game Exploding Kittens. With an original funding goal of $10,000, the project raised more than $8.7 million from more than 200,000 backers. It should be no surprise, given their popularity and relative affordability, that games represented the most-funded project category on Kickstarter as of July 2021 (with about $1.6 billion pledged, according to Statista). Design projects ranked as the second most popular category.

Mini Funds

One of the many advantages available to you as an entrepreneur in the twenty-first century is the recent proliferation of mini funds. As the name suggests, they are smaller funds that invest smaller amounts. The owners of these funds do not invest their own money; instead, they manage money they raise from other investors. Mini fund owners are compensated in two ways, just like venture capitalists. First, they receive a management fee to run the fund and cover overhead costs. This is a percentage (typically 2 percent) of the total amount that they oversee and invest. As their primary mode of compensation, these owners/managers take a share (typically 20 percent) of any profits realized by the fund (this is called the *carry*). Because these funds are small, this option won't be a good fit for your business if you're seeking millions from an investor. But a mini fund can certainly provide a six-figure investment that helps accelerate your growth plans.

While these mini funds can be backed by hundreds of investors, they're typically run by individuals who are well-connected and financially savvy, making this a solid "smart money" option. The due diligence process may be less rigorous than for a traditional VC fund. That's because mini fund managers are basically betting on the founders. They are likely to invest in companies with founders they know and trust, or with founders referred to them by other people they already trust. Sometimes the people who run these mini funds start by using a product they really enjoy, and then they call the founder of the company and have some discussions that lead to an investment.

To invest in mini funds (as is the case with traditional VC funds), individuals must meet the US requirements for an accredited investor; for instance, they must have an annual income of more than $200,000, or $300,000 with spouse (or spousal equivalent) in each of the last two years and an expectation of the same income in the current year.

For a great example of how mini funds have proliferated, consider angel investor Shaan Puri. In September 2020, he launched his mini fund with a tweet:

"Dear Internet, I'm going to raise a $1M+ Rolling Fund for investing in startups -- only from twitter buddies / internet strangers (not counting $ from real life friends)"

Puri asked for a minimum of a $25,000 total commitment, divided into four quarterly payments. Within five days, he raised $1.5 million from people he'd never met. Six months later, Puri's fund, called All Access Fund, was investing about $4 million annually in entrepreneurs around the world. Puri later changed the requirement to a minimum subscription of $10,000 per quarter for at least four quarters.

As an example of how every fund is different, Puri does not charge a management fee (although his fund does have a standard 20 percent carry).

Stages of Startup Funding

Remember the "knee of the curve" startup growth chart (figure 33) I showed you earlier in the "A Workable, Actionable Strategic Business Plan" section of chapter 9? That chart can be tied directly to the different stages of funding. It is an idealized picture—chances are your fundraising process won't be this neat and clean. However, it does serve to illustrate the roles of the various players we've discussed in this chapter.

» **Concept Stage:** After you have an idea for a new venture, you start thinking about developing it into an opportunity. You might be doing online research, asking questions in Reddit or other online forums, talking with people you know, etc. Any small amount of funding required usually comes from the founding team.

» **Seed Stage:** At this point, you've developed a plan and want to start implementing it. You may be building a prototype, mocking up a website to begin beta testing, or starting some initial marketing or other proof of concept. If you can't self-fund this stage, you might start approaching the FFF brigade to help you out (that's friends, family, and fools, in case you've forgotten). If you have a product you can presell, consider crowdfunding as an option.

» **Early Stage:** This is the slow, steady, "organic" growth stage where you're operating the business with just the founding team and maybe a couple of employees or contractors. You will need to invest heavily in infrastructure and marketing to continue the solid growth path. Angel and other individual investors may jump in here, because the risk has been mitigated—you have an actual working product or service that is beginning to sell.

» **Growth Stage:** This is really the domain of this book—the "knee of the curve," when an influx of funding can lead to explosive growth and perhaps domination of a particular sector. This is the preferred realm of venture capitalists and other deep-pocketed professional investors, when the risk/reward ratio is at its best.

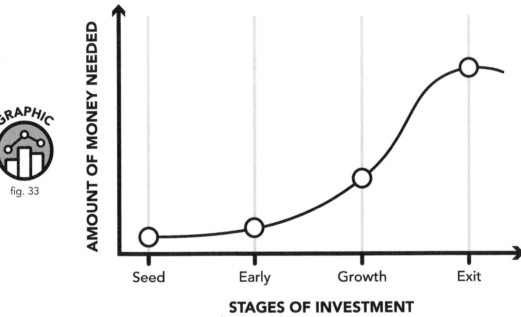

fig. 33

GRAPHIC

» **Mezzanine Financing Stage:** Continued rounds of venture funding take place as needed to fuel continued growth. Other types of more risk-averse partners, like banks and corporate venture arms, may well enter here. The rewards aren't quite as steep as in the growth stage, but the risk is much lower.

» **Exit Stage:** As the firm begins to reach its full potential and can operate without further funding, it's time to put the exit strategy into play. This usually involves a sale to a strategic partner who's in the same space or wants to get into it, or even an IPO.

As you evaluate the debt and equity options available to your company, you may find that the pursuit of funding can distract you from running your business. It is not only time-consuming but stressful. If possible, get the whole team involved so it's not just you making the pitches and filling out disclosures. Although it can feel reassuring to secure a big investment or loan, remember that financing is only useful if it serves your growth and profitability. Otherwise, you've given up a chunk of the equity in your firm or taken on debt that you didn't need.

Chapter Recap

» Debt financing allows you to retain full ownership, but the scheduled payments can create cash flow challenges.

» With equity capital, you don't need to pay back anyone, but you relinquish full control of your business. Your investors will want to help your business succeed—which sounds great until they start pushing for changes you don't agree with.

» Entrepreneurs have several options for borrowing money. Bank loans are typically best suited for businesses with a reliable pattern of revenue and growth.

» One loan option that doesn't involve banks is peer-to-peer (or P2P), where online platforms connect loan-seekers with people willing to provide financing.

» When it comes to equity funding, the amount of money you need (and your growth stage) will help determine which investors make sense for your business. Venture capitalists usually don't make small investments—they often put $10 million or more into a company.

» Although VCs have a big appetite for risk, they also have big expectations for your company's performance. These professional investors have enormous networks that can benefit your business, but they can also pressure you to step down as the company leader.

» Another type of equity investor is the angel investor. Rather than managing other people's money, these investors put their own funds into companies. They usually don't make huge investments like VCs do, but their terms are typically more flexible and they won't seek as much control over your company.

» With crowdfunding, you can have hundreds or thousands of individuals putting money into your project, such as the development of a new product. They won't have ownership in your company, but they will want to have updates on your project's progress.

| 11 |

We Live in a VUCA World

Everybody has a plan until they get punched in the mouth.

— MIKE TYSON

In 2020, the world was upended by a particle ten thousand times smaller than the width of a human hair. The virus (and its numerous variants) that caused the COVID-19 pandemic destroyed lives—and some livelihoods. As lockdowns limited in-person contact, businesses were forced to adapt overnight, with varying success. Sometimes that required overhauling business models or selling products online for the first time or shifting services that would normally take place in person to video sessions. During this time, companies had to protect not only their financial health but also the health and safety of their employees, while continuing to serve the needs of customers.

When faced with a situation that feels unmanageable, it's useful to have a framework that gives structure to the problem and defines specific aspects of the difficulty you face. To that end, consider VUCA, which stands for volatility, uncertainty, complexity, and ambiguity. All four qualities come together to describe situations that are particularly unpredictable and therefore challenging. The term was first introduced in the US Army War College in the 1980s, and the concept reportedly came from the book *Leaders: Strategies for Taking Charge* by Warren Bennis (founding chairman of the Leadership Institute at the University of Southern California) and author/academic Burt Nanus. The VUCA framework is an especially apt way to describe the struggles faced by companies during the pandemic (figure 34):

VOLATILITY
As a result of COVID-19, unpredictable changes were constantly taking place.

UNCERTAINTY
At the start of the pandemic, it wasn't possible to predict how long it would take to develop effective vaccines. Even after vaccines became available, new variants continued to spread and the pandemic did not have a known end point.

COMPLEXITY
The pandemic affected all aspects of business: supply chains, demand for products, and employees' ability to work effectively.

AMBIGUITY
There was no "best practices" handbook for organizations to follow to help them cope with the challenges brought by a pandemic.

GRAPHIC

fig. 34

Change is inevitable. That's a true statement, but it's also trite and useless unless we have strategies for responding to the inevitable. Since VUCA has military origins, let's use another military model to understand what to do about it. Like many, I first heard the term "improvise, adapt, overcome" in the Clint Eastwood movie *Heartbreak Ridge*. But the term isn't fiction—it's an unofficial mantra of the US Marine Corps. Here's the meaning behind those three words: The best-laid battle plans often become unworkable during a combat situation due to changing conditions or incorrect assumptions. The Marines pride themselves on their creativity and ability to adapt rapidly to changing conditions during high-stress situations. Let's use this motto as a way to explore how your business can survive and thrive in our VUCA world.

Improvise

In his classic book *The Lean Startup*, Eric Ries defines a "pivot" as a change in strategy without a change in vision. During VUCA events, that's exactly what you may have to do. But it doesn't take a pandemic to create a need to pivot. Any of the following normal business events can trigger a need for your firm to improvise:

» Regulatory changes
» Product liability
» New moves by your competitors
» Loss of key employees
» Declining sales

Some entrepreneurs fail to pivot because they're in love with their original business idea or they've become too attached to their current operational approach. These founders would have more success if they heeded the immortal words of the rock band 38 Special: "If you cling too tightly, you're gonna lose control." Many people don't realize some of the most successful companies today bear little resemblance to their origins.

Do you know the company Burbn? You probably don't know the name, but I'll bet you're very familiar with what it evolved into. Founded by Kevin Systrom, Burbn was launched as a location-based check-in app. Many apps like this existed, but Burbn had a unique feature: photo sharing. Systrom and his partners reconsidered the focus of their app. Instead of continuing with the original idea, they redesigned the app with enhanced photo-sharing features, removing many of the functions but retaining the ability to comment and "like" photos. They named the redesigned app Instagram and launched it in the Apple Store in October 2010. In 2012, Facebook acquired the company for $1 billion in cash and stock.

Burbn underwent an extremely successful pivot. "Pivot" is a large umbrella term that covers a range of business shifts. Let's explore some of the significant ways you might adapt your strategy (figure 35):

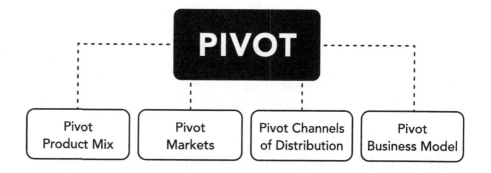

fig. 35

» **Pivot product mix**: Follow the most pressing needs of customers, and change your product lineup accordingly. For some distilleries during the pandemic, that meant producing hand sanitizer when it was in short supply in 2020.

» **Pivot markets**: Your company can boost revenue by exploring new markets and serving customers you hadn't considered in your original business plan. That could include adding B2C capabilities to your B2B business, or vice versa. It could also mean targeting a different demographic; that's what Lululemon did when it shifted some resources to the men's athletic wear market in 2014. At the time, the company's core women's market was starting to plateau. Many observers questioned whether men would shop at a store that had been considered a "women's brand," but Lululemon's shift appears to be paying off. By 2018, 21 percent of Lululemon's $3.3 billion in sales came from men's products, according to the *Wall Street Journal*. In the second quarter of 2021, the company said that revenue rose 61 percent, to $1.45 billion from $902.9 million, year over year. On a two-year basis, Lululemon reported that its men's business was up 31 percent, compared to 26 percent in its women's business.

» **Pivot channels of distribution**: During the COVID-19 pandemic, many business owners changed the way they sold products. For example, when retail stores closed for weeks during the height of the pandemic, some companies began selling direct-to-consumer (also DTC or D2C) and set up their own e-commerce sites for the first time. Traditional wholesale channels produce lower margins, which makes direct-to-consumer sales appealing, but companies should develop a strong digital marketing plan if they intend to make that shift. Some of the largest companies in the world have moved toward DTC in recent years, including PepsiCo. In May 2020, it launched two direct-to-consumer websites—PantryShop.com and Snacks.com—that sell the company's food and beverage brands. Nike has been gradually shifting to DTC for more than a decade. In 2011, direct-to-consumer sales represented 16 percent of its namesake brand revenues; by the end of Nike's fiscal 2020, that number had increased to 35 percent and continues to rise.

When COVID-19 cases spread through Europe in February 2020, Dan Simons began worrying about the business he co-owns, Farmers Restaurant Group. During the second half of March and the first half of April, sales plunged 90 percent compared to the same period in 2019. The pandemic created enormous challenges for his business—and it also helped him spot a new revenue opportunity. "As I started to see restaurants closed for diners, I just thought, the grocery stores are going to get overwhelmed," he said in an interview. Because grocery stores and restaurants have different supply chains, Simons' business had access to products that shoppers couldn't find at their local supermarkets. In less than a month, the company created a retail arm for delivery and curbside pickup of grocery items, prepared foods, and household staples like toilet paper—with an e-commerce platform reliable enough to handle thousands of orders per day. When the unexpected turmoil of COVID-19 forced the company to problem-solve quickly, it sparked an entrepreneurial mindset that will likely persist. As Simons said in an interview, "You know, once you learn you're not resilient or diversified enough, if you think, 'Oh, I learned that lesson, but I won't need to apply it again,' you're just a fool."

» **Pivot business model**: In order to survive, you may find you need to fundamentally change the direction of your business. That was the case for many companies during the pandemic, including bus tour company Milwaukee Food & City Tours. By July 2020, overall tour and transportation revenue was down 95 percent compared with a year earlier, as bus tours for convention groups, weddings, and company outings had been canceled due to COVID. But months earlier, founder Theresa Nemetz had come up with a plan to at least break even and prevent laying off employees in her small business, by shifting from selling a service to selling physical products. When tour cancellations started happening in March, Nemetz began making plans to sell gift boxes featuring food from the shops in her company's bus tours. Inspiration for the new product line struck after she observed many business owners struggling to find ways to boost morale when employees were suddenly forced to work from home. "I thought, wait a second, how could I help other people facilitate that for their staff?" she recalled in an interview. The company also created gift boxes for holidays throughout the year, as well as a product line with a Wisconsin State Fair theme. The specialty food gift boxes were shipped nationwide and also delivered locally by the company's part-time tour-bus drivers. Although the circumstances that prompted the company's business model shift were extremely challenging, the crisis may ultimately benefit the business by providing an additional revenue stream. Nemetz said she plans to keep offering the specialty gift boxes, even as her tour and transportation revenue returns to pre-pandemic levels. "I think it will enhance our business in the long run to be able to offer these products," she said.

Adapt

The ability to make effective decisions will determine your company's ability to thrive. Although those guidelines can still be useful when you find yourself immersed in VUCA, there are other decision-making strategies you'll need to consider in high-pressure situations. You won't be making choices in an ideal scenario. Expanding on Mike Tyson's quote at the start of this chapter, you'll have to revise your plan quickly after your business gets punched in the mouth. Here are some considerations for making informed decisions in high-stress situations:

» **Recognize your biases before they cloud your decisions**: When we're under extreme stress, we're more likely to take mental shortcuts. That can make us more susceptible to common decision-making biases. The best way to combat these errors in thinking is to be aware that they'll likely emerge—and to question them when we hear them from our leadership team or see them in our own thinking. Here are some examples:

- *Confirmation bias*: This happens when we seek out and pay more attention to information that supports our current views. Instead, we should remain curious (a quality we explored in chapter 1) and continually ask, "What assumptions am I making, and how might they be wrong?"

- *Loss aversion*: People like to win, but there's something they like even more: avoiding loss. Some studies suggest that losses are twice as powerful as gains when it comes to influencing our decisions. Another bias that relates directly to loss aversion is the status quo bias. People generally prefer the feeling of business-as-usual, and any shift from that baseline will often register (consciously or not) as a loss.

- *Framing effect*: The way you define a problem can improve or undermine your ability to navigate a crisis. If your approach or description is too narrow—creating an "either/or" scenario, for example—you will unwittingly exclude options that could have been viable solutions. Avoid viewing the situation through the narrow lens of your own experiences.

» **Rely on your board of advisors for candid input**: In chapter 6, we discussed the importance of having a board of advisors that can provide useful guidance. That guidance becomes even more critical for high-stakes, high-stress decisions. Although the decisions will ultimately be yours to make (along with your leadership team), it's crucial to surround yourself with advisors who will speak harsh truths. You don't want a sugar-coated reality. That's particularly true when you need to act swiftly. When people mince words to shield you from unpleasantness, they are really just exposing you to additional unpleasantness by fostering delay of hard decisions.

» **Apply NASA's approach to rapid decisions amid uncertainty:** When a crisis hits your business, it can feel like a life-or-death situation, but that's only true metaphorically. No matter how high the stakes, lives probably don't hang in the balance. That's the case for most organizations, but there are exceptions. NASA is one. When uncertainty strikes and your team members are 200,000 miles from Earth—as was the case when an oxygen tank exploded during the Apollo 13 mission—you need to stay calm and focused and ask the right questions. Having the right problem-solving skills can even help you find a way to fit a square peg into a round hole, and not just metaphorically. For the Apollo 13 crew, Mission Control devised a way to fit a square CO_2 filter into a round space, using cardboard, plastic bags, and duct tape. Without that solution, the crew would have died from carbon dioxide poisoning. It's just one of the high-stakes problems that NASA had to solve quickly to return the crew safely to Earth.

Although Paul Hill didn't serve in that ground crew, he's definitely familiar with NASA's approach to crisis management. Hill worked on twenty-four space shuttle and ISS missions as a flight director and is the author of *Leadership from the Mission Control Room to the Boardroom: A Guide to Unleashing Team Performance.*

He spoke to *Business Insider* about the need to focus on the right questions when catastrophe looms. Instead of panicking, Hill said, NASA's mission control team would ask the following:

- What was everything they knew—and did not know—about the situation at hand?
- What did the data actually say about the situation at hand?
- What was the worst thing that could happen as a result of the situation?
- Did the team have enough information to know for sure? And how could they get more information?
- What immediate steps could be taken to continue making progress in the mission or keep everyone safe?

When you face a crisis, don't assume that strategies you've used successfully in the past will yield the same outcome again. "Where you get in trouble is some bad thing starts happening and you feel the urge to start taking action," Hill told *Business Insider*. "You say, 'Hey, I've been in this situation before. This is what we did the last three times. It's always worked so I'm going to do it again.'" This can lull you into a false sense of security about a particular strategy. As a result, you might unwittingly take shortcuts in your decision-making process and miss important details in a crisis.

When you've arrived at a plan of action, communicate it clearly. As head of Intel, Andy Grove experienced the need for clarity as a leadership essential during dramatic change. He addresses this in his book *Only the Paranoid Survive: How to Exploit the Crisis Points That Challenge Every Company*. "Clarity of direction, which includes describing what we are going after as well as describing what we will not be going after, is exceedingly important at the late stage of a strategic transformation," writes Grove. He observes, "The point is this: how can you hope to mobilize a large team of employees to pull together, accept new and different job assignments, work in an uncertain environment and work hard despite the uncertainly of their future, if the leader of the company can't or won't articulate the shape of the other side of the valley?"

In chapter 7, we looked at the difference between tacit and explicit knowledge, and how the latter can help your business. While tacit knowledge exists in the heads of a few people at your company (or maybe just one), explicit knowledge is codified and accessible to everyone in the organization. This matters for quick, effective decisions in a crisis. When specialized knowledge is broadly available, solutions can come from a wider range of team members. Knowledge isn't power unless you can access it precisely when you need it most.

Overcome

Louis Pasteur once said that chance favors the prepared mind. I'm going to change the quote a little bit and say a VUCA world favors the prepared organization. The more you can do in advance to prepare for the curveballs you know life is going to throw, the better off you will be. Here are some ideas for how you can prepare for VUCA in advance:

Make Contingency Plans

When you make contingency plans to address the unexpected, the goal is not to have a flawless response to chaotic events. Instead, these planning efforts will help you be less reactive and more likely to minimize losses and resume normal operations sooner. Here are some key steps you should take in this process (figure 36):

STEPS TO CREATING A CONTINGENCY PLAN

fig. 36

1 DOCUMENT KEY FORECASTING ASSUMPTIONS

2 CREATE "WHAT-IF" SCENARIOS

3 FORMULATE A PLAN

» **Document key assumptions you're making with your forecasts:** This takes us back to the importance of data management and data analytics, which we addressed earlier in this book. What projections are you making about revenue, customer demand, and growth in new markets, for example? You may feel extremely confident about these projections, but the smartest entrepreneurs recognize that a huge gap can exist between a six-month forecast and what the future actually holds for your company.

» **Model what will happen to your business if you are wrong:** When you run a statistical analysis of "what-if" scenarios, you'll gain a better appreciation for how resilient your company might be if revenue takes a sudden hit. How might a crisis affect your cash flow and liquidity needs, for example? Consider which risks pose a greater threat and have a greater likelihood of occurring.

» **Plan what you can do about it:** There will always be events beyond your control, but by thinking ahead you can prevent a disaster from becoming a catastrophic failure. After you identify key risks that could affect your business, map out a possible response for each one. Here are three elements to keep in mind as you develop plans:

- **Financial concerns**: How will you survive a potential cash flow shortfall, for example, and for how long? (We'll look a bit more at the importance of cash reserves and lines of credit below.)

- **Data backup and recovery**: The role of data will increase as your business grows. We don't even realize how much we rely on it until it's suddenly not available. If your company lacks a data backup and recovery plan, make it a priority to create one.

- **Employee safety**: If the unforeseen event is one that puts workers' health at risk, this bullet point is the one that matters most. Make sure you have in place the necessary procedures to protect employees. Drill them regularly with your employees, and make sure all contact information is up to date. We live in a world where pandemics, extreme weather events, and terrorist attacks have become commonplace. Everyone must know what to do to get to safety when an event occurs, and how to begin the process of getting operations up and running again when it's safe to do so.

Be realistic in the contingencies you plan for. Even though, theoretically, *anything* could happen, there's no sense in wasting time planning for extremely unlikely events. If you live in a hurricane zone, it makes a lot more sense to plan for storm-related flooding and power outages than, for example, a comet hitting earth.

Hold Key Man and Liability Insurance

Did those words make you doze off for a moment? Insurance may strike you as boring, and even a waste of money. You may think, "I'm so busy running my company right now, I don't have time to deal with that." That mentality will set you up for huge regrets. Although no one wants to deal with insurance, you should not be running a growing business without liability insurance. And if you have a team with key people who play an influential role in your company's success, you need key man insurance to protect you in case one of those people unexpectedly leaves the company for any reason.

Have Cash Reserves and Lines of Credit

You might have a great plan to navigate a crisis, but that's not enough. You also need a financial buffer that gives you enough time to implement the plan. A good rule of thumb to consider is six months of cash reserves.

Without that buffer, you're putting your business in a precarious position. Essentially, your boat will capsize immediately if a big wave hits, so all you can do is hope the skies remain storm-free. This is not a strategy. It's wishful thinking. If you don't believe me, ask the many businesses that went under during the pandemic. Too many small companies went bankrupt almost immediately because they didn't have any cash reserves to buy a little time. To avoid that fate, you need some cash on hand and possibly a line of credit to draw on as well. Then if there is a downturn, you won't immediately have to close. When you are starting out, it's easy to say, "I don't have the luxury of saving any money." If you're not saving, start doing it right away. Otherwise, you're just kicking the can of financial disaster down the road. Eventually, you'll trip on that can and fall on your face.

Outsource and Contract as Much as Possible

In chapter 6, we covered general guidelines for deciding what to outsource. In the context of a VUCA world, outsourcing can give you the critical flexibility to respond appropriately in turbulent times. If you need to halt certain projects or if revenue falls off a cliff temporarily—as was the case for a number of businesses during the pandemic—you'll find it's much less complicated to sever ties with contractors than to lay off a significant portion of your staff. When your business thrives, you may think, "Hey, things are going great—now is a good time to hire a bunch of people!" Before you go on a hiring spree, remember that the goal is to maximize flexibility, not head count. Although some roles and responsibilities absolutely belong in-house, make sure you continue to reevaluate and look for opportunities to outsource when they fit your business.

Address Quality and Safety at the Product Development Level

As your company grows, you may find yourself racing to capitalize on new markets and changing customer demands. Although it's important to respond rapidly to industry shifts, it's never a good idea to sacrifice quality for the sake of speed. This can lead to product defects and customer dissatisfaction, or even lawsuits. That's why you need to make quality and safety essential parts of your planning, to ensure you've taken steps to prevent a possible product-quality crisis.

Stay as Lean as Possible

Although this relates to the earlier point about using outsourcing to remain flexible, staying lean means more than judicious hiring. The whole idea of scaling is that your revenues are growing exponentially but your costs are not. Rather, costs should increase in a more linear way and not at the same rate as sales. This is an important distinction that too many entrepreneurs don't understand. If your revenues are increasing exponentially and your costs are going up equally, then you're not really scaling. It's critical to scale properly; otherwise, when any sort of downturn occurs, your company will be dangerously exposed. Reckless spending during the dot-com bubble provides plenty of case studies for how this dynamic plays out. Ad spending during that era provides a great example of what not to do. During the Super Bowl held in January 2000, nineteen dot-com startups paid $1.1 million per thirty-second ad spot. Before the year was over, several of those companies had folded. This included Pets.com, a company that spent more than $20 million on an ad campaign featuring a dog sock puppet. The company went public in February, but in November of that year, it announced it was shutting down. Another startup that ran Super Bowl ads that year was Computers. com. Of the $7 million it had raised, it reportedly spent half on those ad spots. It was sold to Office Depot later that year. Now think about how much crypto and NFT companies spent on Super Bowl ads in 2022.

Think About Your Next Move Constantly

It's a point that has already been emphasized in this book, but it bears repeating. Strategic planning is an ongoing process. It's not a one-and-done exercise where you produce a document, put it on your shelf, and carry on with business as usual. Instead, it should be something you're constantly thinking about and adjusting. Remember: if you're failing to plan, you are planning to fail.

Chapter Recap

» As you grow your business, at some point you'll confront an enormous challenge that reflects the military framework VUCA, which stands for volatility, uncertainty, complexity, and ambiguity. To keep that challenge from feeling unmanageable, draw inspiration from an unofficial mantra of the US Marine Corps: improvise, adapt, overcome.

» To improvise successfully when faced with a significant threat to your company, you'll need to avoid strong attachments to your original business idea. Dramatic shifts may be needed in your product mix, markets, channels of distribution, or business model.

» To adapt during a high-stress situation, make sure you have a plan in place for making fast, effective decisions. That includes an experienced board of advisors to guide you, as well as a problem-solving strategy with specific questions to help you focus and prioritize.

» To overcome adversity, run your business each day with the assumption that eventually you'll get blindsided by an unwieldy problem. That means operating with several months of cash reserves, creating contingency plans that map out risks and how to prepare for them, and staying lean by keeping your costs low (even as your sales skyrocket).

Conclusion

As promised in the introduction, I've covered plenty of ground in this book. That's because you have to cover a lot of ground to grow your business into a truly lasting success. Hopefully, by this point I've convinced you that most stories of instant success are either apocryphal or outliers, or they neglect to account for years of hard work by the founding team (perhaps they failed in their first five ventures before finding "instant success" in their sixth).

By offering my perspective throughout the book, I've focused on giving you a useful alternative to the less-than-ideal discussions that surround business topics. Here's what I mean by that. Academics frequently veer into dry, theoretical territory. They can also rely too much on examples from many years ago that have become "classics" in their field. Another issue I see in newsletters and the Twitterverse is the need to get likes and shares by offering "hot takes" on management topics. These often take the form of "The experts say you need X, but they're all old and don't understand how business works today. Here's what you *really* need." I've tried to take a middle road by showing how the models taught to MBA students, even if they were developed many years ago, can still apply to current issues and have relevance for a rapidly changing business environment. I've also tried to be as holistic as I could, not just covering one business function at the expense of others—a luxury founders rarely have.

When I began by discussing personal development, some readers might have viewed that material as an unrelated detour. I promised it would pay off, and here's why: it's difficult, if not impossible, to scale a new venture if the founder or operator is not fit physically, mentally, and emotionally. For our exploration of mindsets in chapter 1, I kicked things off with the most relevant one—the growth mindset. Then we covered other critical mindsets—optimism, curiosity, persistence, and accountability. These mindsets are not only important for you personally but must be baked into your corporate culture (a topic we returned to in part II). It is difficult to create a culture of, say, accountability in your firm if you don't display it yourself. In chapter 2, I delved into physical and mental health, paying particular attention to rest, fitness, relationships, mindfulness, and task prioritization. In chapter 3, I explored the surprising ways that humor and lessons from the world of comedy can help you (and your team) communicate better and cultivate flexible thinking.

In part II, I switched from the individual to the firm level and applied several commonly used aspects of management to the growth-oriented organization. All are critical, and numerous entire books have been written on each one. My purpose was not to provide an exhaustive treatise, but to present you with some particularly salient issues related to each aspect. I started in chapter 4 with leadership and used John Kotter's definition: the creation of positive, non-incremental change, a vision and a strategy to achieve it, and the empowerment of your team to make it happen. I then reviewed several critical tools leaders use to achieve these ends—delegation, innovation, and transparency. Chapter 5 was a survey of basic management techniques—communicating, organizing, and decision making. Although these may seem routine to many owners, mistakes in any of them can lead to bad outcomes. I tried to provide some very applied models with lots of real-world examples to show relevancy. In chapter 6 I took a deep dive into hiring using the attraction-selection-attrition model as a framework. And chapter 7 was all about SOPs and KPIs and why they are so vital for efficient and effective firm operations.

Part III was about growth—how to think about it, plan for it, and fund it. Chapter 8 addressed different ways to grow and when each makes sense, including make vs. buy, related vs. unrelated diversification, and vertical integration. Then in chapter 9, I moved on to strategic planning and how to approach it in a way that will make your plan a useful, relevant tool for growth rather than a spiral-bound document gathering dust on your shelf. Chapter 10 was devoted to that most elusive of all topics—how to raise funds. It's easier to fund the growth of a successful firm than a startup, but that doesn't mean it's easy. I walked through how you go about the fundraising process for debt and equity funding, including newer sources of funding that continue to proliferate. (No section on crypto yet. Maybe in the second edition.) The final chapter explores some ways to plan for uncertainty and volatility in a world full of both.

My previous QuickStart Guide was about starting a business, which is the backbone of what I teach as an entrepreneurship professor. It is a very difficult thing to do successfully, requiring a scary leap of faith into the unknown and a firm belief in one's vision of the future. Growing and scaling a business has some overlaps with starting a business, in areas like strategic planning and raising funds, but it also includes a whole new set of challenges. The growth and change you're trying to achieve is no longer just about yourself and perhaps a small and like-minded group of friends. Now it affects an entire organization—which requires the management skills that are the crux of this follow-up book. Whether you came to this book directly from my previous writing or are reading me for the first time, I hope that you now feel ready to take the next step in your business venture. However you got here, I wish you every success in the future.

REMEMBER TO DOWNLOAD
YOUR FREE DIGITAL ASSETS!

 Business Valuation Workbook

 Due Diligence Checklist

 Ken's Business Brokers List

 Delegation Decision Matrix

TWO WAYS TO ACCESS YOUR FREE DIGITAL ASSETS

Use the camera app on your mobile phone to scan the QR code
or visit the link below and instantly access your digital assets.

or

go.quickstartguides.com/rungrow

 SCAN ME

💻 VISIT URL

About the Author

KEN COLWELL, PhD, MBA

Ken Colwell, PhD, MBA, is a seasoned strategic and operational leader with extensive experience working within entrepreneurial ecosystems and interacting with relevant private and public sector stakeholders at all levels in order to accomplish objectives.

He has consulted for hundreds of start-up ventures and is the principal of Innovative Growth Advisors.

Dr. Colwell is currently dean of the University of Houston-Victoria School of Business Administration. He has held past decanal posts at School of Business at Central Connecticut State University and the School of Business, Public Administration and Information Sciences at Long Island University–Brooklyn. Prior to taking his current decanal post, he was director of entrepreneurship programs at the University of Miami School of Business Administration and a professor of strategy and entrepreneurship at Drexel University.

Dr. Colwell holds a PhD in strategic management from the University of Oregon and an MBA from San Francisco State University. He has taught strategic management, entrepreneurship, new venture planning, and entrepreneurial consulting at the undergraduate, graduate, and executive levels.

About QuickStart Guides

QuickStart Guides are books for beginners, written by experts.

QuickStart Guides® are comprehensive learning companions tailored for the beginner experience. Our books are written by experts, subject matter authorities, and thought leaders within their respective areas of study.

For nearly a decade more than 850,000 readers have trusted QuickStart Guides® to help them get a handle on their finances, start their own business, invest in the stock market, find a new hobby, get a new job—the list is virtually endless.

The QuickStart Guides® series of books is published by ClydeBank Media, an independent publisher based in Albany, NY.

Connect with QuickStart Guides online at www.quickstartguides.com or follow us on Facebook, Instagram, and LinkedIn.

Follow us @quickstartguides

Glossary

360-degree review
A type of performance review where candid feedback is gathered from a wide range of people one interacts with, including colleagues, direct reports, and others, conducted through online surveys or in-depth interviews.

Agile Development
An iterative approach to software development in which self-organized. cross-functional development teams produce successive deliverables on short time-frames, all while reviewing, testing, and enhancing the work of their counterparts.

Angel investor
An individual who invests their own money in startup firms.

Aquihire
The process of organizations looking for companies to purchase as a way to acquire talent.

Board of advisors
A group of people that provide advice and guidance for a business; preferably people who have strong networks in the business's field.

Cap (capitalization) table
A list of who owns what equity in a company.

Capital structure
The combination of debt and equity that finances an operation.

Confirmation bias
The tendency to seek out and pay more attention to information that supports our current views, rather than challenging ourselves to look at information objectively.

Convertible preferred shares
A type of preferred stock that pays dividends and can also be converted to common stock at a specific time and at a specific ratio.

Debt financing
Paying for some aspect of one's business by borrowing money and promising to pay the lender back, including some rate of interest.

Due diligence
Performing a detailed investigation of a company, including its strengths and weaknesses, to get a clear picture of its potential risks and rewards.

Equity capital
Receiving financing for one's company by exchanging part ownership for funding, thereby diluting one's ownership stake in the company.

Exit strategy
The process of an investor or business owner receiving a return on their investment, usually through selling a company or taking it public.

Explicit knowledge
Information about a business or organization that is codified and organized in a knowledge management system that everyone in a company can access. See also *tacit knowledge*.

First-mover advantage
Having an edge over one's competition by being the first to offer a new and unique product or service.

Fixed mindset
A way of operating mentally that stems from the belief that one's qualities are carved in stone; this drives people to feel the need to prove themselves repeatedly. See also *growth mindset*.

Framing effect
Improvement or undermining of one's ability to navigate a crisis based on how they define the problem at hand.

Grit
A passion and perseverance for very long-term goals, which for entrepreneurs typically means sticking with their primary business goal for years.

Growth mindset
A way of operating mentally that stems from the belief that one's qualities can be enhanced through focused, sustained effort.

GTD
A five-step productivity system developed by David Allen, standing for "getting things done" and including the steps capture, clarify, organize, reflect, and engage.

Improvisational comedy
A type of comic performance in which the performers don't have scripts and instead use audience suggestions to create scenes and dialogue; also a helpful way to learn about teamwork.

Initial public offering (IPO)
When shares of a company are first made available for public purchase on a market.

Key performance indicators (KPIs)
Metrics that support business goals by helping to analyze a company's performance and health. They must be specific, measurable, achievable, relevant, and time-bound to be effective.

Knowledge management system
Software that collects and organizes essential information for a company, so all employees can easily access what they need.

Lean
A methodology focused on eliminating waste and increasing value for the customer, targeting eight wastes that are summed up in the acronym DOWNTIME: Defects, Overproduction, Waiting, Non-utilized talent, Transportation, Inventory, Motion, Excess processing.

Loss aversion
A form of mental bias whereby decision making is guided by the instinct to avoid losses rather than to pursue gains.

Mindfulness
A focus of attention and the ability to quiet one's mind and focus on the present rather than reliving the past or worrying about the future.

Org structure
A business or organization's clearly expressed hierarchy that ensures that all employees understand the purpose of each unit and what it's responsible for.

Policies
Sets of rules for specific decisions that organizations need to make, explaining why the business does things or why it does them a certain way. Policies should reflect a company's culture and overall mission.

Procedures
Sets of steps designed to achieve a particular outcome; in other words, how a business does things. Used interchangeably with *processes* in this book, though they are technically not exactly the same.

Processes
See *procedures*.

Product expansion
The process of a company attempting to grow by offerng new products or services in different categories than its existing product lines.

Product extension
The process of a company attempting to grow by creating new variations in an existing product line.

Psychological safety

The sense of not feeling threatened, a vital part of overall workplace safety.

Related diversification

A form of product expansion whereby a company adds products or services similar to what they already offer.

Six Sigma

An approach to efficiency designed to reduce defects and promote consistency throughout a company's processes. It typically uses five steps to address issues, with two main methodologies, one for existing processes and the other for new processes.

Smart money

Equity investors in a company who are trusted in that company's industry and have a good network of connections they can tap into to help the company.

Standard operating procedure (SOP) manual

Specialized knowledge and information about a company that is gathered in one place and readily available to employees to help make better decisions faster—essentially, an organization's bible.

Tacit knowledge

Information about a business or organization that resides only in the minds of one or a few workers and has not been formally documented. See also *explicit knowledge*.

Unrelated diversification

A form of product expansion whereby a company adds products or services that are significantly different from what they already offer, often appealing to a new customer segment.

Value chain

All the steps involved in a business creating its product or service and providing it to customers.

Venture capitalist

An individual or firm that raises a fund of other people's money and then invests that money.

Vertical integration

A form of unrelated diversification where a company adds capabilities and products up and down its supply chain, either by acquiring companies or developing new capabilities/ products internally.

References

CHAPTER 1

Collison, Patrick. https://patrickcollison.com/bookshelf.

Del Rey, Jason. "Procter & Gamble has acquired the startup aiming to build the Procter & Gamble for people of color," *Vox*. December 12, 2018. https://www.vox.com/2018/12/12/18136744/walker-company-procter-gamble-acquisition-tristan-walker-beve

Drucker, Peter. 1999. "Managing Oneself." *Harvard Business Review*.

Easter, Michael. "These Two Men Are on a Mission to Save CrossFit," *Men's Health*. February 1, 2021. https://www.menshealth.com/fitness/a35142700/crossfit-ceo-eric-roza-dave-castro-transformation

Gates, Bill, interview by Eric Schmidt. *YouTube*. https://www.youtube.com/watch?v=XLF90uwII1k.

Gorman, Alyx, and Josh Taylor. "CrossFit CEO Greg Glassman resigns after offensive George Floyd and coronavirus tweets," *The Guardian*. June 9, 2020. https://www.theguardian.com/us-news/2020/jun/10/greg-glassman-crossfit-ceo-resigns-george-floyd-protest-coronavirus-tweets-conspiracy-theories

Grant, Adam. "The Problem with All-Stars," *LinkedIn*. May 1, 2018. https://www.linkedin.com/pulse/problem-all-stars-adam-grant/

Greene, Robert. "Be Like Henry Ford: Apprentice Yourself in Failure," *Fast Company*. https://www.fastcompany.com/3002809/be-henry-ford-apprentice-yourself-failure

Gregersen, Hal. "Bursting the CEO Bubble," *Harvard Business Review*. March-April 2017. https://hbr.org/2017/03/bursting-the-ceo-bubble

Guth, Robert A. "In Secret Hideaway, Bill Gates Ponders Microsoft's Future," *Wall Street Journal*. March 28, 2005. https://www.wsj.com/articles/SB111196625830690477

Hawkins, Andrew J. "Uber's CEO caught being a jerk on camera by one of his own drivers," *The Verge*. February 28, 2017. https://www.theverge.com/2017/2/28/14766868/uber-driver-argument-ceo-travis-kalanick-video

Landsverk, Gabby. "CrossFit gyms around the world are rebranding after the CEO's insensitive comments about George Floyd: 'They don't own the workout'," *Insider*. June 9, 2020. https://www.insider.com/gyms-are-dropping-crossfit-brand-after-glassman-george-floyd-comments-2020-6

Molokhia, Dalia. "The Importance of Being Curious," *Harvard Business Publishing*. May 24, 2018. https://www.harvardbusiness.org/the-importance-of-being-curious

Morse, Gardiner. "Behave Yourself," *Harvard Business Review*. October 2002. https://hbr.org/2002/10/behave-yourself-2

Raz, Guy. *How I Built This: The Unexpected Paths to Success from the World's Most Inspiring Entrepreneurs*. Mariner Books,

2020.

Rego, Arménio et al. "Leader Humility and Team Performance: Exploring the Mediating Mechanisms of Team PsyCap and Task Allocation Effectiveness," *Journal of Management* 1009–1033. 2017. doi:https://doi.org/10.1177/0149206316688941

Santana, Marco. "Fattmerchant marks 5 years, mayor's office reports its revenue," *Orlando Sentinel.* July 18, 2019. https://www.orlandosentinel.com/business/os-cfb-fattmerchant-five-year-anniversary-20190718-5qendlibfjdcfeqsrlydob43ga-story.html

Schmidt, Eric, Jonathan Rosenberg, and Alan Eagle. "The bear-hugging football coach who became Silicon Valley's go-to guru," *Fast Company.* April 4, 2019. https://www.fastcompany.com/90331367/bill-campbell-silicon-valley-trillion-dollar-coach-book

Warshawsky, Jon. "Predictably Irrational: Beer, Pricing and the Human Mind," *Deloitte.* August 2, 2008. https://www2.deloitte.com/us/en/insights/deloitte-review/issue-3/predictably-irrational-beer-pricing-and-the-human-mind.html

Wischhover, Cheryl. "Why CrossFit Devotees Leaving the Brand Behind Is Such a Big Deal," *Vox.* June 12, 2020. https://www.vox.com/the-goods/2020/6/12/21289151/crossfit-greg-glassman-black-lives-matter-box-katrin-davidsdottir-games-reebok

CHAPTER 2

Barbosa, Brenda. "Billionaire Richard Branson Does This at Every Meeting. Here's Why You Should Do It Too," *Inc.* June 9, 2017. https://www.inc.com/brenda-barbosa/the-habit-billionaire-richard-branson-swears-by-and-how-you-can-cultivate-it-to.html

CNN Business Traveler. "Richard Branson Shares His Travel Tips," *CNN.* May 5, 2006. http://edition.cnn.com/2006/TRAVEL/04/25/branson.tips/index.html

Dyson, Brian. Georgia Tech Commencement Speech. September 6, 1996. https://apps.npr.org/commencement/speech/brian-j-dyson-georgia-tech-1996

Entrepreneurs' Organization. About. https://hub.eonetwork.org/Web/About_Public/Our-Values/Web/About%20Public/Our-Values.aspx?hkey=b7ce9b0b-14b0-4ccc-8e5b-9e94cf467afb

First Round Review. n.d. "The Founder's Guide to Discipline: Lessons from Front's Mathilde Collin." *First Round Review.* https://review.firstround.com/the-founders-guide-to-discipline-lessons-from-fronts-mathilde-collin

Fogarty, Philippa. "Why Walking Makes You a Better Worker," *BBC.* March 3, 2019. https://www.bbc.com/worklife/article/20190304-why-walking-makes-you-a-better-worker

Getting Things Done. https://gettingthingsdone.com/what-is-gtd

Gregersen, Hal. *Questions Are the Answer.* 2018, Harper Business.

Hubbard, Caryn. "Shareholder Update: Q4, 2020 — 2020 Results and What's Ahead," *Buffer.* 2020. https://buffer.com/resources/shareholder-update-q4-2020

La Roche, Julia. "How Meditation Makes Ray Dalio Feel 'Like a Ninja in a Fight'," *Business Insider.* February 12, 2014. https://www.businessinsider.com/ray-dalio-2014-2

Salzberg, Sharon. "Meditation Is About Recovering and Starting Again," *Mindful.* February 7, 2019. https://www.mindful.org/meditation-is-about-recovering-and-starting-again

Valencia, Jordana. "How Founders Can Recognize and Combat Depression," *Harvard Business Review*. February 17, 2017. https://hbr.org/2017/02/how-founders-can-recognize-and-combat-depression

Widrich, Leo. "How Much Sleep Do You Really Need to Work Productively?" *Lifehacker*. August 10, 2012. https://lifehacker.com/how-much-sleep-do-you-really-need-to-work-productively-5933568

Wilding, Melody. "The Essential People Every Entrepreneur Needs in Their Life, According to a Certified Love Expert." *Thrive Global*. https://thriveglobal.com/stories/the-essential-people-every-entrepreneur-needs-in-their-life-according-to-a-certified-love-expert

Winfrey, Oprah. "What Oprah Knows About the Power of Meditation," *Oprah.com*. https://www.oprah.com/inspiration/what-oprah-knows-about-the-power-of-meditation#ixzz6ugtYYWQD

CHAPTER 3

Aaker, Jennifer. *Humor, Seriously: Why Humor Is a Secret Weapon in Business and Life*. Currency, 2021.

Albert-Deitch, Cameron. "Why Dollar Shave Club Co-Founder Michael Dubin No Longer Believes in DTC," *Inc*. March 31, 2021. https://www.inc.com/cameron-albert-deitch/michael-dubin-dollar-shave-club-lessons-ecommerce.html

Costolo, Dick. "How to Run Your Company Like an Improv Group, by Twitter CEO Dick Costolo," *Bloomberg*. April 11, 2013. https://www.bloomberg.com/news/articles/2013-04-11/how-to-run-your-company-like-an-improv-group-by-twitter-ceo-dick-costolo

Elkins, Kathleen. "The surprising dinner table question that got billionaire Sara Blakely to where she is today," *Business Insider*. April 3, 2015. https://www.businessinsider.com/the-blakely-family-dinner-table-question-2015-3

Fried, Jason. "Want to Know What Your Employees Really Think?" *Inc*. October 2011. https://www.inc.com/magazine/201110/jason-fried-on-learning-what-your-employees-think.html

Frieswick, Kris. "The Serious Guy Behind Dollar Shave Club's Crazy Viral Videos," *Inc*. April 2016. https://www.inc.com/magazine/201604/kris-frieswick/dollar-shave-club-michael-dubin.html)

HBR IdeaCast (podcast). "How Many Managers Does It Take to Change a Lightbulb?" *HBR*. February 2021. https://hbr.org/podcast/2021/02/how-many-managers-does-it-take-to-change-a-lightbulb

McCaffrey, Tony, and Jim Pearson. "Find Innovation Where You Least Expect It," *Harvard Business Review*. December 2015. https://hbr.org/2015/12/find-innovation-where-you-least-expect-it

McGraw, Peter. "Dropping Babies with Anthony Jeselnik" podcast. *PeterMcGraw.org*. April 3, 2020. https://petermcgraw.org/dropping-babies-with-anthony-jeselnik/

McGraw, Peter. *Shtick to Business: What the Masters of Comedy Can Teach You about Breaking Rules, Being Fearless, and Building a Serious Career*. Lioncrest, 2020.

Stevenson, Seth. "Getting to 'Yes, And,'" *Slate*. March 30, 2014. https://slate.com/business/2014/03/improv-comedy-and-business-getting-to-yes-and.html

Tabaka, Marla. "Don't Be So Serious about Sales and Marketing: How Sara Blakely Shaped Spanx Success with Humor," *Inc*. July 16, 2019. https://www.inc.com/marla-tabaka/dont-be-so-serious-about-sales-marketing-how-sara-blakely-shaped-spanx-success-with-humor.html

CHAPTER 4

ActionDanBro. https://www.actiondanbro.com/

Amabile, Teresa M., et al. "IDEO's Culture of Helping," *Harvard Business Review*. January-February 2014. https://hbr.org/2014/01/ideos-culture-of-helping

Bharadwah Badal, Sangeeta, and Bryant Ott. "Delegating: A Huge Management Challenge for Entrepreneurs," *Business Journal*. April 4, 2015. https://news.gallup.com/businessjournal/182414/delegating-huge-management-challenge-entrepreneurs.aspx

Bigger Pockets Podcast #480. "Making $200K a Month after Being on the Verge of Bankruptcy." *Bigger Pockets*. June 2021. https://www.biggerpockets.com/blog/biggerpockets-podcast-480-dan-brault

Brown, Brene. https://daretolead.brenebrown.com/

Catmull, Ed. *Creativity, Inc.: Overcoming the Unseen Forces That Stand in the Way of True Inspiration*. Random House, 2014.

Hammett, Gene. "Agile Culture Improves Growth with Andrew Paradise at Skillz." *genehammett.com*. September 15, 2019. https://www.genehammett.com/459-agile-culture-improves-growth-with-andrew-paradise-at-skillz

Harrison, Spencer, et al. "Research: 83% of Executives Say They Encourage Curiosity. Just 52% of Employees Agree," *Harvard Business Review*. September 20, 2018. https://hbr.org/2018/09/research-83-of-executives-say-they-encourage-curiosity-just-52-of-employees-agree

Hoffman, Reid. "If There Aren't Any Typos in This Essay, We Launched Too Late!" *LinkedIn*. March 29, 2017. https://www.linkedin.com/pulse/arent-any-typos-essay-we-launched-too-late-reid-hoffman

IDEO Design Thinking. "The Secret to Your Success? Make Others Successful," *Design Thinking Blog*. July 3, 2013. https://designthinking.ideo.com/blog/the-secret-to-your-success-make-others-successful

Lurie, Zander. "SurveyMonkey's CEO on Creating a Culture of Curiosity," *Harvard Business Review*. January-February 2019. https://hbr.org/2019/01/surveymonkeys-ceo-on-creating-a-culture-of-curiosity

Quickbase.com. "What Is Servant Leadership?" https://www.quickbase.com/blog/what-is-servant-leadership-thoughts-from-southwest-airlines-president-colleen-barrett

Rozovsky, Julia. "The Five Keys to a Successful Google Team." *re:Work*. November 17, 2015. http://rework.withgoogle.com/blog/five-keys-to-a-successful-google-team

Seppälä, Emma. "What Bosses Gain by Being Vulnerable," *Harvard Business Review*. December 11, 2014. https://hbr.org/2014/12/what-bosses-gain-by-being-vulnerable

CHAPTER 5

Brunswick Group. "2021 Connected Leadership." *Brunswick Group*. https://www.brunswickgroup.com/media/8059/connected-leadership-2021-report.pdf

Bryant, Adam. n.d. "How to Run a More Effective Meeting," *The New York Times*. https://www.nytimes.com/guides/business/how-to-run-an-effective-meeting

Crook, Jordan. "Canva Raises 200 Million at a 40 Billion Valuation," *TechCrunch*. September 14, 2021. https://techcrunch.com/2021/09/14/canva-raises-200-million-at-a-40-billion-valuation

Cutter, Chip. "Even the CEO of Zoom Says He Has Zoom Fatigue," *Wall Street Journal*. May 4, 2021. https://www.wsj.com/articles/even-the-ceo-of-zoom-says-he-has-zoom-fatigue-11620151459

Felton, Ryan. "Tesla Switching to 24/7 Shifts to Push for 6,000 Model 3s Per Week By June, Elon Musk Says," *Jalopnik*. April 17, 2018. https://jalopnik.com/tesla-switching-to-24-7-shifts-to-push-for-6-000-model-1825335216

First Round Review. n.d. "How Fast-Growing Startups Can Fix Internal Communication Before It Breaks." *First Round Review*. https://review.firstround.com/How-Fast-Growing-Startups-Can-Fix-Internal-Communication-Before-It-Breaks

Jen Su, Amy. "Do You Really Trust Your Team? (And Do They Trust You?)," *Harvard Business Review*. December 16, 2019. https://hbr.org/2019/12/do-you-really-trust-your-team-and-do-they-trust-you

Joyner, April. "Superhuman CEO Rahul Vohra explains how Tiger Global's John Curtius is very different from other VCs," *Business Insider*. August 11, 2021. https://www.businessinsider.com/how-startup-superhuman-raised-75-million-from-tiger-global-ivp-2021-8

Know Your Team podcast. "Episode 21: Interview with Katrina Markoff, Founder + CEO of Vosges Haut-Chocolat." *Know Your Team*. June 14, 2018. https://knowyourteam.com/blog/podcast/episode-21-interview-with-katrina-markoff-founder-ceo-of-vosges-haut-chocolat

Leonardi, Paul, and Tsedal Neeley. "What Managers Need to Know About Social Tools," *Harvard Business Review*. November-December 2017. https://hbr.org/2017/11/what-managers-need-to-know-about-social-tools

Poctzer, Sharon. "This Fundamental Problem Can Kill Your Startup—Here's How to Avoid It." *Inc.* https://www.inc.com/sharon-poczter/how-to-do-org-design-right-at-startups.html

Rampton, John. n.d. "Ways to Participate in Social Media Strategy as CEO." *The Economist*. https://execed.economist.com/blog/career-hacks/ways-participate-social-media-strategy-ceo

Rogelberg, Steve G. "The Science of Better Meetings," *Wall Street Journal*. February 15, 2019. https://www.wsj.com/articles/the-science-of-better-meetings-11550246239

Shi, Diana. "9 CEOs share their best tips for successful remote work," *Fast Company*. 2021. https://www.fastcompany.com/90595007/9-ceos-share-their-best-tips-for-successful-remote-work

Steer, Derek. "We're Sharing Our Slack Guidelines and How They're Helping in an All-Remote Culture," *Mode*. https://mode.com/blog/mode-slack-guidelines

Vohra, Rahul. "How to Make Your Meetings Twice as Fast," *Superhuman*. September 24, 2020. https://blog.superhuman.com/how-to-spend-50-less-time-in-meetings

Zipkin, Nina. "She Was Told 'No' 100 Times. Now This 31-Year-Old Female Founder Runs a $1 Billion Business," *Entrepreneur*. June 12, 2019. https://www.entrepreneur.com/article/310482

CHAPTER 6

Bryant, Adam. "In Head-Hunting, Big Data May Not Be Such a Big Deal," *The New York Times*. June 20, 2013. https://www.nytimes.com/2013/06/20/business/in-head-hunting-big-data-may-not-be-such-a-big-deal.html.

Connley, Courtney. "Black and Latinx founders have received just 2.6% of VC funding so far in 2020, according to new report," *CNBC*. October 8, 2020. https://www.cnbc.com/2020/10/07/black-and-latinx-founders-have-received-just-2point6percent-of-vc-funding-in-2020-so-far.html

Deloitte. n.d. "Diversity, Equity & Inclusion in the VC Industry." *Deloitte*. https://www2.deloitte.com/us/en/pages/audit/articles/diversity-venture-capital-human-capital-survey-dashboard.html

Gage, Deborah. "The Venture Capital Secret: 3 Out of 4 Start-Ups Fail," *Wall Street Journal*. September 20, 2012. https://www.wsj.com/articles/SB10000872396390443720204578004980476429190

Knight, Rebecca. "7 Practical Ways to Reduce Bias in Your Hiring Process." *Harvard Business Review*. June 12, 2017. https://hbr.org/2017/06/7-practical-ways-to-reduce-bias-in-your-hiring-process.

Koerth, Maggie. "Most Personality Quizzes Are Junk Science. I Found One That Isn't," *FiveThirtyEight*. January 2, 2018. https://fivethirtyeight.com/features/most-personality-quizzes-are-junk-science-i-found-one-that-isnt

Law.com. "CVS, Best Buy End Job-Applicant Personality Tests Amid EEOC Probe," *Yahoo! News*. June 7, 2018. https://www.yahoo.com/news/cvs-best-buy-end-job-072408349.html

Meinert, Dori. "What Do Personality Tests Really Reveal?" *SHRM*. June 1, 2015. https://www.shrm.org/hr-today/news/hr-magazine/pages/0615-personality-tests.aspx

Nguyen, Janet. "Five Things You Didn't Know About the History of the Myers-Briggs System." *Marketplace*. October 30, 2018. https://www.marketplace.org/2018/10/30/5-things-you-didn-t-know-about-history-myers-briggs-system/

O'Boyle, Ed. "4 Things Gen Z and Millennials Expect From Their Workplace," *Gallup*. March 30, 2021. https://www.gallup.com/workplace/336275/things-gen-millennials-expect-workplace.aspx

Raymond, Joan. "How to know if you're the rarest personality type," *Today*. November 15, 2017. https://www.today.com/health/personality-type-infj-rarest-myers-briggs-combination-t118739

Wharton. "Is Cultural Fit a Qualification for Hiring or a Disguise for Bias?" *Knowledge at Wharton*. July 16, 2015. https://knowledge.wharton.upenn.edu/article/cultural-fit-a-qualification-for-hiring-or-a-disguise-for-bias

CHAPTER 7

EEOC Small Business Requirements. US Equal Employment Opportunity Commission. https://www.eeoc.gov/employers/small-business/small-business-requirements

EOS Entrepreneurial. https://www.eosworldwide.com/eos-model.

Federal Trade Commission. "CAN-SPAM Act: A Compliance Guide for Business." *FTC*. https://www.ftc.gov/tips-advice/business-center/guidance/can-spam-act-compliance-guide-business

Liao, Shannon. "Riot Games agrees to pay $100 million in settlement of class-action gender discrimination lawsuit," *The Washington Post*. December 28, 2021. https://www.washingtonpost.com/video-games/2021/12/27/riot-discrimination-100-million-settlement

Oldroyd, James B., et al. "The Short Life of Online Sales Leads," *Harvard Business Review*. March 2011. https://hbr.org/2011/03/the-short-life-of-online-sales-leads

CHAPTER 8

Blake, Alex. "The Mac's Apple Silicon processor transition: Everything you need to know." *DigitalTrends*. April 7, 2021. https://www.digitaltrends.com/computing/mac-apple-silicon-transition-explained

Campbell, Dakin. "How WeWork spiraled from a $47 billion valuation to talk of bankruptcy in just 6 weeks," *Business Insider*. September 28, 2019. https://www.businessinsider.com/weworks-nightmare-ipo

Carr, Austin. "Jimmy Buffett Has Just What New York Needs Right Now: A $370 Million Monument to Frozen Drinks," *Bloomberg*. June 9, 2021. https://www.bloomberg.com/news/features/2021-06-09/jimmy-buffett-opens-370-million-margaritaville-in-new-york-city-s-times-square

Condon, Stephanie. "AWS hits $54 billion annual run rate," *ZDNet*. April 29, 2021. https://www.zdnet.com/article/aws-run-rate-hits-54-billion-annual-run-rate

First Round Review. n.d. "What I Learned From Developing Branding for Airbnb, Dropbox and Thumbtack." *First Round Review*. https://review.firstround.com/what-i-learned-from-developing-branding-for-airbnb-dropbox-and-thumbtack

Hyundai Newsroom. "The Story of Steel: Strengthening Car Safety." *Hyundai*. February 6, 2017. https://www.hyundai.news/eu/articles/stories/the-story-of-steel-strengthening-car-safety.html

Musk, Elon. Twitter account. https://twitter.com/elonmusk/status/1117144865299501056?s=20

O'Brien, Sara Ashley. "WeWork's losses doubled to $1.25 billion last quarter," *CNN*. November 14, 2019. https://www.cnn.com/2019/11/13/tech/wework-losses-ipo/index.html

Reichart, Corinne. "Amazon buys 11 more jets for its delivery fleet," *CNET*. January 5, 2021. https://www.cnet.com/tech/services-and-software/amazon-buys-11-more-jets-for-its-delivery-fleet

Swanson, S. A. "Merchants of Efficiency," *Middle Market Growth*. September 3, 2019. https://middlemarketgrowth.org/cover-merchants-of-efficiency

Wiltermuth, Joy. "Here's a look at how WeWork's $50 billion pile of office leases could unravel," *MarketWatch*. October 14, 2019. https://www.marketwatch.com/story/heres-a-look-at-how-weworks-50-billion-pile-of-office-leases-could-unravel-2019-10-10

Wolverton, Troy, et al. "WeWork opened 400 locations in three years. In some cases, it used deep discounts to convince existing customers to relocate to help fill them," *Business Insider*. September 30, 2019. https://www.businessinsider.com/wework-used-disounts-to-convince-tenants-to-relocate-new-locations-2019-9

CHAPTER 9

First Round Review podcast. n.d. "CEO Jeff Lawson reflects on the peaks and valleys of Twilio's growth story," *First Round Review*. https://review.firstround.com/podcast/episode-14

Jobs, Steve. Interview with CNBC: Defending His Commitment to Apple. *YouTube*. 1997. https://www.youtube.com/watch?v=xchYT9wz5hk

Tung, Liam. "Google erases 'Don't be evil' from code of conduct after 18 years," *ZDNet*. May 21, 2018. https://www.zdnet.com/article/google-erases-dont-be-evil-from-code-of-conduct-after-18-years

Twilio. "Twilio Announces Fourth Quarter and Full Year 2020 Results." *Twilio*. February 17, 2021. https://investors.twilio.com/news/news-details/2021/Twilio-Announces-Fourth-Quarter-and-Full-Year-2020-Results/default.aspx

CHAPTER 10

Bazerman, Max H., and Patel Paresh. "SPACs: What You Need to Know," *Harvard Business Review*. July-August 2021. https://hbr.org/2021/07/spacs-what-you-need-to-know

Clark, Kate. "Uber's First Day as a Public Company Didn't Go So Well," *TechCrunch*. May 10, 2019. https://techcrunch.com/2019/05/10/ubers-first-day-as-a-public-company-didnt-go-so-well

Cornelius, Philipp, and Bilal Gokpinar. "Crowdfunding Can Deliver More Than Just Money," *Harvard Business Review*. March 23. 2021. https://hbr.org/2021/03/crowdfunding-can-deliver-more-than-just-money

DNS Capital. "DNS Capital's Investments." https://www.dnscap.com/investments

Grigely, Emily. "Nutpods Founder Shares How She Continues to Grow Her Business Amidst COVID-19," *Small Business Journal*. July 28, 2020. https://thesbjournal.com/featured/nutpods-founder-shares-how-she-continues-to-grow-her-business-amidst-covid-19

Kleiner-Perkins. "Google Case Study." https://www.kleinerperkins.com/case-study/google

Kolodny, Lora. "Uber losses narrow as delivery growth outpaces fall in ride-sharing," *CNBC*. February 10, 2021. https://www.cnbc.com/2021/02/10/uber-earnings-q4-2020-.html

Metcalf, Tom. "These Are the World's Richest Families," *Bloomberg*. August 1, 2020. https://www.bloomberg.com/features/richest-families-in-the-world/?sref=BLKWHazc

Sacra. n.d. "How Shaan Puri's podcast landed him a $4M rolling fund," *Sacra*. https://sacra.com/p/shaan-puri-myfirstmillion-interview

Schroter, Will. "Beware the Absentee Landlord of Equity," *StartUps.com*. August 25, 2021. https://www.startups.com/library/expert-advice/beware-absentee-landlord-of-equity

Schultz, Abby. "Direct Investing Is Rising Among Family Offices," *Barron's*. August 7, 2020. https://www.barrons.com/articles/direct-investing-is-rising-among-family-offices-01596832423

Shaan's All Access Fund. https://angel.co/v/back/shaans-all-access-fund

Swanson, S. A. "DNS Capital's Family Values," *Middle Market Growth*. October 24, 2018. https://middlemarketgrowth.org/cover-dns-capital-family-values

Vizard, Sarah. "How Coca-Cola, Lego and Gillette tapped into the wisdom of crowds," *Marketing Week*. February 13, 2019. https://www.marketingweek.com/coca-cola-lego-gillette-crowdfunding

CHAPTER 11

Cain, Áine. "A former NASA flight director explains how to stay calm in a crisis," *Business Insider*. November 13, 2017. https://www.businessinsider.com/nasa-flight-director-stress-crisis-2017-11

Grove, Andrew. *Only the Paranoid Survive: How to Exploit the Crisis Points That Challenge Every Company*. Currency, 1999.

PepsiCo. "PepsiCo Launches New Direct-to-Consumer Offerings to Deliver Food & Beverage Products and Meet Increased Demand Amid Pandemic." *Pepsico*. May 11, 2020. https://www.pepsico.com/news/press-release/pepsico-launches-new-direct-to-consumer-offerings-to-deliver-food--beverage-prod05112020

Planes, Alex. "The Biggest Waste of Money in Super Bowl History," *The Motley Fool*. January 20, 2013. https://www.fool.com/investing/general/2013/01/30/the-biggest-waste-of-money-in-super-bowl-history.aspx

Richtmyer, Richard. "Pets.com at its tail end," *CNN Money*. November 7, 2000. https://money.cnn.com/2000/11/07/technology/pets/index.htm

Scott, Charity. "Lululemon Leans into Men's Apparel as Segment Expands," *Wall Street Journal*. December 11, 2019. https://www.wsj.com/articles/lululemon-tests-how-far-men-will-stretch-11576069203

Swanson, S. A. "Curbside Enthusiasm," *Middle Market Growth*. September/October 2020. https://middlemarketgrowth.org/cover-curbside-enthusiasm

Index

Emotion(s)
    decisions based on, 104
    judging of, 47
    meditation for control of, 46
    non-identification of, 47
    underestimation of, 21
Emotional availability, 74, 86–88
Empathy, 64, 87–88
Employee(s). *See also* Job candidates; Team(s); Team members;
        Workforce
    antidiscrimination laws for, 148
    appreciation of, 80
    attracting of, 116–119
    attrition of, 127–128
    behavioral questions for, 119–121
    compensation for, 117–119
    delegation to, 75
    empathy for, 87–88
    guidelines for, 76
    hiring of. *See* Hiring
    incentive structures for, 117–119
    initiative taking by, 76
    interview process for, 119–121
    kindness toward, 88
    motivating of, 109
    overexpansion effects on, 166–167
    over-specificity in finding, 117
    personality tests for, 122–125, 124*f*
    proactivity in finding, 116
    psychological safety for, 79–83
    questions from, 84
    recruiting of, 116
    remote work by, 118
    safety of, 224
    selection of, 119–127
    in team-based organizational structure, 107, 108
    termination of, 128
    training of, 137
    valuing of, 75
    wellness programs for, 118
    younger, 118–119
Employee handbook, 139
Employment antidiscrimination laws, 148
Enthusiasm, 26
Entrepreneur, 37, 42–43
Entrepreneurial Operating System, 143–144, 157
Entrepreneurs' Organization, 40
EO. *See* Entrepreneurs' Organization
EOS. *See* Entrepreneurial Operating System
Equal Employment Opportunity Commission, 123, 147–148
Equity capital, 197
Equity clawbacks, 203–204
Equity financing, 197. *See also* Equity funding
Equity funding
    advantages of, 203
    angel investors, 205–207
    business valuation for, 197–199

description of, 197
    disadvantages of, 203
    private equity firms, 205–206
    term sheet traps, 203–204
    venture capital, 206–207
Equity investors
    due diligence by, 202
    feedback from, 201
    "No" from, 201
    pitching to, 199–205
    rejection from, 201
    vetting of founders by, 202
Euphemisms, 104
Executive coach, 22, 24
Exercise, 38
Exit stage, of startup funding, 212
Exit strategy, 181
Experimentation, 54–55
Explicit knowledge, 136–137, 222
Exploding Kittens, 209

F
Facebook, 22, 40, 131, 159, 206
Facebook Messenger, 52
Failure
    approaches to, 13
    case examples of, 15–17, 81–82
    humor approach to, 65–66
    laughing at, 66
    learning through, 79
    planning and, 172, 177, 226
    psychological safety and, 79–83
    reframing of, 10
    three-part approach to, 81–82
Family and friends
    company involvement by, 43
    depression assessments by, 41
    scheduling time with, 42
    Family office funding, 208
Farmer's Fridge, 208
Farmers Restaurant Group, 218
Fast Company, 95
Fatigue, 37
Fattmerchant, 14
FBA. *See* Fulfillment by Amazon
Fear, culture of, 32
Federal employment antidiscrimination laws, 148
FedEx, 164
Feedback
    in 360-degree review, 20
    company example of, 101
    from equity investors, 201
    in team meetings, 99
Ferriss, Tim, 37
Fey, Tina, 58
Feynman, Richard, 24
Finance software, 150

Financial concerns, 224
Financial Fridays, 141, 149
"Find Innovation Where You Least Expect It," 63
FINTRX, 208
First-mover advantage, 173–174
First Round Review, 101, 170, 187
Fishkin, Rand, 24, 39–40, 49, 103–104
Fitbit, 95
Five balls of life, 36
Five-factor model, 124
Fiverr, 130
Fixed mindset
    growth mindset versus, 10, 11f, 12–13
    origins of, 10
    triggers for, 13–14
Fixed-mindset persona, 13
Flaubert, Gustave, 37
Flexibility, 110
Flippa.com, 160
Floyd, George, 32
Focusing on the present, 44, 59
Follow-up questions, in conversations, 43
Ford, Henry, 15–17, 30
Ford Motor Company, 15–17
Forest bathing, 38
Forgiveness, 48
Founders
    business acquisitions and, 162
    first-mover advantage, 173–174
    growth-related questions for, 169
    lack of delegation by, 75
    support from, 40
    vetting of, by equity investors, 202
Framing effect, 220
Frankl, Viktor, 46
Fried, Jason, 66
Friends, family, and fools, 191, 211. See also Family and friends
Front, 53
Frontline workers, 100–101
Fulfillment by Amazon, 129, 164
Functional and project/issue organizational structure hybrid, 109
Functional fixedness, 63
Functional organizational structure, 105–106, 106
Funding
    crowdfunding, 208–210
    debt. See Debt funding
    equity. See Equity funding
    family offices for, 208
    mezzanine financing, 205, 212
    mini funds, 210–211
    raising money for growth, 191–192
    self-funding, 191
    startup, 211–213
Funding Circle, 196

G
Gartner, 174

Gates, Bill, 19, 207
General Electric, 124
Gen Z, 119
Getting Things Done. See GTD
Ghandour, Fadi, 12
Gillette, 209
GIPHY, 159
Glassman, Greg, 31–32
Gmail, 149
Goals
    factors that affect, 187
    SMART, 185–186, 186f
Goldsmith, Marshall, 22–23
Google, 22, 80, 88, 110, 120, 183, 207
Google Docs, 149
Google Sheets, 149
Google Workspace, 149
Government compliance, 146–148
Grant, Adam, 30
Greene, Robert, 16–17
Greenleaf, Robert K., 85
Greenroom, 172
Gregersen, Hal, 44
Greiner, Lori, 43
Grit, 15, 25, 27–28
Groundlings, The, 60
Grove, Andy, 207, 222
Growth
    by acquisition, 158–162
    "at all costs" approach to, 166, 171
    competitors and, 168
    explosive, 180
    factors that affect, 179
    industry factors, 179
    management factors, 179
    market factors, 179
    overexpansion issues. See Overexpansion
    product expansion for, 156–157, 158f
    product extension for, 156, 158f
    raising money for, 191–192
    setbacks during, 26
    strategies for, 169
    sustainable, 167
    timing for, 172
    underexpansion, 171–173
    by vertical integration, 162–165
Growth mindset
    case example of, 14
    cultivating of, 12–14
    fixed mindset versus, 10, 11f, 12–13
    humility for, 30
    optimism, 14–17
    overview of, 9–10
    persistence and, 11, 25–28
Growth stage, of startup funding, 212
GTD, 52, 53f

WHAT DID YOU THINK?

We rely on reviews and reader feedback to help our authors reach more people, improve our books, and grow our business. We would really appreciate it if you took the time to help us out by providing feedback on your recent purchase.

It's really easy, it only takes a second, and it's a tremendous help!

——— NOT SURE WHAT TO SHARE? ———
Here are some ideas to get your review started...

- *What did you learn?*
- *Have you been able to put anything you learned into action?*
- *Would you recommend the book to other readers?*
- *Is the author clear and easy to understand?*

TWO WAYS TO LEAVE AN AMAZON REVIEW

Use the camera app on your mobile phone to scan the QR code or visit the link below to record your testimonial and get your free book.

 SCAN ME

or

www.quickstartguides.review/rungrow

 VISIT URL

GET YOUR NEXT
QuickStart Guide®
FOR FREE

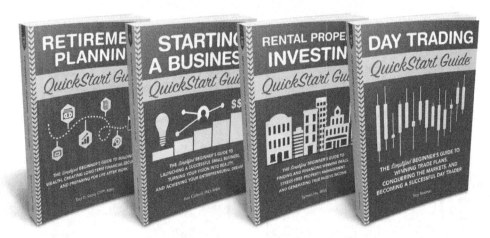

Leave us a quick video testimonial on our website and we will give you a **FREE *QuickStart Guide*** of your choice!

RECORD TESTIMONIAL   **SUBMIT TO OUR WEBSITE**   **GET A FREE BOOK**

SAVE 10% ON YOUR NEXT
QuickStart Guide®

USE CODE: QSG10

www.quickstartguides.shop/business

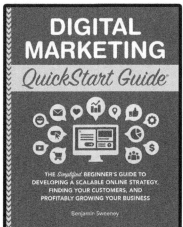

www.quickstartguides.shop/dmarketing

www.quickstartguides.shop/investing

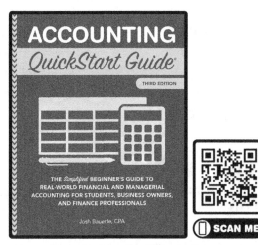

www.quickstartguides.shop/accounting

Use the camera app on your mobile phone to scan the QR code or visit the link below the cover to shop.
Get 10% off your entire order when you use code 'QSG10' at checkout at www.quickstartguides.com.

LISTEN TO *QuickStart Guides* ON THE GO

NEW AUDIBLE MEMBERS
GET THEIR FIRST AUDIOBOOK
FREE!

DIGITAL MARKETING *QuickStart Guide*

FOREX TRADING *QuickStart Guide*

FLIPPING HOUSES *QuickStart Guide*

REAL ESTATE INVESTING *QuickStart Guide*

INVESTING *QuickStart Guide*

TWO WAYS TO SELECT A FREE AUDIOBOOK

Use the camera app on your mobile phone to scan the QR code or visit the link below to select your free audiobook from Audible.

or

www.quickstartguides.com/free-audiobook

 SCAN ME

 VISIT URL

CLYDEBANK MEDIA

QuickStart Guides®

PROUDLY SUPPORT ONE TREE PLANTED

One Tree Planted is a 501(c)(3) nonprofit organization focused on global reforestation, with millions of trees planted every year. ClydeBank Media is proud to support One Tree Planted as a reforestation partner.

Every dollar donated plants one tree and every tree makes a difference!

Learn more at www.clydebankmedia.com/charitable-giving or make a contribution at onetreeplanted.org.

Made in the USA
Middletown, DE
23 August 2023

37220813R00157